STORYTELLER

STORYTELLER

TALES FROM A FASHION INSIDER

JEFFREY BANKS

POINTED LEAF PRESS

This book is dedicated to the sassiness, brilliance, and unconditional love my mother, Eleanor M. Banks, has shown, and continues to show me, well into her 104th year. She has always given me the courage to be who I am and championed who I hoped to be.
—Your loving son

CONTENTS

Of course, the immediate question that comes to mind when seeing the title of this book is why *Storyteller*? As a child, when given this nomenclature, it was not a good thing.

It meant you told fibs, if not outright lies as in "Don't believe him, he's a storyteller." However, the dictionary defines "storyteller" as: "A person who tells, writes, or reads stories to others. Storytellers can also be people who relate anecdotes or recite tales. Storytelling can often involve being vulnerable and exposing anxieties, fears, and shortcomings."

People have often marveled at the way that I remember certain situations, conversations, and details from decades earlier, and when I retell them, have remarked about my ability to relay them in storytelling form. "You tell the best stories," they say, as if these tales were fabricated from thin air when, in truth, they are just vivid memories, which remain with me always.

In the past, when I have been asked to permanently record them, I always demurred, believing that it would be narcissistic and self-serving to assume these stories would be of interest to anyone but me. But recently, I have had a change of heart and think that writing these stories down might be a way of honoring the incredibly interesting, special, and unique characters I have come to know on this fascinating journey we call life. So herewith, the storyteller tells all, well...almost all.

I. EARLY DAYS

From my earliest memory my right hand was always attached to a pencil, a pen, or a crayon. It's as if they were an appendage to my arm. I don't really ever remember being without one. I was always drawing. A six-hour car trip? No problem. Just give me a stack of paper and this five-year-old was completely happy in the back seat. I have never been carsick, drawing or reading.

Drawing and books seemed to always satisfy me as a child. In fact, the toy box my father built for me never held toys, only books and magazines. I could read at the age of four and constantly annoyed the hell out of my parents by rattling off every billboard and street sign, every time we were in the car. I am still a voracious reader and enjoy hours poring over an interesting biography of a historical figure.

I distinctly remember my very first trip to a museum. It was the National Gallery of Art, with my mother, when I was about five or six. One of the first things I saw was an Edgar Degas painting of ballet dancers at the barre. I was fascinated, gobsmacked if you will, staring at this magnificent depiction of dancers. My mother says I stood there for almost half an hour, completely transfixed. Soon after, I wanted to know everything I could about Degas.

As soon as I got my first library card, the library became my second home. On Saturdays, I would walk the few blocks to my local branch, often waiting outside before it opened. *The Reader's Guide to Periodical Literature*—a precursor to Google—became my best friend, leading me down a rabbit hole to everything about Degas and his world, along with Jean-Auguste-Dominique Ingres, John Singer Sargent, and others.

I thought that I wanted to be an artist, because after all, it was my favorite thing to do at school, but then I read what a difficult life so many artists led, and I began to rethink what I wanted to become when I grew up.

Suddenly it hit me: fashion design. It was like instant gratification. In art you could create a painting, and it might take years, if ever, to be appreciated. But with designing, you would know within months, even weeks, if your creation was embraced or not by the buying public.

OPPOSITE With all the expectations of the world ahead of me, I ascended the steps of my boyhood home in Washington, DC.

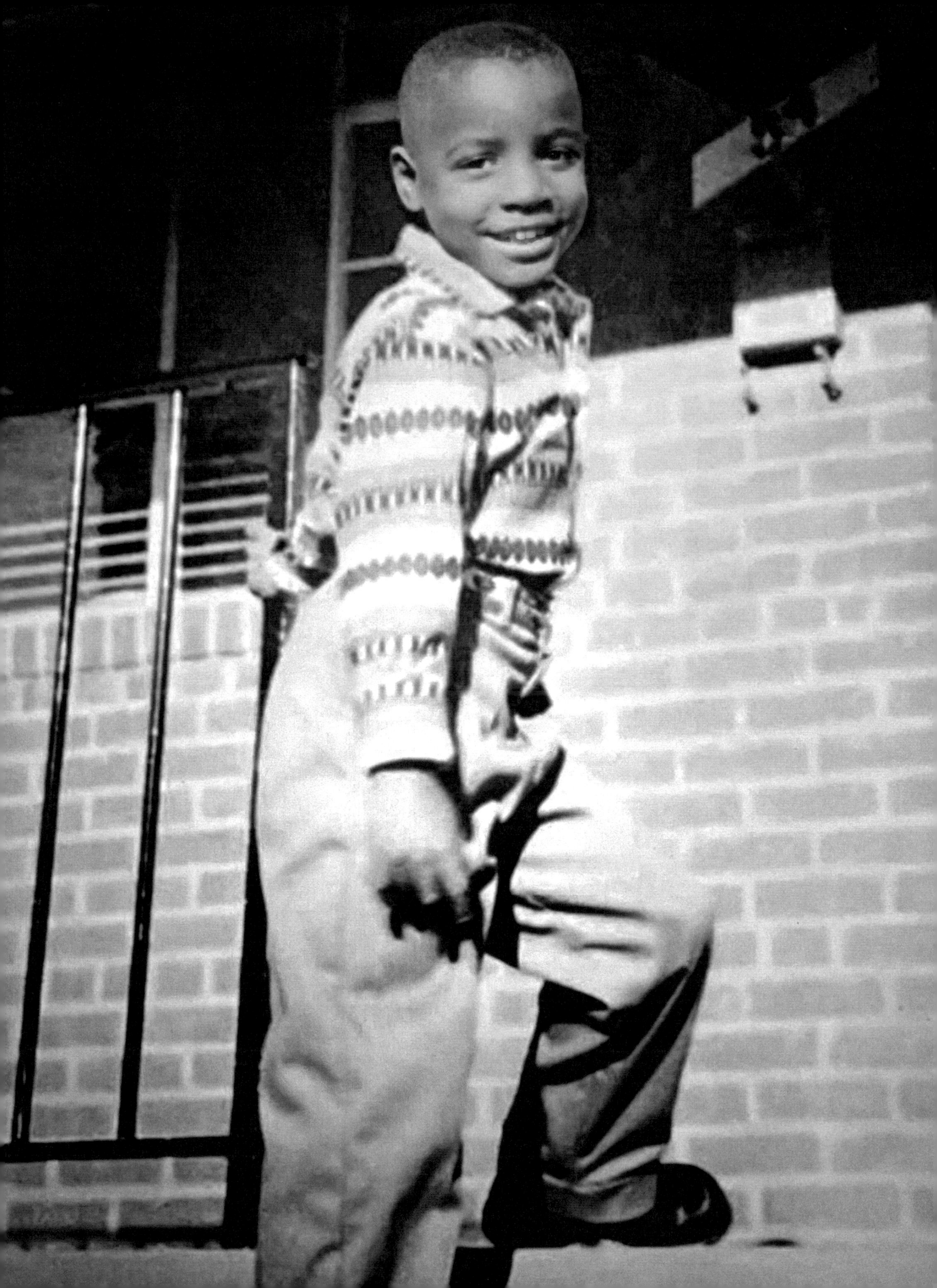

( ) Duke of Windsor

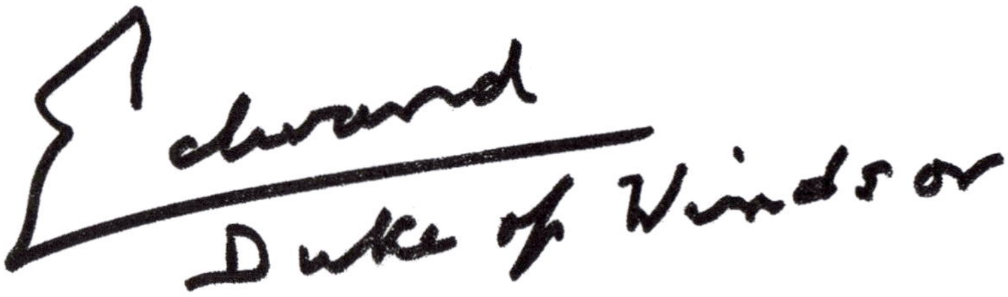

( ) Duchess of Windsor

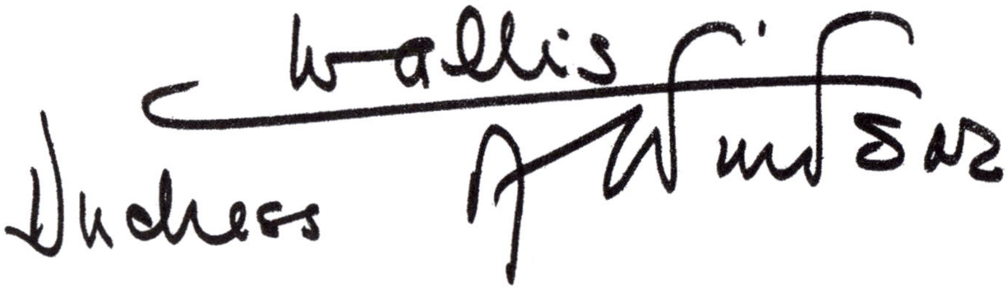

(✓) Fred Astaire

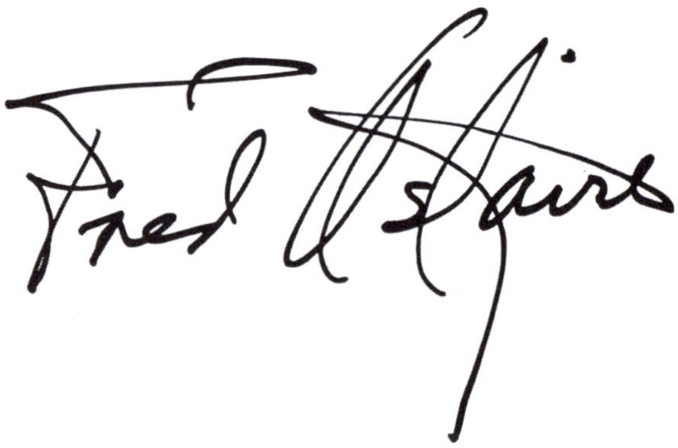

(✓) Hubert de Givenchy

(✓) Ralph Lauren

OPPOSITE When I was 13 years old, I made a list of the 10 people I most wanted to meet by the time I was 23. Well, I almost got there. I never met the Duke and Duchess of Windsor or Truman Capote, but I'm happy to say that I checked off all the rest of those boldface names.

And so, when I was 10 years old, I knew it was going to be fashion for me. By the age of 13, a truly pivotal age for me, I got my own set of keys to our house and could stay home by myself. I made a 10-year career plan, vowing that I wanted to win the Coty Award, the Oscar of the fashion world, by the time I was 23. I also put together a list of the 10 people I most wanted to meet in the next 10 years. I didn't get to meet the Duke and Duchess of Windsor or Truman Capote, but I did succeed with the other seven. I was driven and committed, and I thought that was completely normal for a 13-year-old kid. Maybe I wasn't so normal, but I was definitely dedicated.

(✔) Richard Avedon

( ) Truman Capote

(✔) Norman Norell

(✔) Audrey Hepburn

(✔) Barbra Streisand

ELEANOR M. BANKS

Having been born the youngest of six siblings and the only girl, my mother, Eleanor M. Banks, had to be scrappy from day one, and she was. I loved her telling me the story of wearing a white organdy dress her mother had made for her elementary school graduation and having the boy sitting behind her dip her long braids into an inkwell and ruin the back of her dress. When she found out what he had done, she summarily beat the crap out of him.

She learned to type early on, still has the most wonderful handwriting, and sews beautifully. During World War II, Eleanor worked for the government in Little Rock, Arkansas, moonlighting on weekends as a bartender on the local train lines. In 1945 she heard that there were better government jobs in Washington, DC.

So she borrowed $500 from her uncle and, knowing not a single soul in Washington, moved there and promptly became the first female and only Black person in the Coast Guard stenography pool. Very quickly, she rose through the ranks, happily taking on more and more responsibilities.

Originally living at a government-funded housing facility, nicknamed "The Dormitory," where she met her best friend Mary Washington, my mother focused primarily on work. Both Mary and my mother met their respective spouses, Louis Christophe and Clarence Banks, at "The Dormitory." Marrying soon after, my parents lived in an apartment that was part of a two-family home. Mary and Louis Christophe married and, when I was born, became my godparents. Often this is just an honorary title, but in this case, my godparents were like a second, wonderful set of parents whom I saw regularly, on an almost weekly basis.

My mother was determined to live in her own home. My father, who was now working as a cartographer for the United States Naval Oceanographic Office, insisted that they could not afford a house. Without telling him, Eleanor visited several banks and loan offices and also spent what little free time she had looking at affordable housing and new development areas, finally finding an area where homes were being built in the southeast section of Washington that she liked. She went from bank to bank until she found one that could support her plan to purchase this newly built home in a mostly Black area. She got all her ducks in a row and then presented the plan to my father, insisting that he sign the papers. She had it all figured out and was not going to be deterred. I guess that is where I get it from, a no-holds-barred determination when I go for something I want.

Mom encouraged my artistic ambitions from day one, and she and my father always instilled in my sister and me that we could become

OPPOSITE A glamor gal, my mother and the famous legs my father fell in love with first, early on in their postwar relationship.

OPPOSITE On Good Friday in 1962, my mother came home with fabric for a skirt suit, blouse, and plaid coat. After dinner, she laid out the fabric and the pattern pieces, and cut the garments. This photograph shows the finished result on Easter Sunday morning. Note the perfectly matched plaid seams.

and achieve anything we wanted as long as we were willing to work hard for it. My mother trusted my judgment when it came to stylistic choices from a very early age, and I was constantly accompanying her on shopping trips downtown. My mother has extraordinary taste when it comes to clothing, and she has always been particularly keen about her appearance—wearing gloves of cotton, suede, leather, jersey, and cashmere—of which she owned many varieties and wore every day when she worked. And because she felt the greatest sin a woman could commit was to be in public with soiled gloves, every time she purchased a pair of gloves, she bought an exact duplicate pair which she kept in her purse inside its plastic sleeve. As the day wore on, if her gloves became soiled, she changed into the fresh pair inside her handbag. On Thursdays, she would take a week's worth of her soiled gloves to Woodward & Lothrop department store at 11th and F Streets which, believe it or not, had a glove cleaning department. She would also pick up the previous week's group of gloves. My mother never entered her church, the 19th Street Baptist, without a hat, and she owned dozens of them. Blessed, or perhaps cursed, with a very narrow foot (she is an 8AAAA), she could not wear cheap shoes; they just didn't fit. So her salesman at I. Miller, who became a good friend of hers, would hoard, collect, and call her when he received shoes in her size, and invariably, when she found shoes that fit properly, she bought them in every color available.

My mother has a very sharp sense of humor. As a five-year-old on a shopping expedition with her downtown, I saw two blond boys dressed and looking exactly alike.

"Mommy, look!" I shouted, "Those boys look just alike!"

She explained, "That's because they are identical twins." I asked, "How come I wasn't identical twins?"

"Because one of you is two too many," she replied.

Another time, years later, while reading a biography of Humphrey Bogart, I discovered that he died on the afternoon that my sister was born. "Why did you never tell me this?" I phoned, asking my mother.

"I was busy, OK?" she retorted sharply.

Shortly after my father died, I went home on a particularly warm and sultry day before Thanksgiving. The train from Penn Station was so crowded that I had to stand all the way to Philadelphia before I could get a seat. Hot, tired, and hungry, I was not in a good mood to say the least. When I finally arrived at Union Station in Washington, there was a very, very long taxi line. After what seemed an eternity, I finally got a cab. In Washington, there exists a share-a-ride system if all the passengers are going in the same direction, but only if the first passenger is asked about it and agrees. Too tired to argue when the cab driver proceeded to pick up two other passengers without asking me, my trip home was prolonged further. When I got there, I exited quickly with bag in hand as the driver pulled up across the street from my home. I intended to pay the driver at his open window, definitely depriving him of a tip, as I prepared to dress him down.

"I know the rules, and you broke them," I yelled, standing by his open window and preparing to pay him.

"Look, you goddamn faggot . . ."

I didn't let him finish, I had dropped my bag and reached in through the open window with both my hands at his throat, when suddenly he stepped on the gas and sped away. As I retrieved my bag, I turned, and there standing in the open doorway was my mother.

"Have you been standing there for a while?" I asked.

"Yes," she answered.

I added, "And you heard everything that went on?"

"Yes," she said.

"So I know what you're thinking," I said.

"You do?" she answered quizzically.

"Yes, you are wondering if what he said is true, aren't you?" I asked.

"I am?" she said, quietly.

"And you know what? It is true! And you know what else, I know what you are thinking right now!" I said.

"You do?" she asked.

"Yes, you are blaming yourself."

She asked, "I am?"

I answered, "Yes, you are. And you know what? You are to blame! You are to blame for my great school record. You are to blame for the fact I am the youngest Coty Award winner. And you are to blame that I am a successful designer, so if you are going to blame yourself, you are going to have to take all the blame."

She laughed out loud and asked if I was hungry.

"Starving," I answered. We sat at the kitchen table; she fed me and talked and talked until 3am. I don't remember what she made that night, but it was probably my favorite, her meatloaf. I crave it so much that every year at Christmas she sends me home with a care package of at least two frozen ones. When the Council of Fashion Designers of America (CFDA) issued a designer cookbook, there were only two meatloaf recipes in it: Bill Blass' and Eleanor Banks'.

A few years ago, shortly before my mother turned 100, we had an hours-long telephone conversation, and she said that her whole life all she wanted was to become a wife and mother, and through me she got to experience things she had never dreamed of—travel all over the world, visits to the White House, and seeing her son become successful and well known were more than she could have ever imagined.

Given that I believe I have the best mother in the whole wide world, I couldn't ask for any more than that.

OPPOSITE Ann Stock, Hillary Rodham Clinton's social secretary at the White House, arranged to have a photographer record my mother's first meeting with the First Lady, who arrived minutes later dressed in the identical shade of pink.

OPPOSITE BOTTOM Mom and I met President Bill Clinton at the White House at the unveiling of the White House Christmas tree in December 2000. I had been asked, along with 75 other designers, to create an ornament for the tree, giving my interpretation of Santa Claus' suit.

OPPOSITE On Mother's Day, I surprised my mother by getting to her church in Washington, DC, before her. Of course, per usual, she was dressed to the nines.

Eleanor Banks' Meatloaf

Prep time: 20 minutes
Total time: 1 hour, 30 minutes
Oven temperature: 350°F (175°C)
Serves: 4

Ingredients

Vegetable oil or nonstick spray, for the baking dish
1 pound ground chuck
½ pound pork breakfast sausage
¾ cup fine plain breadcrumbs
2 to 3 celery stalks, finely chopped
1 medium onion, finely chopped
½ green bell pepper, finely chopped
Celery salt, to taste
Salt and freshly ground black pepper, to taste
2 small (8-ounce) cans tomato sauce

Preparation

Preheat the oven to 350°F (175°C). Grease a 9-by-13-inch loaf dish with oil.

Combine the chuck, sausage, breadcrumbs, celery, onion, green pepper, some celery salt, and salt and pepper to taste in a large bowl. Add 1 can of the tomato sauce and mix very well. Pour the remaining can of tomato sauce in a large measuring cup. Add half a can of water, stir to combine, and set it aside.

Shape the chuck mixture into a loaf (approximately 9-by-5 inches) in the Pyrex or metal baking dish. Insert a meat thermometer into thickest part of the loaf and bake for 30 minutes.

Reduce the oven to 325°F (165°C). Spoon off the excess fat from the baking dish and baste the meatloaf with the tomato sauce mixture that was set aside. Continue to bake the meatloaf until cooked through and the internal temperature registers 160°F, about an additional 40 minutes.

Tent the meatloaf with aluminum foil and let it rest for 5 minutes before slicing.

Note: This meatloaf is especially great for next-day sandwiches since it stays very moist.

For a fancier version, arrange ¾ pounds of bacon in a lattice on top of the loaf before baking. You can also substitute ground turkey for the chuck for a healthier variation.

My father, Clarence Lorenzo Banks, was a mix of many contradictions. With two much older sisters, Anna and Lillian, he was the only son of Joseph and Carrie Johnson Banks and was, in fact, a change-of-life mistake. His parents were devout Roman Catholics in Baltimore, Maryland, who attended mass every morning and were in their fifties when he was born. Obviously, the rhythm method failed. Because his parents were elderly by the standards of the time, they lacked the energy to play with a young toddler. His older sisters were both married and out of the house when he was born. Early on, he learned to depend on himself and become very self-reliant. He could do woodwork, fix a car, do plumbing, paint houses, iron anything, and even hem his pants or sew slipcovers for furniture. He was in the army during World War II, although he never discussed the scar by his hip, or how he got it during the war. He was, like many of his generation, very tight-lipped with his emotions, with one exception: he had a very short fuse. He was not a violent man but he did not suffer fools or disobedient children.

After his military service and on the GI Bill, he began to study and pursue his dream of becoming an architect. Like many of his army friends, he stayed in government housing in Washington, DC, that was nicknamed "The Dormitory." My mother was living in the female version of "The Dormitory" while working for the Coast Guard. One day while cruising by the tennis courts with a male friend, he spied my mother and her girlfriend playing tennis. My mother was clad in shorts that showed off her shapely gams. "You see that gal with the great legs," he exclaimed to his buddy. "I am going to marry her!" he stated confidently, especially given the fact that they had never actually met.

And marry they did, in 1947. Mom wore a tailored grey flannel skirt suit, a large picture hat, and platform-sole sling-back shoes. Years later, when I remarked to my mother about how unattractive I thought YSL's 1940s collection was, especially the platform shoes, she was visibly hurt by the comment considering that she had been married wearing them.

My father put aside his dream of becoming an architect for the more practical job of working as a cartographer for the United States Naval Oceanographic Office in Suitland, Maryland. Drawing precise maps of our overseas operations and installations, many of which were top secret, was a job perfectly suited to the most anal man I have ever met.

My father could show you the exact angle to place a dish in the dish rack to have it dry in the least amount of time. He had me in tears at

OPPOSITE My father proudly served in the United States Army in World War II but, like most men of his generation, he never discussed his time in the service, nor the small scar on his lower back that I suspected came from the war.

OVERLEAF LEFT This photograph of my parents was taken at their wedding in Washington, DC in 1947. When I was a child, I remember remarking to my mother how much I disliked the platform shoes she wore at the ceremony. My father, on the other hand, looked quite dashing in his pin-striped suit.

OVERLEAF RIGHT A newly discovered picture is of my father bottle-feeding me. I guess I was that little once.

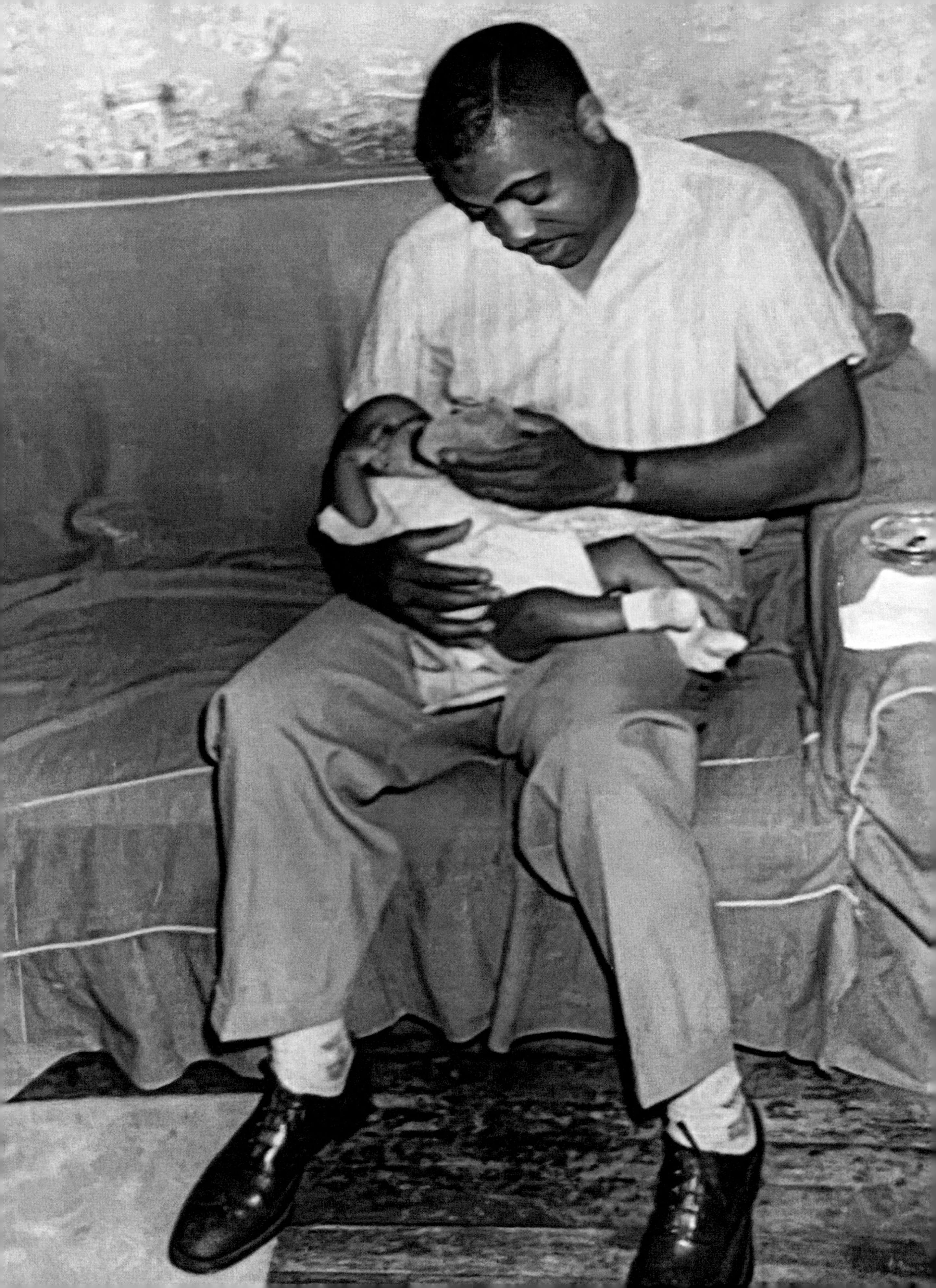

OPPOSITE This family portrait was taken in front of our Washington home. I am about five or six years old and my sister Adrienne is about three or four years old.

the age of five when I was learning to tie my shoes because the double-knotted ends were not exactly even. Dad felt that if one were going to do a job, it had better be one's best effort, and perfection was preferred.

Surprisingly, or maybe not so surprisingly, his penchant for perfection led to his favorite hobby, which he practiced almost daily: baking—a precise science that requires meticulous attention to detail and exact measurements. That was really right up his alley. Every night for dinner we had his homemade baked culinary delights: the usual cakes, pies, tarts, and fritters, but also more extravagant confections like profiteroles, eclairs, Napoleons, and bread puddings with raisin-filled hard sauces. All of them were entirely homemade. He was most proud of his pie crusts, which he worked on constantly to perfect. He said that anyone could make a sweet pie filling, but the measure of a true baker was if his pie crust was entirely flaky and delicious. And his was. I was so used to these nightly delicacies that at around the age of six, I had my first overnight sleepover at a friend's house, and when the hostess presented a bowl of wobbly red gelatin as the after-dinner dessert, I loudly proclaimed, "That's not dessert, that's Jell-O."

I know Dad was not pleased that his son wanted to be a fashion designer, but in his defense, he never outlawed my desire and, in fact, took me to art lessons and bought whatever art supplies I wanted. He did, however, draw the line, when early on, I tossed *Vogue*, *Glamour*, and *GQ* into the cart when we went grocery shopping on Thursday nights. Somewhat embarrassed, he said to my mother, "Just get him subscriptions!"

Both my parents were great providers for me and my sister. We were never aware of not having anything we really needed. In later years, I really came to appreciate something they did almost every weekend. Many people grow up and work for years in Washington without ever seeing or discovering the many historical monuments and treasures that are part of the fabric of that city. Not the Banks family. We went to the Washington Monument, the Capitol Rotunda, the White House, the United States Mint, the Folger Shakespeare Library, and many more places. Those weekend trips, however, were never couched as appreciating history, but were always presented simply as fun things to do, and they were. Of course, two of our annual events were going to see the National Christmas tree on the Ellipse and, probably my father's favorite, going to see the cherry blossoms in bloom. That usually entailed dressing up, often in our Easter finery, for portraits Clarence took himself.

Typical of the stoic 1950s-era masculine man, my father was never one to heap praise on me. No matter how many A's or awards I got, he never said congratulations or, more importantly, "I love you," the three words I craved. As a toddler, I always kissed my parents goodnight before going to bed. One night, when I was about five years old, and Dad was in his favorite armchair reading the newspaper, I leaned over to kiss him goodnight and he stopped me, saying, "Don't do that anymore, boys don't kiss." Those words stunned me, and I felt utter rejection as that moment was forever emblazoned in my mind.

Despite this, my father did have a wicked sense of humor that I like to think I inherited. When we visited friends or relatives, and it was time to leave, he called my mother's leave-taking "the long goodbye," and he would say to her, "I am going out to start the car. . . . I'll see you in a half an hour." He said my predilection for minutiae was "a font of useless information. You can remember every damn dress Audrey Hepburn ever wore, but you never remember to tie your shoelaces." My pithy retort was always, "Dad, some things are important, and some things are not."

Dad was always the family photographer. Prints, slides, home movies, everything was always documented. It's as if the camera was an extension of his arm. Although I always had a camera from an early age—first a Kodak Brownie and later an Instamatic—I was definitely intimidated by his prowess and rarely took pictures myself until after his death.

OPPOSITE I was captured cradling my baby sister, Adrienne, for a formal portrait in those innocent days long ago.

Adrienne, my younger sister, was born a little over three years after me. Since my parents had waited almost eight years for me to join the family, they were overjoyed when I got a sibling. Although we resembled my mother and each other physically, our personalities could not have been more different. I took after my mother—patient, forgiving, and nonconfrontational. My sister, on the other hand, had a short fuse and a volatile temper, similar to my father, but she could make friends easily with almost anyone.

Her greatest fault was being almost too trusting and eager to give away all her worldly goods to people who did not deserve them. This caused her to be taken advantage of time and time again, because she was so eager to please. Unfortunately, she attended many of the same schools that I did, and given that I was an overachiever, the inevitable comparisons by teachers did not help my sister's confidence in her studies. Although my parents and I pleaded with my former teachers not to compare my sister to me, they continued to do so. It was not until she attended a brand-new high school where no one knew me that she began to flourish.

OPPOSITE As was the custom in middle-class Black homes, through the years, Easter meant dressing up in all our finery. All the photographs were taken on Easter Day.

Despite everything, my sister was enormously proud of me and maintained dozens of scrapbooks of any and all press clippings about her big brother.

Adrienne was the exact opposite of me when it came to fashion and clothing. Her idea of getting dressed up was a pair of jeans and a vintage leather jacket bought at a thrift store. As an adult, she just did not care that much about clothing. What she did care about was her large coterie of friends, as well as my mother, especially after my father died. She saw herself as my mother's protector even though my mother was entirely capable of taking care of herself well into her nineties.

As in many families, addiction visited our family in the wake of a tragic car accident, in which my sister was involved in 1985. Through a mechanical failure of her car, it jumped the lane she was driving in and went into an oncoming lane. My sister's leg was severely injured in the accident and when she woke up in the hospital after surgery and inquired about the car that had been heading toward her, she was told by a not very bright nurse that the person in the other vehicle had been killed. Sinking into a deep depression because she blamed the accident on herself, she began to abuse the pain medication she had been given. Although insurance adjusters confirmed that the crash was not Adrienne's fault and that, in fact it, was a mechanical issue with the car, she continued to blame herself. Prescribed pain medication soon led to stronger illicit drugs and, eventually, stints in rehab.

Needless to say, this caused tremendous tension among my sister, my mother, and me. And there were a few years when we barely spoke. Fortunately, Adrienne went into recovery, got her own apartment, relieving a lot of the strain on my mother, and things began to greatly improve between us. Just when things started to go well, disaster struck again, when Adrienne had a stroke. The stroke left her unable to walk on her own as she was now wheelchair-bound. She received years of physical therapy at a rehab hospital to improve her upper-body strength in anticipation of being able to return to and function in her own apartment.

From New York, I was consulting with doctors, psychiatrists, physical therapists, and social workers on my sister's condition and her imminent release after many years when she was suddenly diagnosed with acute leukemia and died within a couple of days.

I loved my sister despite our difficult relationship, and I know that she loved me. She is free at last of physical and emotional pain, and for that I am glad.

My mother claims that I could draw before I could walk—recognizable things and never stick figures. I do not know if that is true, but what I do know is that I do not ever remember a time when I was not drawing—even when I was six or seven years old, I was not only drawing hairdos on a dummy head block but also the rollers and setting diagrams to achieve the different hairdos. Just shy of my 10th birthday, I asked my mother if I could design her Easter outfit. Now you must know that in Black families in the 1960s getting dressed to the nines for Easter Sunday was a cultural ritual, one in which my family certainly participated.

OPPOSITE I recreated a sketch of my mother's Easter outfit that I designed when I was 10 years old.

My mother was an expert sewer who could mend or sew practically anything. When it came to sewing, she was fairly fearless. One Good Friday evening I remember her coming home from work with some fabric and, after dinner, laying out all the fabric on the dining room table and cutting out a 9/10th plaid coat, tweed skirt suit, and blouse. She spent all day sewing it with my father, then marking the hemline with one of those old-fashioned ruler-and-chalk hemline markers. On Easter Sunday morning she very proudly strolled into church looking magnificent.

Although, when I was nine, I didn't know how to sew, I knew enough about fashion to know exactly how I wanted my mother to look, and so I sketched her ensemble, a banana-colored wool jersey asymmetrically closed coat with a matching banana-colored raw-silk-empire-waist sheath dress underneath it. Both the dress and the coat were detailed with faux jet-beaded buttons.

Because my mother worked full-time, and even though she was an expert seamstress, she had little time for serious sewing. What she did have, however, was Annie, her dressmaker, a genius when it came to sewing. Annie could make anything from a quick sketch, a photograph, or a torn-out newspaper page, including the pattern. Everything she created was always amazing. And so, these two accomplished women let this precocious little boy, with his hand-drawn sketch and his definitive ideas about exactly what he wanted, direct them in making my mother's Easter outfit.

I went to the fittings and directed them both about bust lines and hem lengths and, surprisingly, they both listened to this bossy little kid. I must say, I was very pleased with the results. Then it was on to the accessories. I told my mother she must carry a black alligator handbag and wear black patent-leather sling-back shoes. I was insistent that the two black textures be distinctly different. Next, was the question of what hat to wear. My mother never entered church on Sunday without a hat. I decreed that she should wear a perfectly

plain chapeau, with a small crown and a large brim—but without flowers, ribbon trim, or veil.

With a swatch of coat and dress fabric firmly enclosed in her handbag, mother and son began a three-weekend tour of virtually every store in Washington, searching for the perfect hat. We went to Woodward & Lothrop, the Hecht Company, S. Kann, Sons & Co., and every small independent millinery store in between. I was not satisfied with any of the offerings. Finally, having exhausted the list of Washington retailers, there remained only one, Julius Garfinckel and Company, the finest and most expensive specialty department store in town.

With some hesitation from my mother, we entered the store on F Street. The millinery department was at the back of the first floor behind cosmetics and perfume. Down the long center aisle about 75 feet forward, I spied it . . . the holy grail of hats. "That's it. That's the one!" I said excitedly.

My mother was not convinced, "How can you be so sure from this far away?" she asked.

But I was determined in my conviction that this was the one as we swiftly approached it. My mother is quite petite, and so candidly, I did fear that this simple cardinal's hat of fine Italian straw might overwhelm her small frame, but my fears were soon allayed when she tried it on, and it was perfect. She was convinced right away. But then, she flipped the hat over and saw the $75 price tag. Seventy-five dollars then was like $300 today.

"Your father will kill me if I buy this hat!" she said.

I folded my little arms across my chest and said resolutely, "I am not leaving here unless you buy that hat!"

And so she did and wore it with the outfit I had designed for her to church on Easter Sunday, and we both basked in the acclaim. My career path, as far as I was concerned at 10 years of age, was firmly set.

Almost immediately upon joining the workforce at the Coast Guard, my mother met June. This tall, elegant white woman with beautiful, long white hair became one of my mother's best friends. Older by some years than my mother, they soon seemed to be joined at the hip. June made my mother's work experience as a singular Black woman in a mostly white male workplace so much more pleasurable.

Both June and my mother enjoyed sewing, and my mother talked about once going together to the Woodward & Lothrop department store in Washington at lunchtime to look for fabric to make a coat. After a while, they became separated between the bolts of fabric and the extensive pattern department. Asking a salesperson for help in locating my mom, June said, "I am looking for my daughter," and just then spotting her, she exclaimed, "There she is! There's my daughter." The gobsmacked sales associate could not believe her eyes that this petite Black lady could somehow belong to this tall white woman.

Another time, a few years later, when my parents purchased their first home in a newly developed Black neighborhood, June was invited to dinner and decided to take a taxi from her home to their new house. Directing the white cab driver to this new address, he kept insisting that she must be mistaken.

"Are you sure the address is correct?" he kept asking.

"Oh, yes, that's it," June said, until they pulled up, right in front, where my mother was sitting on the steps waiting for her. "There she is, there's my daughter," June screamed upon seeing Mom, leaving the perplexed cab driver scratching his head.

When I graduated from elementary school, my parents had a celebratory dinner the night before. My mother's godparents, whom I called Grandpa and Grandma Martin, drove all the way from Youngstown, Ohio, to be there, and June also attended. She brought me what was at the time the best graduation gift ever, my very own television set! It was just in time because the nightly squabbles between my sister and me over whose night it was to watch what they wanted on the family television set had reached a fever pitch, and we were always close to blows. Now all that was in the past, and I could close my bedroom door and watch whatever I wanted on the six or so channels that existed at the time. That television set stayed with me all the way to college.

BURGUNDY FARM COUNTRY DAY SCHOOL

I am still astonished that my parents found out about the extraordinary private school where I began my formal education. Remarkably, the school was founded only a year before I started there. Burgundy Farm Country Day School, in Alexandria, Virginia, was established, chiefly by members of the diplomatic corps who wanted a multiracial, multiethnic educational system for their children to attend. One of the founders was Eric Severeid, the esteemed CBS news journalist. The school got its name because the founders bought a dairy farm with its requisite traditional red farm buildings. Modern classrooms were created inside the shells of what remained from the original structures. The farmer who had owned the farm to raise and maintain farm animals stayed on doing his work for all of us kids to observe. The school was the very first racially integrated school in Virginia. We had kids from Israel, France, and many other countries, along with Americans. We did not wear uniforms and we called the principal, Earl Sargent, and all the teachers by their first names. My first-grade teacher, Paula Heywood, was from British Guiana, and my second-grade teacher was Camay Calloway, the jazz musician Cab Calloway's oldest daughter. I simply loved school. I couldn't wait to go every day, although, because of the distance from Washington, it meant I needed to be dressed, fed, and ready to be picked up in those old-fashioned Volkswagen buses at 7am. I remember learning cursive writing being especially thrilling. It was to some degree like drawing, which I think is why I liked it so much. We also had a swimming pool and a potter's wheel with pottery classes and a very active drama department that involved the whole school. I actually was the Mikado in one production. I had my first crush on a classmate—Royce Davis from Israel. At the age of five, I became so enamored with her that when her family put on a Passover Seder service at school, I went home and told my parents that I wanted to become Jewish. My second and much more serious crush was, I believe, in the second grade on the college student teacher's aide from Antioch College named Alan, who was so very kind to the kid who was not the least bit interested in playing football. I got teased because of it. Alan took such great care talking with me every day that I came to think of him as my great protector. The day came when he told me he wasn't coming back to school for the next semester. I was inconsolable, feeling I was being abandoned, and I couldn't stop crying. Fortunately, my love of learning, especially reading, overtook the sadness of Alan's leave-taking. I was like a sponge, lapping up everything that was fed to me and loving it all.

Unfortunately for me, just as I was about to enter the fourth grade,

OPPOSITE The familiar red farm buildings in Alexandria, Virginia, once held animals but were transformed into modern, air-conditioned classrooms in the school where I started my formal education.

LEFT Camay Calloway, my second-grade teacher, was one of the very first African Americans to teach in white schools in Virginia. She was the daughter of Cab Calloway, the famed entertainer and bandleader. In 1978 she became the principal at Ashlawn Elementary School, where she remained until her retirement in 1993. She was one of several teachers who stimulated my love of learning in a big way.

my sister was ready to start grade school, and my parents deemed it too expensive to send us both to Burgundy Farm. So to be fair, we were both sent to public school in Washington. I was, to say the least, not happy. In fact, I was furious and full of resentment toward my parents and my sister. I was leaving my friends and a very familiar situation for something new and I was not amused.

What I learned then and what I have come to know about myself very well is that I am by nature a creature of habit and oh so resistant to change. This change at such a young age was seismic. But what I also began very slowly to learn is that in life one must adapt or die. At public school I was being teased constantly for speaking well and for loving learning. This torture, along with the fact that I was in a different and sometimes hostile environment, was definitely impinging on my love of learning.

Eventually, I came to realize that I was better and smarter than my tormentors and that I would just have to establish some long-term goals to ignore those people and, in some cases, the teachers who were giving me a hard time. By middle school, things had changed somewhat, and there were a couple of great teachers whom I not only looked up to but who also inspired me.

In 1966 in the sartorially barren wasteland that was known as Washington, DC, there arose a phoenix on the Potomac that would challenge this conservative three-button sack coat town. It was called the Georgetown Slack Shoppe. Created by David Pensky and Rick Hindin, it was, for a fashion-starved teenager, simply nirvana. Everything about it was of quality and, although primarily bottoms were sold, I fondly remember my very first purchase, a pair of heavy wool, dark hunter-green trousers that I wore to death. Future purchases included flared bottom bois-de-rose corduroy pants and a treasured maroon leather motocross jacket with an asymmetric zipper.

The next year, the owners opened a new, larger emporium just down the block on Wisconsin Avenue. It was called Britches of Georgetowne. The store offered tailored clothing, dress furnishings, sportswear, footwear, and antique jewelry. Everything was housed in beautiful vintage display cases that were mounted on pale sage-colored carpets with brass-trimmed lighting. It was elegant and modern, and I was astonished. From the moment I first entered the store, I knew I was never going to shop anywhere else.

In addition to its many different resources from Italy and France, Britches was one of the very first stores in the country to carry Polo by Ralph Lauren—initially just ties and shirts. I had read all about Ralph Lauren in *Daily News Record*—the bible newspaper of menswear, the brother of *Women's Wear Daily* and *Gentleman's Quarterly*. I really loved the Ralph Lauren point of view about dressing men, especially its wide, luxuriously fabricated neckwear.

On one of my first shopping excursions alone to Britches, I spotted what I deemed to be one of the most beautiful ties I had ever seen. It was a navy and maroon regimental tapestry weave punctuated by thin white stripes and intricate white snowflakelike designs. I had to have it. I proudly carried out my treasure and when I returned home was questioned by my father as to what I had purchased. "It's a Polo tie," I said, carefully unwrapping it to show it to him.

"That's a nice tie," he said. "How much did you pay for it?" "Twenty-five dollars," I said proudly.

"TWENTY-FIVE DOLLARS!!!" He exclaimed: "A Countess Mara tie is $5; that's an expensive tie! Take it back!"

I replied, "No, I love it."

His retort was, "You don't have $25 worth of neck, so take it back!" Of course, I refused.

Thereafter, whenever I needed an article of clothing, much to my parents' dismay, I headed to Britches. The fact that it was probably

MEN'S WEAR

A FAIRCHILD PUBLICATION JULY 26, 1974 $1.00
THIS ISSUE IN TWO SECTIONS SECTION I

THESE MEN ARE THE TALK OF THE 'TOWNE'

Retail Issue Featuring
MRA Annual Business Survey

TENNIS AT 100 YEARS

OPPOSITE Rick Hindin and Dave Pensky who, along with the assistant manager Danny Latham, took a chance on a fashion-obsessed 15-year-old teenager and, in the process, changed the trajectory of my life.

OVERLEAF A glimpse inside the unique, original Britches store offers the look of its antique display cases, brass fittings, endless mirrors, eau-de-Nil carpeting, and luxurious haberdashery. I thought it was one of the most beautiful spaces I had ever seen and I literally couldn't wait to go to work every Saturday.

the most expensive men's store in Washington did not deter me. One day after school, I was browsing the new arrivals at Britches when Danny Latham, the assistant manager, came up to me and said, "I've seen you in here before. I think you must be one of our youngest shoppers. How old are you? 18?"

I replied, "No, I'm 15!" Latham added: "Wow! I am going to let you in on a little secret. We are going to open a second Britches location next year." I said that I already knew that it would be on Connecticut Avenue in the old Saks Pasternak building. "How the hell did you know that?" he asked.

"I read it in *DNR*. I've had a subscription since I was 12!"

Instantly, he exclaimed, "Would you like to come work for us?"

I excitedly said, "YES," and that very Saturday I started my very first job, as a salesman at Britches. I was beyond elated.

Although I had never held any kind of job before, except for doing chores around the house, I was unbelievably excited to be working at Britches. All of the other salespersons were in their twenties and thirties. I, however, was being paid a straight salary but I didn't care. I was having so much fun waiting on men with their wives and/or girlfriends, putting together combinations of shirts and ties and learning about the stock in the store. On that first Saturday, I was having so much fun that I truly lost track of time and suddenly became very hungry, and asked Danny if I might go out for lunch.

"Jeffrey," he said, "it's five minutes to six. We are closing soon. What have you been doing?" I said, "I was having fun." It was at that point that I learned of an everyday ritual at Britches. Each salesperson's sales were totaled and the person who achieved "high book," or the highest dollar figure in sales, got a perk or small bonus. I was shocked when I found out that I had beaten these established sales associates. It was then that I learned an important life lesson: How to make friends with people who might hate your guts. I took pains to explain to the other salespersons, especially Natasha, the ravishing Russian brunette who could wrap a man around her little finger just with her gaze, that I was only part-time—initially, only on Saturday. Exhilarated, I felt that next Saturday could not come fast enough.

Eventually, I added Thursday evenings to my after-school work schedule and became very friendly with John Ablon, Mark Snyder, Michael Zeitlin, and Robert Marin, all of whom worked at the store. I truly loved working there and amassed a great list of clients who only wanted to work with me. Nothing pleased me more than when a wife or girlfriend said, "I don't know what you did before, but please do it again. He's never looked so good."

By my second year at Britches, I was so established that Rick and David thought that I should be transferred to the brand-new store on Connecticut Avenue, which was even more opulent and dramatic

with its grand staircase, mezzanine, and mirrored dressing rooms. I worked full-time in the summer, as well as on Saturdays and after school during the school year. One day, a casually dressed Black man came into the store and my fellow salesmen eyed him up and down as not really a potential sale and backed away from him. I took the initiative, went right up, and introduced myself, asking if I could help him. "I'm Earnie," he said, "and I am looking for an alternative to a tuxedo, as I have to attend many black-tie affairs." I proffered that Ralph Lauren had just introduced a velvet evening suit. It came in black, brown, navy, and bottle green. Earnie tried on the size 38 regular in the black, and it fit him perfectly. He then asked to try on the brown. It was the same thing as I spied the other salespersons rolling their eyes thinking I was clearly wasting my time. Subsequently, after trying on the remaining two colors with similar perfect fit results, Earnie exclaimed, "I'll take them all." As I rang up the enormous sale that included several different tuxedo shirts, I asked Earnie what he did for a living. "I am a Secret Service agent at the White House," he said. Lesson learned. Never judge a book by its cover.

OPPOSITE I was looking somber and serious in my McKinley Technology Senior High School yearbook picture. I was probably not smiling because my braces had yet to be removed.

Since childhood, I had always been proud of two things: first, that I was a daily member of the clean plate club—without which, I would get no dessert—and second, that I had perfect attendance in elementary school, junior high school, and high school. Even when I was sick or not feeling well, I begged my parents to let me attend school so as not to blemish my perfect record. However all this was about to change on Friday, February 13, 1970. That was the day I found out that Ralph Lauren was coming to Washington for a Red Cross Valentine's Day fashion show. I was bound and determined to meet him. I told my parents that I was not going to be attending school that day and that they should write a note making some excuse, because I was going to meet Ralph Lauren. They ended up writing a note saying that I had an all-day orthodontist appointment. Off I went to my part-time job at Britches. I got to the store early, dressed head-to-toe in Polo: burgundy double-breasted blazer, grey flannel trousers, equestrian-print necktie, and brown suede kiltie shoes.

David Pensky and Rick Hindin, the owners of Britches, noticed my early arrival, asking me if I had my driver's license yet. As a matter of fact, I had only received it a month or so beforehand. "Here," they said, handing me the keys to the company station wagon. "Go pick Ralph up at the airport."

OPPOSITE I was photographed with Mom on Mother's Day, wearing one of the early Ralph Lauren ties that incorporated the polo player logo.

I answered, "Are you kidding me?" They were not, so off I went to National Airport. Halfway there, the car rumbled to a stop. I realized that I had a flat tire, and panic set in. What the hell did I know about fixing a flat, and did I even have a spare in the car? Fortunately for me, there was a spare in the car, and as I stood by the side of the road, I was able to flag down another motorist who helped me change the tire.

By now I was late, and even though it was February, I was *schvitz*ing. Luckily for me—my second save of the day—Mr. Lauren's—that's what I called him initially—plane was late, too, and the Eastern Airlines shuttle landed just as I got to the airport. Mr. Lauren, accompanied by Joe Barrato, his vice president of sales, was not in a good mood. As gifts for David and Ricky, they had brought framed silk scarves with mounted polo players printed by Ratti in Italy. They had wanted to bring the aluminum-framed scarves on board with them, but Eastern Airlines insisted that they check them as baggage. The result was that the frames broke, and the broken glass shredded the scarves, ruining them completely. I spent the entire car ride from the airport telling every joke I knew to lighten the mood.

When we arrived at the store, I had lots of time to talk to the man I had idolized since purchasing that first jacquard silk tie. He asked me what I wanted to do as a career, and I said that I wanted to be a fashion designer like him. We talked about Fred Astaire, Cary Grant, Grace Kelly, and the Duke of Windsor. And when I told him that I wanted to go to design school in New York, he said, "When you come to New York to look at schools give me a call, I might have a job for you." Well, that was all I needed to hear. That one sentence kept me going for an entire year, in the hope that one day I might work for Ralph Lauren.

Very early on a warm summer July morning in Washington, my father and I loaded up the car with what seemed to be all my worldly possessions—lots of books, magazines, records, a television, a stereo, and clothes, lots and lots of them. The car was so chock-a-block with all my stuff that my sister had to stay home because there was no room for her in the car.

I cannot tell you the excitement I was feeling at that very moment. Although I had just graduated from high school three weeks earlier, I wasn't the least bit homesick about leaving Washington, not one damn bit. New York was beckoning, and I was its willing suitor. The long drive went very quickly for me, with my father taking the wheel

LEFT This photograph shows a view of the quaint and welcoming campus of Pratt Institute in Brooklyn, New York. It is particularly wedded to the surrounding neighborhood with its historic brownstones and sheltering trees.

and my mother sitting silently, sewing identification labels into all my clothes. I didn't have the heart to tell her that I did not think any of my classmates would have Polo by Ralph Lauren clothes. I still recall the Carpenters singing "Close to You" on the radio as we crossed into New Jersey. When we finally arrived at the Pratt Institute in Brooklyn, I found out that the dorm room I had rented for the summer was indeed a three-bedroom apartment on the fourth floor that I now had all to myself. My parents were a lot less thrilled. My mother thought the bathroom was disgusting and immediately set about scrubbing it from top to bottom. She continued with the kitchen, including the refrigerator, before a visit to the local grocery store to stock up. My father decided that what I really needed was a toolkit and set out to find the nearest hardware store. I tried to persuade him that the superintendent at the dorm building could take care of emergencies, but he would not hear of me not having my own tools.
Finally, I realized it was about 4:30pm, and they were still there fussing about. I said, half jokingly, "Don't you people have a home to go to?" My mother, who is most definitely not the crying type, burst into tears and I suddenly realized what a difficult transition this was for her, so I tried to console her as they prepared to finally depart to go back to Washington. As the car slowly pulled out of the semicircular driveway, I walked quickly in the opposite direction

RIGHT My college colleague Leland Neff did this beautiful pen-and-ink drawing of the Pratt campus.

toward the subway and the beginning of my Manhattan adventure. I got onto the subway full of high hopes and a little bit of anxiety as to which trains to catch, I realized that I had made a big mistake as I ended up somewhere in Queens and not in the desired Manhattan. Luckily, a fellow rider on the platform took pity on me and told me which train I needed to take to get to Midtown. Who says New Yorkers aren't kind? Following his instructions to the letter, I soon emerged at 57th Street and Sixth Avenue—learning a bit later that Sixth Avenue and Avenue of the Americas are one and the same. Halfway up the stairs to the street with rush-hour pedestrians passing by, I spied an older man sprawled across the steps as if he were sleeping. I moved closer and saw that there was a pool of blood around him and an aged woman bent over him, begging him to wake up. All the while, the passersby seemed unfazed and kept going without even glancing down. I quickly approached the woman and told her not to move him at all. I took his wrist and detected a faint pulse. I told her to stay with him, and I would go find help. Racing up the remaining steps I ran up and down Sixth Avenue until I found a policeman, explained the situation as he called for backup and an ambulance, and we ran back to the subway. I waited for what seemed like an eternity for the ambulance to come and take away the man and his wife, as the police questioned me, while the bystanders ogled. The thought that blared through my head was . . . Welcome to New York!

II. TAKING ON NEW YORK

On a chilly March day in 1971, my mother and I arrived to look at colleges in New York. Our first foray was to Brooklyn to see the Pratt Institute and its campus. Though it was my second choice, the Pratt Institute had a very amiable atmosphere bustling with students and a collegial vibe. I was very impressed that the dorm facilities were two full-size apartment buildings on Willoughby Avenue, directly across the street from the school. The school definitely fit my idea of what a college campus should look and feel like. Not so for Parsons School of Design, my first choice, located at the time on several floors of an office building on East 54th Street in Manhattan. It was a bit of a visual letdown as the Fashion Department was incredibly overcrowded with students who were literally cutting out their projects on the floor in front of the elevators. With no campus or dormitories to speak of, the student handbook suggested that freshmen should live at the YMCA for the first month or so until they made friends with classmates and then look to rent an apartment together. Given that Parsons was as expensive as it was, and also the fact that my mother was not keen on her 17-year-old son living at the Y for a month, I knew I faced an uphill battle in parental approval of Parsons. I decided not to do my normal push for my first choice because I had something much more exciting pending.

The next day, March 17, was my appointment to speak with Ralph Lauren about a part-time job. I was so very excited that not only I but also my mother had forgotten that it was St. Patrick's Day. Coming from the East Side, we had to cross through the parade at Fifth Avenue to get to the Polo offices. On a typical New York spring day, the previously chilly weather had blossomed into balmy spring. I was wearing an outfit I had planned for weeks, a camel's hair bi-swing back sports coat, tic-weave Harris tweed trousers, a shirt and tie, a canvas tartan-lined raincoat, and brown-suede kiltie shoes . . . all by Ralph Lauren, of course. And I was *schvitz*ing! At the building entrance, I instructed my mother to go to Bonwit Teller, and I would meet her in the Safari Room in an hour's time. "Oh, no," she said, "I have to meet this Ralph Lauren. I can't have you working for someone I don't know!"

I retorted, "Mom, I am going on a job interview, and you are *NOT* going with me, you are going to Bonwit's." The two of us stood there for a few moments arguing until I suddenly turned, entered the building, and left my mother standing outside.

I took the elevator to the fifth-floor reception area, and the receptionist, who was ensconced behind her desk with the famous blue-and-white china bowl filled with M&Ms, asked me to be seated and said

OPPOSITE Ralph Lauren was photographed in the Polo offices at 40 West 55th Street in New York, where it all began.

BONWIT
TELLER

OPPOSITE The now-gone Bonwit Teller department store, which was located in New York on Fifth Avenue and 56th Street, was an elegant emporium of good taste, with great Art Deco lines. In 1971 I told my mother to take refuge there while I interviewed with Ralph Lauren.

that Mr. Lauren would be down in a few minutes. She gestured to a denim-covered loveseat where I noticed that a very attractive Black man was already seated. As I took my seat next to him, I took a closer look. "Aren't you Bobby Short?" I gasped.

"Why yes, I am," he said happily as I think he was thrilled to be recognized, especially by one so young. We began to converse, quite animatedly. It seemed that Mr. Short had come for a new tuxedo fitting for his engagement at the Café Carlyle, and then, all of a sudden, there was Ralph Lauren standing in front of us.

"Jeffrey, have you met Bobby?" he said.

"Why, we are old friends," Bobby said.

I said a quick goodbye to my new "old" friend as Mr. Lauren whisked me up one floor to his office. Using a large vintage pine table in front of the window as his desk, Ralph gestured for me to sit opposite him as I held my small, newly purchased portfolio filled with fashion sketches at my side. We proceeded to pick up where we had left off a year ago, discussing our mutual love of Fred Astaire, Audrey Hepburn, Katharine Hepburn, and Cary Grant. It was as if two like-minded people were discussing quantum theory but, instead, we talked of fashion and film. We were so deep in conversation that I lost all sense of time. Suddenly I glanced at my watch and realized we had been speaking for an hour and a half and I had yet to even open up my portfolio. I suddenly realized that my poor mother probably thought I was dead or that some other misfortune had befallen me. Fortunately, we had discussed, albeit briefly, the possibilities of my school schedule and working part time. "Mr. Lauren, I really have to go and meet my mother now," I said, somewhat sheepishly.

"I will call you within two weeks to let you know if you have the job," he said, reassuringly.

I hastily took my leave and practically flew the block and a half to Bonwit's to find my mother, who was calmly waiting for me in the Safari Room at the store. A sigh of relief swept over me that she was neither angry nor worried about me and, as we departed New York on the bus from Port Authority, a feeling of euphoria swept over me. I felt my dream of coming to New York and working for Ralph Lauren might actually be coming true.

After two years of working for Ralph Lauren and attending Pratt, I decided I needed to be more challenged in school if I was going to remain there so I made the decision to transfer to Parsons School of Design.

Once I had made the decision to leave Pratt Institute and go to the Parsons School of Design, I was sure that I definitely wanted to live in my own apartment. Surprisingly, I got no pushback from my parents—especially my father. He had one proviso: he would pay for an apartment as long as the rent was $400 a month or less. The only problem was that the apartment I found on 16th Street, three blocks away from school, was $414 a month, and my father was not about to budge on the amount. I decided to invite my parents up for the weekend to schmooze them and try to change their minds. I took them to the Metropolitan Museum, two Broadway shows, and finally the Café Carlyle on Saturday night to see Bobby Short. Bobby did two shows a night, and we had reservations for the second one. Arriving just as he was finishing the first show, we waited to be seated and, while Bobby was playing his final number, he looked up from the piano, saw us, and gave a quick wave. Of course, I returned his wave with my mother whispering to me, "Who are you waving at?"

I said, "Why Bobby, of course."

She exclaimed, "You don't know Bobby Short!" as he quickly finished and exited to thunderous applause.

"Yes, Mom, I do," I said, as the waiter showed us to our table right next to Bobby's piano, an indication that I had some pull in the place. My father, who never drank a drop of liquor, ordered his customary root beer, and my mother ordered her regular scotch, neat. "It's awful dark in here," said my father, tourist camera with a long lens hanging prominently around his neck.

"Dad," I said, "it's a nightclub. It's called atmosphere, just drink your root beer!" Suddenly, a waiter appeared out of nowhere with a jeroboam of champagne.

"Did you order that?" my mother asked anxiously.

"No," I replied. "Bobby must have sent it over."

My mother then repeated in an alarmed voice, "You don't know Bobby Short!" At that moment, she received a small tap on her shoulder and, turning around, there stood Bobby, grinning wildly.

"Why you must be Mrs. Banks!" he said. Watching my parents melt under Bobby's gaze was a real pleasure, to be followed by the joy of hearing him perform so splendidly close up, and then pose endlessly for my father's camera at the end of the show. As we stood on Madison Avenue, and I tried to hail a cab for them to go back to their hotel, my father turned to me and said, "How much is that apartment, again?" I said, excitedly, "$414!" And, with a short okay, the apartment was mine. Monday morning I called Bobby to tell him that he had gotten me my very first apartment.

OPPOSITE High atop Manhattan, as well he should be, Bobby Short sits at his piano with the Chrysler Building looming large behind him.

HIRSCHFELD

OPPOSITE Al Hirschfeld was for decades the documentarian in illustration of all things artistic in New York. His take on Bobby Short, the "king of Café Society," has the subject at his beloved piano.

It is sad to me that many young people today have no idea who the great Bobby Short was. I remember first experiencing him as a child on the *Today Show* where he seemed to croon the American Songbook standards several times a year. He helped me develop my love for George and Ira Gershwin.

The great thing about Bobby was not only his delivery of songs by the Gershwins, Cole Porter, Richard Rodgers and Lorenz Hart, Irving Berlin, Harold Arlen, Billy Strayhorn, and Duke Ellington, but also the fact he knew so many of these composers personally, as well as the back stories of how so many of these songs came to be. That is why when I finally met him, when I was 17, he was already so well known to me.

Robert Waltrip Short was born in Danville, Illinois, on September 15, 1924. His childhood classmates included Donald O'Connor and Dick Van Dyke. He was a prodigy on the piano and began performing in saloons and dance halls, leaving home at the age of 11 to perform in Chicago.

Bobby became the king of New York Café Society in 1968 when he took up residence at the Café Carlyle on the Upper East Side of Manhattan. Filling in for the Carlyle regular George Feyer for a two-week stint, he quickly became a fixture at the nightclub. For New York swells wanting to cap off a glamorous evening, nothing beat sitting at the crowded little tables at Bemelmans Bar and hearing Bobby's witty interpretation of Porter's "Katie Went to Haiti" or his version of Vernon Duke's "I Can't Get Started." Accompanied by Beverly Peer on bass and Dick Sheridan on drums, every performance was unique, special, and so sophisticated. The set list varied from night to night, which made seeing Bobby live very interesting.

Bobby broke so many barriers performing not just in this country, but all over the world. Once, when I was traveling to London on the Concorde, as I was checking in, I heard a familiar voice behind me say, "Is that Jeffrey Banks I see?" It was Bobby, who was also going to London for a stint at Pizza on the Park, an unlikely name for a nightclub. He promptly invited me and my traveling companions as his guests on opening night, two days later.

As a Black man, Bobby epitomized the elegant erudite gentleman, but not even all the awards and accolades he amassed protected him from facing racism. His close friendship with the socialite and fashion designer Gloria Vanderbilt once prevented her from buying a New York apartment. Still, he was named to the International Best-Dressed List and was inducted as a laureate into the Lincoln Academy of Illinois.

I once made a few outfits—several pairs of pastel-hued pinwale corduroy trousers and a tuxedo, I believe, for him to take to his home in the South of France.

Every year at Christmastime, my friend and coauthor Doria de La Chapelle and her husband, Philippe, would, instead of exchanging gifts, treat us to dinner and a Bobby Short performance at the Café Carlyle. In August 2004, I spied on "Page Six" in the *New York Post* an item saying that Bobby, then at the age of 80, was planning to retire after his New Year's Eve performance. I immediately called the Carlyle and made a dinner reservation for the three of us for the week before Christmas.

Several months later, on the appointed date, we got all dolled up to attend Bobby's performance. Once again we were given the prized table next to the piano. We swooned and loved every minute of his performance, Doria reminding me that her parents would often take her as a young woman to see Bobby whenever they came to visit New York from their home in Springfield, Massachusetts. At the evening's end, Bobby came over to say hello and I chided him, "So Bobby, this is your swan song, right?"

He laughed heartily and said, "Don't tell me you read that 'Page Six' item?" I did, I admitted. "Nothing to it," he said, still laughing.

Little did we know that it was the last time we would see him perform, as just a few short months later, Bobby died of leukemia in March 2005, in New York.

The day he died, I raced up to the Carlyle to purchase multiple copies of his CDs for Doria and me. Bobby Short, the man I had admired for so long as a model of sophistication and a wonderful credit to his race was gone. He represented all that I wanted to become: a respected master of his craft held in high esteem by his colleagues.

OPPOSITE This is the way Barbra Streisand looked when I met her–with long, flowing hair cascading past her shoulders. The cover art by Robert Redding for her album *Live Concert at the Forum* was taken from a photograph and was originally part of the poster for "Four for McGovern," a concert that also featured Carole King, James Taylor, and Quincy Jones.

OVERLEAF In Los Angeles, on April 14, 1969, Fredrick Glaser prepped Barbra Streisand on the set of *On a Clear Day You Can See Forever* as she was getting ready to attend the Academy Awards ceremony that evening.

Once, when I was ten years old, I came home from Sunday school to a telephone call from my godfather, Louis Christophe. He implored me not to miss the *Ed Sullivan Show* that evening—there was a singer he wanted me to see who he knew I would just love. Boy, was he right. Barbra Streisand opened her mouth to sing, "When the Sun Comes Out," and I was instantly smitten.

I was enchanted with everything about Barbra—her looks, her voice, her manner. And being the obsessive kid that I was, I immediately wanted to know everything about her and hear and own every record she had ever made. Soon thereafter came her television specials, *My Name Is Barbra*, *Color Me Barbra*, *A Happening in Central Park*,

Barbra
Streisand
Live
Concert At The Forum
featuring
Sweet Inspiration / Where You Lead &
Sing / Make Your Own Kind Of Music

and the albums that accompanied them. Still later came Richard Avedon spreads in *Vogue* and the *Life* magazine cover stories. I was, as far as I was concerned, her number one fan.

Much later, in fall 1972, I was now working for Ralph Lauren, and we launched his first full women's collection. One of the first stores to pick up the collection was Henri Bendel. To launch the collection, Bendel's gave Ralph both of their semi-curved windows on 57th Street. Bob Currie, the genius window and display director at the store, fashioned an intriguing display that, like most of his windows, told a witty story. In the left-facing window was a pantsuit-wearing mannequin facing the wall with her back to us. The lighting was focused on two things: her fingers, with their chipped nail polish, and the floor, with the remains of said nail polish. If you looked closely, you would also notice that the wallpaper had been strategically shredded right beside the mannequin. In the right-side window were several haughty female mannequins, also clad in Ralph Lauren man-tailored pantsuits. They stood in front of a carved wooden bar, looking askance at the solitary facing mannequin. Standing behind the bar was a lone male mustachioed mannequin in a white shirt and black bowtie. Gazing at the windows for a few minutes, it suddenly hit me what was happening. The setting was a lesbian bar and the single lady had been spurned by the others, taking out her frustration by raking her nails against the bar's wallpaper. It was very racy and very funny, too!

A couple of days after the windows were installed, Barbra Streisand, who was in town for some voice rerecordings and meetings, passed by the windows, and, intrigued by them, wandered inside Bendel's. She fell in love with the clothes, but there was only one problem, they didn't quite fit her. Somehow, she got the office number and called, asking if Ralph Lauren might indeed make custom clothes for her. Needless to say, Ralph was over the moon! It was his very first full women's collection, and Barbra Streisand wanted some things. Of course she could come up to the office! Calls were made, and it was agreed that Barbra would arrive that Saturday at 40 West 55th Street at 10am. Very quickly word got out among our very small office staff that Barbra Streisand was coming on Saturday morning. And just as quickly, everyone it seemed had such an increased workload that it was imperative that they come into the office on Saturday. By Thursday afternoon, Ralph had to issue an edict that only Buffy Birrittella and I could come into the office on Saturday.

On Saturday, Ralph and his wife Ricky, Buffy, and I were in early, anxiously awaiting Ms. Streisand. The hour of engagement came and went, and then about 45 minutes past the arranged time, there was a knock at the door. Ralph told me to answer it, and there stood Barbra Streisand replete with a *Rosemary's Baby*-type of haircut. Now you must remember this was the early 1970s when Barbra wore her bone straight hair parted in the middle, cascading way past her shoulders. As soon as they were introduced, virtually the first thing Ralph said to Barbra was, "I can't believe you cut your beautiful hair!" Of course, being the little *wisenheimer* and tremendous Barbra fan that I was, I knew immediately that Barbra was wearing a wig, but far be it from me to burst her bubble. I could tell Barbra was enjoying fooling everyone but me. Ralph, however, bereft at the presumed loss of Streisand's lovely locks, would not let up until finally, he said, "You look like a Hadassah lady!" With that, Barbra, somewhat annoyed, ripped the wig off, her attractive tresses tumbling down. The tension was so thick you could cut it with a knife. I instantly thought that I needed to change the mood right away. So I suddenly exclaimed, "Barbra, I remember when you first cut your hair in 1965 at the Frederick Glaser salon in Chicago."

She suddenly brightened up and said in her best Mae West-like imitation, "Oh, this boy, he knows everything about me." From that moment on we were best buddies, and not long afterward, I found myself in the dressing room, taking Barbra Streisand's measurements, as she stood before me in her bra and panties. And I will tell you this, she had the most beautiful skin I had ever seen on a human being—not a blemish, mole, or freckle. Her flesh was almost translucent, like fine Limoges porcelain. She also had a gorgeous chest and shoulders, and long, long thin legs.

When Barbra emerged for Ralph's inspection, I had dressed her in not only the samples we had on hand, but also the accessories we had used at the fashion show—sweater knit hat, and boots from Shoe Biz at Bendel's. Ralph took note of what Barbra wanted, and she changed back into her own clothes. Ralph asked Barbra if she was hungry, and she said she was. She eagerly asked me if I knew McDonald's. In 1972 there were only two McDonald's restaurants in Manhattan of which I was aware. One was a drive-through at 34th Street and 10th Avenue that was only recently demolished, and one was on Second Avenue in the East 60s. "I'd like a Big Mac, fries, and a strawberry shake," Barbra said. I took everyone else's orders and jumped in a cab to go to Second Avenue. I bade the driver to wait while I quickly ran inside, giving him a big $5 extra incentive to do so. When I returned with lunch, a much more relaxed Barbra polished off not only her order, but also half of mine. Going back to her hair, it seems that she had been wanting a different look for an upcoming film. A girlfriend had suggested that she consult with a hairdresser, who had proposed that she try out the short-haired wig as opposed to cutting her hair outright. His name was Jon Peters, and the rest, as they say, is history.

The morning moved swiftly into the late afternoon and La Streisand realized that she was running late for her tennis lesson. She asked me to call and let them know she was on her way and to call her chauffeur to pick her up. I packed up the accessories Barbra had worn; Buffy went into the bathroom to retrieve Barbra's coat and the much-maligned wig. In her haste, she had accidentally dropped the wig in the toilet so she emerged with the wet hairpiece wrapped in a terrycloth towel. This time, however, laughter rang out and Barbra was a very good sport about the mishap. As her car had arrived, and she was saying her goodbyes, I offered to escort Barbra downstairs and I helped her into the car and closed the door. She rolled down her window, crooked her finger at me, and as I leaned over, she kissed me lightly on the cheek. Needless to say, a certain schoolboy's fantasy had been duly fulfilled.

OPPOSITE Kenneth Battelle, known as Mr. Kenneth, was photographed tending to Marilyn Monroe's platinum locks. The movie star was just one of the many celebrated heads he coiffed that included Kay Graham, Jacqueline Kennedy Onassis, Brooke Astor, and Audrey Hepburn.

A few short weeks after joining Ralph Lauren, I found that going to Bloomingdale's several times a week was one of the aspects of the job I loved the most. It was almost like being a junior divisional to make sure the Polo Shop on the first floor was in tip-top shape. I am sure the salespersons grew weary of this tiresome teenager continually saying, "Mr. Lauren doesn't like it that way!" about the arrangement or outfitting of the mannequins. Ralph loved it when I reported back to him about how the Polo Shop looked.

One Saturday afternoon, as the summer sale of spring merchandise started, I surveyed the bargain hunters as they perused what was left in the department. I spotted someone I recognized immediately—Mr. Kenneth, the world-famous hairdresser who coiffed the heads of both Jacqueline Kennedy Onassis and Marilyn Monroe. I went over to him to offer my help as he fondled a white jacquard cotton shirt with playing-card motifs. I knew the shirt well, since I owned one myself. "I see you seem to like that shirt a lot," I said.

"Yes, it's quite lovely," Kenneth said.

"Let me show you the perfect tie to go with it," I said, as I scurried to find the navy tie with matching colored card motifs that would complement the shirt. The tie was not on sale, it was $25, but the shirt, which had been $35, was reduced to $27.50. Kenneth agreed the shirt and tie combo was terrific. But handing me back the tie, he took one more long lingering look at the shirt and then replaced it on the sales table saying, "I think it's a little rich for my blood, but thank you so much for your help." As he walked away, I carefully made note of his shirt size.

First thing Monday morning, I called Bruno at our warehouse in Chelsea and asked him to please send me the aforementioned shirt and matching tie in a navy-blue Polo shirt box. I then wrote a letter that said, in part:

> *Dear Mr. Battelle,*
> *I think it a shame for anyone who is such a fan of Mr. Lauren's work not to have the perfect shirt and tie combination.*
> *Please accept these with my compliments,*
> *Jeffrey Banks*
> *Assistant to Ralph Lauren*

I messengered the box and letter to Kenneth's salon at 19 East 54th Street. A few days later, a letter arrived at the office addressed to Ralph. Mr. Kenneth somewhat sheepishly apologized for what he said was his cheapness in not buying the shirt outright. He was astonished that Mr. Lauren's young assistant actually knew his last name, but he nonetheless thanked him profusely for the gift.

Ralph called me into his office to dress me down, "Who gave you the authority to send a free shirt and tie to him?" he asked. I stood my ground, "It's the greatest PR ever," I said. "He will be wearing your clothes while working on all the best society ladies in New York—Pat Buckley, Annette Reed, Mica Ertegun, Chessy Rayner, and Jackie Kennedy Onassis. They are all going to go home and tell their husbands to buy your clothes. After a moment, Ralph had to concede that I was right, and that it had been a smart move. I was absolved. I guess reading all those *Glamour*s and *Vogue*s had paid off.

OPPOSITE Mr. Kenneth's legendary five-story salon, in a 17,000-square-foot brownstone on Manhattan's East 54th Street, was designed by the interior decorator Billy Baldwin and dramatically tented with thousands of yards of opulent fabric.

I was very familiar with this Renaissance man from a very early age. I knew that he had gone to the Parsons School of Design in New York when he was 16 years old. I also knew that, upon graduating, he had an enormous contract with Revlon to create one-off looks to be used in their advertising. Eventually, Joel Schumacher became the window designer at Henri Bendel. Unfortunately, he fell into a pattern of drugs and disco that became very problematic for him.

I was quite surprised that the man I had just met was so completely candid with the teenager who was helping him dress George Segal for the film *Blume in Love*. Joel told me that with drug dealers in hot pursuit, he had escaped to California from New York with the hope of breaking into the movie industry. Falling asleep in the early morning on a deserted beach in Los Angeles, he awoke hours later to see a couple on a blanket nearby. The couple introduced themselves as Frank and Eleanor. When they asked Joel what he was doing in Los Angeles, he told them he wanted, as a former designer, to break into costume design in the movies. As it turned out, the couple was Frank and Eleanor Perry, the great filmmaker and screenwriter husband-and-wife duo, and they were seeking a costume designer for their film *Play It As It Lays*. And the rest, as they say, is history.

Joel Schumacher very quickly rose from being simply a costume and production designer to an extremely successful film director with films including *Sparkle*, *St. Elmo's Fire*, *The Lost Boys*, and *Batman Forever*. However, in all the ensuing years, with the big highs and considerable lows of the film industry, Joel maintained a wonderful friendship with me. I will never forget that, years after he had achieved great success as one of Hollywood's go-to directors, he spied me across the plaza at Lincoln Center and literally ran across it to greet me. Another time, after he had left California to move back to New York, I spotted him on 17th Street and yelled "Hello!" as he

OPPOSITE A young Joel Schumacher squired the actress and model Marisa Berenson to yet another black-tie affair.

darted between moving cars just to cross and embrace me. Joel maintained his lean, lanky physique and was always handsomely dressed, even when he just wore jeans, which were always adorned with his collection of turquoise and silver jewelry.

Joel was an anomaly in Hollywood of the 1970s, an openly gay man who was respected not only for who he was, but for his ability to deliver commercial vehicles for the studios that hired him. He was responsible for launching the careers of Colin Farrell, Demi Moore, and Kiefer Sutherland. I always admired him for conquering the dual demons of drugs and alcohol and rising above them to creative heights. I found Joel to be exactly the same kind and funny man at the end of his life as he was when I first met him decades earlier. Sadly, we lost Joel just a few short years ago, but he left an indelible mark on me about what it is to conquer, survive, and ultimately thrive.

When I decided to make my big switch from Pratt Institute to Parsons School of Design, it was a major change for me. First of all, the chair of the department, Ann Keagy, decreed that I must attend classes every day from 9am to 2:30pm. That meant no more school only two days a week as when I had attended Pratt. After 2:30pm, my life was my own, and I would hop on the subway and race uptown to go to work at Polo. On many days that meant working from 3pm to 10pm or later, going home to do schoolwork, getting a few hours of sleep, and then, going back to school all over again. Often, that routine would be shortened, as we might be preparing for a show, so my time for homework and sleep might be decreased by hours. After about six months, I found myself falling asleep at school and/or at work, which was definitely not good, not good at all. Enter Frank Rizzo, my teacher at Parsons. Frank was a former Parsons student himself, who was a successful bridal designer, and took a special interest in my plight. I was on the verge of leaving school. "After all," said Ralph, "the whole reason to go to school is to get the kind of job you already have." It was hard to argue with that reasoning, but I was really torn between that and the fact that I had so little time left before getting my degree.

I spoke to my parents and they were okay with whatever decision I made, though I was sure that they secretly wanted me to stay in school and graduate. Frank Rizzo's wise and careful counsel led me to finally make my decision to stay in school. Frank's gentle but firm advice was laced with humor, which made him a favorite with all the students in my class. But I think the quality of his that really resonated with me was that he truly cared about each and every student in the class. That interest was so important because the chair of the department was not exactly cut from the caring cloth. Keagy was a strict educator who was pretty inflexible when it came to her version of a Parsons fashion design education. It was definitely her way or the highway. She was the exact opposite of today's "woke" educators. She always favored boys in her classes, and her descriptions of certain students as "Yellows" and "Blacks" would certainly get her dismissed from today's academic world. Keagy disliked me from day one because I was not beholden to her for a job, as I already had one. She resented seeing me at the black-tie industry events she attended and then in class in jeans the very next morning. Frank was the sympathetic buffer between the students and Keagy's militaristic reign. You could discuss everything with him, from your love life to the fact you were out of funds for school supplies. He was always there for you, and it was Frank, who we alternately called "Riz" or "Rizzo," whom listened and advised you as to what to do.

Frank carefully laid out all my options and in his own quiet way, convinced me to finish school. My respect and admiration for him in helping me grew in spades. Although I was happy with my choice, Ralph was not, because it involved quitting my job with him and concentrating solely on school. When I told him about my decision it was very difficult because I think he took it as a betrayal of sorts, since Ralph had always said I was like another son to him. I was very despondent and, despite Rizzo's counseling, I began to doubt if I had done the right thing.

A couple months after quitting, I was in class one morning and a very displeased Keagy entered, saying to me "Calvin Klein is on the phone for you in my office." As I left my stunned classmates and followed Keagy into her office, I picked up the receiver to speak with him. Somehow, it seemed Calvin had heard that I was no longer working for Ralph and wanted to hire me. I knew Calvin only slightly from being at some of the same social events and decided to enrage Keagy by trading on our familiarity. I said loudly that I couldn't possibly work for him as I was now a full-time student. Calvin did not take no for an answer, and he urged me to have lunch with him the next day at Bill's to discuss his offer. I agreed to meet him the next day as a chagrined Keagy heard me bid him goodbye.

Bill's was the fashion world's version of Sardi's, where designers grabbed a quick lunchtime meal in the garment center on 40th Street or savored their scotches as they reviewed the comings and goings of the rag business after work. Like at Sardi's, designers sat in booths under framed and signed press kit photographs of themselves, after being greeted by name by Sis Kantrankowitz, the owner. I knew about Bill's but this was my first time there when I met Calvin Klein

OPPOSITE Frank Rizzo in his role as both teacher and fashion chair was captured in a critique session at Parsons.

OVERLEAF LEAF I sketched my sophisticated take on a child's jumper dress that was done in a Donegal tweed lined with a challis foulard print.

OVERLEAF RIGHT My menswear project at Parsons was a mix of a corded Indian cotton jacket, a multi-textured striped T-shirt, and polished cotton drawstring pajama pants, all in shades of ivory. John Weitz was my design critic, and his only comment was that I needed to sign my sketches "bigger."

Gladstone
red
black knee socks
7½
J. BANKS — JR. HIGH — DRESSES
95

18
39

SAGA— J. BANKS "SISAL" MINK REVERSE TO DONEGAL TWEED

OPPOSITE This is my sketch of my prize-winning Parsons SAGA reversible Donegal tweed/mink jacket.

RIGHT The knit trim on the finished mink jacket was made to resemble tweed and match the coloration of the mink skins.

on my lunch break from school. He was beyond charming as he tried to convince me to come and work for him. Although I was hugely flattered, I was just as resolute that school was my most important job. As we finished lunch, Calvin urged me to cross Seventh Avenue and come up to see his showroom. He had recently expanded from designing coats and suits into a full sportswear range, and he was eager to show me his efforts. As I entered 205 West 39th Street and his all-white showroom, Calvin proudly displayed his sportswear separates, blouses, gabardine pants, leather jackets, and skirts. He held up a tic-weave four-panel gored A-line skirt and excitedly exclaimed, "This is my Harris tweed skirt."

I looked at the dark green and rust skirt and said, "Calvin, that isn't Harris tweed. It's not even 100 percent wool! What is this, wool and acrylic? Did you buy this fabric from Anglo?"

Calvin, not masking his surprise, quietly answered, "Yes, it was from Anglo, and it was wool and acrylic."

Before he could say anything else I said, "Calvin, Harris tweed is 100 percent wool, hand-woven on looms in the Outer Hebrides Islands of Scotland in 28-inch-wide widths, and that is *not* Harris tweed." Well, that sealed the deal. Now Calvin wanted me more than ever. And then he offered me the proverbial offer I couldn't refuse. He would pay me a weekly salary regardless of the time I spent in the office. I would go into the office only when I had the time, be it one day a week, only on the weekends, or five days a week. I reasoned to myself that this arrangement enabled me to keep one hand in the industry and also finish school.

Shortly after I graduated from Parsons, Keagy stepped down as the department chair of fashion, and Frank Rizzo was elevated to that position. As chair, he breathed new life into the department while maintaining most of the teaching staff and adding new talent. A few years after he took the reins of the office, he asked me to become a critic for the senior class. This involved coming in at least three times per semester to critique sketches, muslin mock-ups, and final fabric fittings. I was flattered, but after the Keagy regime, I had vowed never again to enter the halls of Parsons. Frank persisted and had me come down to school to discuss it further. I told him that I would happily write a check to the school in his honor, but to please not ask me to be a critic. "Just do it one time, for me," he pleaded. How could I say no? I revered this man and everything he had done for me so much that I had to acquiesce, but I did it very reluctantly.

When the day came, I went back to Parsons, now located on Seventh Avenue, with much trepidation. About 15 minutes into it, I was hooked. I found myself simply loving critiquing and teaching the kids and hopefully helping them not make the kinds of mistakes I had made. What I loved most about working with these budding designers was that I was trying to help their vision not mine. Over the next 13 years or so, I was so lucky to be a critic for designers such as Martin Cooper, Karen Suen, Michael Ward, Mark Badgley, and James Mischka, among so many others. Once again, Frank Rizzo saw in me something I did not see in myself: teacher.

Many years and many critique sessions later, Frank called me and asked if I could come down to the school that afternoon to discuss something important. I was available so off I went. When I got there, Frank truly surprised me by saying, "I have decided to retire." I had heard this from him several times before, and I certainly did not believe it.

"Oh, Frank, you aren't going anywhere," I replied.

"No, it's true," he said. "And that's what I want to discuss with you." I thought that he had a list of possible successors he wanted to run by me.

"So who are you thinking of?" I asked.

"Why you, of course," he answered. I suddenly had the wind knocked out of me. "You're the best teacher we have," he continued. Suddenly, I began to bawl like a baby and the waterworks would not stop. The man I so revered as a teacher, but more importantly as a friend, somehow felt I was capable of filling his enormous shoes. It took me a while to compose myself, and I told Frank that I would certainly

OVERLEAF With its time-worn pages, Frank Rizzo's Filofax silently speaks volumes about the history of the fashion industry.

think about his proposal. But I truly thought then, as now, that I had been paid the highest compliment of my life.

After much reflection and many sleepless nights, I turned Frank down, feeling I wasn't ready for the responsibility of running a department at my alma mater. Frank, in retirement, moved full-time to a small town in Tennessee with his partner, Richard Hatler, yet, we continued to speak often. Frank was my greatest cheerleader when I first decided to write books, and I was always happy to send him early copies of every volume. He was particularly happy that I decided to write about Norman Norell since he had worked for years at Parsons with Norell and was, like me, outraged that no one had written extensively about him. He became an active participant, suggesting different resources for researching my book. He was particularly pleased that I had reached out to Michael Vollbracht, his former student, to include his beautiful work in my tome.

Sadly, Frank did not live to see the publication of the book he was so very keen to see written. His death left a deep chasm that will never be filled.

A couple of years ago I received a box from Frank's widower, Richard. Carefully packed inside was Frank's address book and diary with a life's worth of students' names and addresses from before his time as chair at Parsons until his retirement. Along with it, came a note from Richard expressing that he felt there was no one more deserving than me to be the guardian of such a treasure.

JOHN BRY-SMITH
Gramercy Park Hotel
2 Lexington Avenue 10011
GR5-4320

DR. THOMAS KOWAL
4000 Gypsy Lane, Apt. 547
Philadelphia, Penn, 19144
(215)438-5058
SS# 149-20-2083
School: Philadelphia College of
Textiles & Sciences
School House Lane
Philadelphia, Penn., 19144
(215)843-9700, VI8-1300

FLORENCE EISEMAN
301 North Water Street
Milwaukee, Wisc., 53202
3 weeks in May, Sept, Jan, & 1 week
in Nov.
279-3358

ERIKA ELIAS
(MRS. BERT STAHL)
400 E56th Street
New York, N.Y., 10022
758-7916

PERRY ELLIS
575 7th Avenue
New York, N.Y., 10018
921-8500

EMBASSY GOURMET
CAROL HADDAD
1431 Broadway
New York, N.Y., 10018
354-0550

ENCORE
1132 Madison Avenue (84th St.)
New York, N.Y., 10028
TR9-2850

ARTHUR L. ENGLANDER
220 Madison Avenue
New York, N.Y.
685-9300

MR. ED ENGLISH
208 E87th Street (home)
New York, N.Y.

MRS. LEE ENNIS
136 Roosevelt Street
Garden City, L.I., N.Y., 11530
(516)FL2-4755

As a child, my life was ruled by my very regimented father. Thursday nights were grocery-store nights. My father did all the grocery shopping. Staples from one store, Safeway, with produce and meat from another, Giant. Every other Thursday, after grocery shopping and dinner, was haircut night. Off my dad and I went to Mr. Ruff's barbershop for our biweekly trim. Usually when we would get there, the one television would be set to wrestling or boxing. Much to my father's embarrassment, I would ask Mr. Ruff that the channel be changed to NBC and the *Dinah Shore Show* to see what Ms. Shore was wearing. More often than not it was Norman Norell. By the time I was in high school, my main act of rebellion was to grow my hair out in a small Afro. Rigidly maintained in a neat and fastidious fashion, I was very proud of what I considered a cutting-edge style. Flash forward a couple of years to my first week in New York after my high school graduation. As I caught my reflection in the Fifth Avenue department store windows, I was horrified at what looked back at me. My hair looked like Sly's of Sly and the Family Stone, and

LEFT BELOW I have entrusted Laurent de Louya or, as I have nicknamed him, "Monsieur de Vacances," with my greying tresses, going all the way back to my teenage years.

that is definitely not the image I wanted to project. Although I am sure my heightened anxiety exaggerated my appearance, I decided I could not go another day with all that hair. As I traversed 57th Street between Fifth and Madison Avenues on the lookout for a tonsorial parlor of some sort, I spied a second-story salon with the improbable name of Cinandre. As I meekly ventured inside, I quietly asked the receptionist if, by any chance, there was a stylist familiar with cutting Black hair. Without missing a beat, she called out the name of Laurent de Louya. This quiet French Moroccan Jew indicated, "Sure, no problem" as I was in his chair under the care of his adept haircutting skills, which used what looked like small manicure scissors. The finished haircut was sensational, and Laurent has been the only one to cut my hair ever since.

Laurent has become the go-to men's stylist for politicians, actors, dancers, and titans of industry. *New York* magazine once did a major piece on him and his celebrity clientele. But to me, Laurent is my playful, hard-working friend who years ago I dubbed "Monsieur de Vacances," because he rarely takes a day off. It has been our running joke for years. His fascinating stories about moving to Paris when he was quite young and working his way up the ladder from sweeping the floors of hair salons to running errands for Parisian mobsters for extra cash are spectacular.

We have lived life in tandem for decades, through his marriage, his children, his grandchildren, and his divorce, and several different salon addresses. On the anniversary of our 40th year, as friends with a client relationship, I surprised Laurent by showing up at his salon with a celebratory cake. I even designed a mother-of-the-bride dress for his longtime colleague and stylist Renata. I know many of his clients from friendly invitations made during salon visits and have sent several friends to him who have become long-term clients themselves. We laugh ourselves silly at every session, and he has never lost his tonsorial touch. He still cuts every hair with those little scissors.

Perry Ellis and I started our careers at precisely the same time. I think it was kismet that we ever met at all. I was a design assistant at Calvin Klein and, Charles Suppon, one of Calvin's assistants, invited me to a summer backyard cookout at the Upper West Side townhouse he shared with the interior designer John Stedila. As we were enjoying ourselves on a warm afternoon, their neighbor, whose backyard abutted theirs, was putting out his garbage.

"Hey, Perry, come here!" Charles shouted to Perry Ellis, his lanky long-haired neighbor. "I want you to meet my friend Jeffrey," Charles said cheerfully. Introductions were made, and we quickly discovered that we were from the same part of the world—Perry from Virginia and the perfect southern gentleman and me from Washington, DC—which I have never really considered a southern city.

That quick conversation became the basis for a burgeoning friendship. Perry, then working as a merchandiser at Vera, had briefly gone on a few dates with Calvin, who quickly became somewhat enamored of this guy with the quick, slightly naughty sense of humor. Finding out that Perry was fond of Rigaud Cypress candles with a very expensive piney scent that at the time were only available at Bergdorf Goodman and Henri Bendel. After one such date, Perry later told me, Calvin, in hot and heavy pursuit, sent a case of the candles from Bendel's to Perry's house. Unfortunately for Calvin, a love match was not to be. Fortunately for me, my friendship with Perry flourished.

I fondly remember going to Perry's very first show for his namesake brand that opened with football players, a marching band, and models dressed in pleated cheerleader skirts and shrunken little sweaters that spelled out P-E-R-R-Y E-L-L-I-S when the models all stood together. I was so thrilled for him, because he had single-handedly put the fun back into fashion.

Over the next few years, Perry and I spent hours together at dinners in New York or at his home on Fire Island. Once, as we sat on the rail, watching the dancers at teatime, I asked Perry to name his favorite food. He answered without hesitation, "Spare ribs!" I laughed heartily.

"What's so funny?" he asked.

"I happen to make great spare ribs," I replied. That was a big mistake on my part, as thereafter, I was summoned to Perry's house on Water Island to make them quite often. Perry had a habit of calling me late on a Saturday afternoon to come the next day and make spare ribs. The problem was that usually the calls were made way after 5pm and the Pines Pantry closed at 6pm. One Saturday, as I was poised to go to tea dance at about 5:45pm, the phone rang, and it was Perry asking me to come and make spare ribs the next day.

OPPOSITE Perry Ellis' long, lean 1920s-inspired dresses from the spring 1982 collection, which was dubbed the "Chariots of Fire" collection based on the movie score by the Greek composer Vangelis that Perry used for his show. The Bloomingdale's advertisement features models Eva Voorhees, Lisa Ryall, and Esme Marshall.

OVERLEAF This photograph offers a rare glimpse of a friend of Perry Ellis' gazing out of the window of the designer's idyllic home on Water Island, which was designed by the architect James Terrell.

OPPOSITE Perry Ellis was captured with Carrie Donovan, the style editor of the *New York Times Magazine*, who was a very early champion of his innovative work.

"You have to come," he said. "Carrie Donovan is my weekend guest, and I told her all about your ribs."

I said, "But Perry, I have less than 10 minutes to get to the store!" He then shouted, "Well, hang up now!" I remember sprinting as fast as I could to the store, arriving just in time to purchase the ribs.

The next day, I dragged everything for the almost-two-mile trek along the beach to Perry's house. Sure, I could have taken a water taxi, but in those days, the taxi was very unreliable and always time-consuming. Perry actually owned two houses, one that faced the ocean and the other, a somewhat smaller house directly behind it, where his guests usually stayed. There was a little deck that faced the bay where residents could pick up their copies of the *New York Times* that were delivered. There was just about enough room for a single deck chair. I was inside, cooking away, as Perry was outside entertaining his guests who included his assistants Jed Krascella and Patricia Pastor and, of course, Ms. Donovan.

Carrie, who had been a longtime editor at *Vogue* and *Harper's Bazaar,* was now the fashion editor at the *New York Times.* She had been among the first fashion editors to champion Perry and Donna Karan, and was extremely close with Perry. She was known for three things: her oversized black eyeglasses, booming voice, and gumball-sized pearl necklaces that she was rarely seen without. In the early 1990s, she was also known for her starring spots in Old Navy commercials.

Shortly, after sending out the first batch of ribs, Perry raced back into the kitchen. "Jeffrey, you've got to come out. Carrie wants to tell you how much she loves your ribs." I stepped out onto the little deck, and there was Carrie, topless with a wee bikini bottom and barbecue sauce cascading over her pearls and down between her ample cleavage.

"Oh, Jeff," Carrie said, licking her fingers, "these are absolutely the best spare ribs, ever!"

There you have it: I had the Carrie Donovan seal of approval and a vision of her burned into my brain forever.

When Perry met Laughlin Barker, who worked as a lawyer for one of the law firms Perry had hired, sparks flew, and soon they were a couple. Perry, who had been involved in several intimate relationships prior to Laughlin, seemed to me truly happy for the very first time. To see them together, standing next to each other, was to witness true love. Three years later, Laughlin was diagnosed with AIDS, and a year later, it was clear he was dying. Perry, however, the eternal optimist, was in denial about Laughlin's condition. A short time later, Perry himself was diagnosed with AIDS. Laughlin died on January 2, 1986.

I vividly remember advising Perry that he should sign with Alixandre, the company that made my furs, when he wanted to go into the fur business. I also explained the mechanics and timetable of the

LEFT Although he was not a cook, Perry Ellis thoroughly enjoyed fine dining.

menswear industry, which ran counter to the women's calendar. Perry could not understand how I was finalizing fall fabrics for menswear at the beginning of the summer, but he got the hang of it. In those days, we wanted our friends and colleagues to succeed in business and I, for one, was thrilled to see Perry flourish.

In March 1986, the very first AIDS fundraiser backed by the fashion community was held at the Jacob K. Javits Convention Center. Although Perry had participated in its inception, it was doubtful he would attend. He was still in mourning for Laughlin and not well himself. We did not expect to see him. He surprised us by showing up, looking very gaunt, with an overcoat draped over his shoulders and wearing thick eyeglasses. One side of his face was drooped due to Bell's palsy, and he barely spoke to anyone.

At that time I thought that it was one of the bravest things I had ever witnessed. Particularly then, the stigma of AIDS was one of terror, and the admission of having the disease was considered a death knell of one's business. And yet, there stood Perry among his peers, shoulder to shoulder in the fight against AIDS.

A few weeks later that spring, I attended Perry's fall show as I had done for every show since that very first one. He came out at the end barely able to stand and supported by his assistants. Instead of his usual skipping down the length of the runway, he waved faintly and then disappeared down a back elevator into a waiting ambulance, without receiving his well-wishers. Perry died in the early morning hours of May 30.

I often liken Perry's legacy to that of Alexander McQueen's. Both designers created almost a lifetime of design ideas in the span of a decade or so. For Perry, that included womenswear, menswear, childrenswear, hosiery, furs, home, and fragrance.

Perry's death from AIDS, one of the very first major names in the fashion world to succumb to the disease, affected me deeply. Years later, it is why I wanted to tell his story for the legions of people who did not have the great pleasure of knowing the amazing talent that he was.

Jeffrey's Oven-Baked Spare Ribs

Tender, fall-off-the-bone ribs with homemade barbecue sauce, no grill required
Prep time: 20 minutes
Total time: 4 hours, 30 minutes
(Please note: Total time encompasses the longest time possible for doneness–i.e., the worst-case scenario the ribs cook 3 hours, 30 minutes in oven until tender)
Serves: 4

Parboil the ribs

The "silverskin" on spare ribs is a thin, tough membrane of connective tissue covering the back of the ribs. Removing it before cooking is recommended, as it can make the ribs chewy and rubbery, and prevent seasonings from fully penetrating them.
After removing the silverskin, put the ribs in a large pot with enough water to cover them. Add seasonings (if you prefer) such as 2 tablespoons of whole peppercorns or 3 bay leaves and bring it to a boil.
Simmer the ribs until they are just tender, about 30 minutes.

After parboiling, place the ribs on a foil-covered sheet tray, (I bake my ribs in a 275°F oven for 2 to 3 hours.)

For the ribs

2 to 2½ pounds spare ribs (yields approximately 10-13 ribs)
Salt and pepper, to taste

For the barbecue sauce

1 tablespoon olive oil
¼ cup finely chopped onion
1 teaspoon ground cumin
1½ cups ketchup
½ cup pineapple juice
½ cup apple cider vinegar
½ cup water
¼ cup light brown sugar

Combine all the ingredients above. Stir and bring the mixture to a boil, then lower the heat to a simmer.
Continue to simmer uncovered for about 30 minutes, stirring occasionally, or until the sauce has thickened.

After the ribs have cooked to the desired doneness, slather them with sauce and place them back in the oven for at least 10 more minutes.
Serve ribs by cutting them as you desire.
Leftover barbecue sauce can be stored in an airtight container in the refrigerator for no longer than one week.

OPPOSITE In the early 1970s, Tom Fallon, in the black bathing trunks, was surrounded by friends at a pool in Fire Island Pines.

OVERLEAF LEFT TOP Pool Time: Michael Vollbracht, Bethann Hardison, Victor Fernandez, a friend, Candy Pratts Price, and I were lounging on a summer day in The Pines.

OVERLEAF LEFT BOTTOM The designer Stephen Burrows and Victor Fernandez, who later became Stephen's assistant, were catching rays by the pool.

OVERLEAF CENTER Tom Fallon, Bill Blass' trusted associate, enjoyed sunbathing on Fire Island.

OVERLEAF RIGHT TOP The model and entrepreneur Bethann Hardison and Victor Fernandez were deep in conversation.

OVERLEAF RIGHT BOTTOM Jeffrey Frisch and I were photographed on Fire Island Pines in what seems a lifetime ago.

Fashion's raconteur hardly begins to describe the charismatic designer Tom Fallon. Tom attended the Fashion Institute of Technology in New York at night, during the waning days of his enlistment in the army. Meeting Halston, who was then the head milliner with his own department at Bergdorf Goodman, Tom ended up helping to establish Halston's first ready-to-wear line. When Halston's backer suddenly pulled out, he suggested that Tom speak to designer Bill Blass, who almost instantly offered him a position as an assistant, a job that lasted over 20 years.

It was Tom who, after discovering the model Billie Blair on a train to Philadelphia, persuaded Blass to use her at the famous Battle of Versailles show, to thunderous applause. In fact, it was Tom who conceived of the Bill Blass tableaux at Versailles, not Kay Thompson. Inspired by the Ascot sequence in *My Fair Lady*, the horse races at Longchamp, and the Cotton Club, he brought Blass' "Café Society" looks to life for the Parisians. Tom's flair for the dramatic stood Blass in good stead, as he traveled extensively, putting on, over the years many highly successful trunk shows.

I met Tom shortly after coming to New York right out of high school. Robert L. Green, the razor-tongued fashion director of *Playboy*, gave a sumptuous barbecue every year for all the menswear designers at his home in Bucks County, Pennsylvania. That year, just to be contrary, the menswear designers were disinvited. Only their assistants were invited, and that's how I met Tom.

We shared many mutual friends such as Michael Vollbracht, and Tom eventually left Blass to become a fashion executive at the Carlisle Company for many successful years, before finally becoming an interior designer.

Listening to Tom recall important fashion history is a true treat. Who else can tell of attending a Norell black-tie opening with Halston and emerging from their limousine and stepping directly into dog shit? Or how on his very first trip to Paris, he caught the eye of Hubert de Givenchy, who demanded to meet him. He is indeed living history, and I feel privileged to know him.

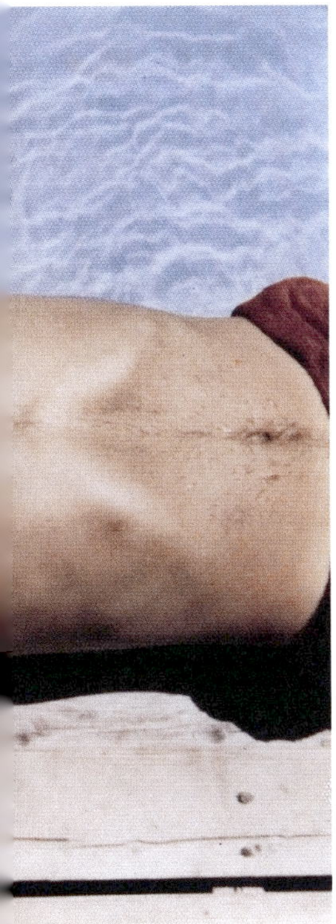

Working for Calvin Klein was a completely different situation from my job as an assistant designer at Ralph Lauren. It was a calculated move on my part to stay involved with the fashion industry while I was still finishing school. I was the third-ranked design assistant after Charles Suppon and Zack Carr. Calvin was always my boss, which was an entirely different relationship than the one I had with Ralph.

However, I will say that Calvin gave me tremendous leeway in the areas I was responsible for. I worked on his burgeoning licensing—scarves, belts, umbrellas, furs, and home line. It was challenging but fun. I remember speaking with the scarf licensee about how important prints were to the scarf business and then trying to translate that into a line with a designer who wasn't particularly fond of prints. I remember my first success was with a cream-colored cotton voile scarf with navy and orange polka dots and a navy striped border, which was simple and clean enough to satisfy Calvin, but decorative enough to sell thousands of pieces in two sizes. I was extremely proud of the innovative umbrella designs I did for Mespo, which included suede and lizard-handled models and shoulder-strapped, double-faced, trapunto-stitched, and completely waterproof designs that were perhaps way ahead of their time from a design standpoint. I particularly loved designing luxurious furs with Alixandre, whom I had worked with during my time at Parsons. I remember expressing to Calvin how important I thought furs were in helping him transition from a mere coat and suit designer to a full-fledged collection designer. "You don't want one of your customers putting a Bill Blass or an Oscar de la Renta fur over one of your evening gowns, do you?" I recall saying to Calvin.

Of course, the story of how I came to work at Calvin Klein has become sort of a Seventh-Avenue legend. As a small present of gratitude for hiring me, I had taken the CK logo from a press kit and asked my friend Tommy Gingerella to silk-screen Calvin's name in white on the bicep of a couple brown T-shirts. Tommy was silk-screening T-shirts in his loft in SoHo and drying them in his oven. On my first day I brought them to Calvin, who graciously accepted them with the caveat: "I don't think I could ever wear my name on my sleeve."

Calvin left the open box with the shirts in it on the breakfront cabinet behind his desk. A couple of days later, Barry Schwartz, Calvin's business partner, spied the shirts in Calvin's office and asked if they were part of the new resort collection. Calvin explained that no, they were just a gift from me. Later, Barry confided in me that he was a bit disappointed that they were not part of the line. A few weeks later,

OPPOSITE This portrait of Calvin Klein was taken about the time I went to work with him, just as he was transitioning from a "coat and suit" guy to a full-fledged sportswear designer.

Calvin Klein

OPPOSITE The commercial evolution of my first-day present to Calvin: the logo T-shirt that started it all.

the night before the show, I did something that might have gotten me fired right off the bat. I took one color of each of the T-shirts from the collection—both brights and pastels—and went down to Tommy's loft in SoHo and had him print the Calvin Klein logo in white on the bicep of each one. The next morning, I asked the salesgirls who were going to seat the guests for the show to wear the T-shirts with the logos. The T-shirts in the show were without the logo. The day after, when the market appointments began, all the buyers said that they wanted the T-shirts with the logos that the salesgirls had worn at the show. My friend Tommy suddenly found himself having to hire more help to keep up with the overwhelming demand from Bert Browse, Calvin's production guy. Soon afterward, jeans and underwear followed.

Calvin was an amazing marketing genius with an innate perception of what people wanted before they even knew they wanted it. Witness the success of his jeans, underwear, and fragrances: they all were made to promote an underlying feeling of sexiness. Calvin never questioned his decisions regarding marketing and merchandising and almost always was ahead of the zeitgeist.

The Calvin Klein T-shirts with the logos were just the beginning. Calvin reimagined blue jeans with his name on the back, aligning them with a clever, sexy commercial fronted by a barely legal Brooke Shields that had the television censors quaking. Then, taking the idea of basic Fruit of the Loom tighty-whities, streamlining the fit, and sexing up the waistbands with his name, Calvin revolutionized the underwear industry for both men and women. The pole vaulter Tom Hintnaus sunbathing in only his CK briefs looming seven stories above Broadway stopped traffic and drove millions of dollars worth of sales. Men envisioned wearing the briefs would grant them Greek-god status.

The one area he had not really ventured into was menswear. Sure, we had done a few looks to accessorize the women's shows, but we never planned to produce or sell the looks. I had encouraged Calvin to take the plunge. One day he surprised me by saying he and Barry had negotiated a deal with Irving Selbst, a major salesman in the menswear industry, with Yves Saint Laurent and Cardin track records, as well as with Bond Clothing, a very large domestic tailored clothing company. The biggest surprise of all was that Calvin said he was going to relieve me of all of my present design responsibilities and make me vice-president of menswear design. I was thrilled and excited and immediately began putting together mood boards and making fabric appointments. However, a couple weeks passed, and the deal fell through. Calvin told me not to worry and that I would just continue to work at everything I had done before. A few days later, I received an early morning call at home from Selbst.

"Yeah, hi," he began with his strong *basso profundo* voice. "I knew that you were going to be the designer of the men's line for Calvin, and we are all set up, so we would like to back you."

I was stunned and for once lacked the words to respond. "I'll have to get back to you, Irving," I stammered.

I went into the office somewhat shell-shocked but was able to corner Calvin alone by midafternoon.

"Calvin, I need to discuss something with you. Are you free for dinner tonight?" I asked.

"Sure," he responded.

We ended up going to Texarkana in the West Village, a restaurant owned by Abe and Alene de la Houssaye, known for its tasty Cajun-Louisiana Creole cooking. It was one of our favorite places.

"First of all, I am very happy and am not hitting you up for a raise," I began. "I got a call from Irving Selbst, and he and his partners want to back me," I said "And I just don't know what I should do."

Calvin looked at me very earnestly and said, "You would be a fool not to take it." He added, "And, if it doesn't work out, you can always come back!"

I was stunned and pleased that Calvin was so encouraging, and a new exciting path for me had just opened up. I am forever grateful that Calvin saw in me something that I did not yet see in myself. Months later, at my first show, I invited both Calvin Klein and Ralph Lauren to attend, seating them next to each other. The photographers had a field day, and I have never looked back.

OPPOSITE Photographed by Bruce Weber, Olympic pole-vaulter Tom Hintnaus' heroic body, clothed in Calvin Klein underwear, inspired a generation and changed an industry forever.

III. ON MY OWN

The Coty Awards show, in a change of venue from Lincoln Center, was to be held in the large auditorium of the Fashion Institute of Technology in 1977. I was nominated for Best Menswear Designer, but I had no illusions that I might win. After all, I had been in business for only a year, and my competition was quite formidable. However, the special award for men's furs was extra important to me as it had never been given before. I was the first and the youngest designer to be on the list. I decided that I must make the very best of this award and decided the only way to do that was to have all the styles of the collection come out on that stage at the same time. Although at that point I had no real money to speak of, I had become friendly enough with most of the top male models and Edie Raymond Locke, the editor-in-chief of *Mademoiselle*. My slot on the bill was the next-to-last place, the last award being yet another one for the designer Geoffrey Beene.

I sat in the audience in an aisle seat directly across from Mr. Beene. As my section of the program began, one by one the handsomest men in New York filled the stage, each wearing my hypermasculine furs, and each looking drop-dead gorgeous. Eventually, the stage was filled on two levels with 31 men in my fur coats. The audience went berserk. After what seemed like a joyful eternity, the applause died down, and Ms. Locke stepped to the podium to announce the final award. "And now," she said, "for the most beautiful women's clothes in the world . . . Jeffrey Banks!"

Mr. Beene shot me a murderous glance as he sat across the aisle from where I was. I shrugged sheepishly at Edie's mistake. I understand he never spoke to her again, and it took years for him to speak to me after that. Nonetheless, it was a glorious evening, and I was thrilled to be recognized by so many of the same people I had admired for so long this early in my budding career.

OPPOSITE Here I am, receiving my very first Coty Award for Men's Furs–the first of its kind–from FIT's vice-president Shirley Goodman. I was the youngest recipient to do so.

OVERLEAF Part of the group of 31 male models who displayed my entire men's fur collection onstage at the same time during the 1977 Coty Awards Show. The 31 included Bob Menna, Tony Sanchez, Renauld White, Denis La Marsh, Michael Taylor, and Greg Bauer.

Irving Selbst was known in the menswear industry as a legend. Having introduced both the menswear of Yves Saint Laurent and, before that, Pierre Cardin to the United States, he was responsible for millions of dollars in tailored clothing sales in the 1960s and 1970s, and was at the time working to promote me. At about six feet and four inches and around 300 pounds, he was a large man with big appetites. In addition to his clothing sales prowess, he was a partner in several restaurants, among them Nickels, an Upper East Side haunt. There he plied garmentos with food and drink while cajoling large orders from buyers as they dined and tried to pry off the buffalo-head nickels that were glued and polyurethaned onto the tabletops.

Irving had such a large personality and presence that he was enlisted to play the head of the Jewish mafia in *The Gang That Couldn't Shoot Straight*. He also had bit parts in the films, *Birdy* and *Watermelon Man*. Irving used these film appearances as talking points to help drive menswear sales while pitching to buyers.

Irving had long been separated from his wife, Nancy, and was in a relationship with Linda LaMotta, the fighter Jake LaMotta's beautiful niece. Jake was portrayed by Robert De Niro in the film *Raging Bull*.

It was Linda who accompanied Irving and me on my very first trip to Europe. I was incredibly excited to be going, first to Paris and then to London. Taking the Friday evening flight to Paris, we arrived very early Saturday morning, but there was just one problem: when we landed, Irving was stuck in his seat! Eventually, mechanics had to board the plane and remove the sides of his seat to release him.

I was all agog as we traveled into the city, passing the Cathedral of Notre-Dame. I noted a chicly dressed older woman in Sonia Rykiel whom I would see two more times during my stay in Paris, wearing essentially the same outfit but each time styling it with different accessories as only the French can do.

When we got to the legendary Le Meurice hotel, our rooms, of course, were not ready, so we went out for breakfast. When we returned, I entered my room only to see the maid ironing the thick linen sheets directly on the bed. Okay, I thought, I have finally arrived. But the best was yet to come.

That evening, Irving said that he was going to take Linda and me to a super place for dinner. It was called Le Sept and was located at 7 rue Saint-Anne. There was a restaurant on the ground floor and downstairs, one of the first discotheques in France. Although he did not dance at all, Irving insisted that we all go downstairs after we finished a delicious dinner. Halfway down the stairs, I heard Irving

OPPOSITE Three examples of 1970s Yves Saint Laurent menswear, which, along with Pierre Cardin's designs, ushered in the peacock revolution with its aggressively shaped silhouette.

LEFT Irving Selbst had a dynamic personality that not only aided his ability to be a great menswear salesman, but contributed to his career as a successful character actor.

yell out, "Hey, Pierre! It's Irv, over here!" To my complete surprise, there was the designer Pierre Cardin and his partner, André Oliver, to whom Irving introduced me on the landing. As we reached the bottom of the stairs, once again I heard Irving bellow out over the thumping disco beat, "Yves, Pierre, over here, it's Irv!"

And there before me stood Yves Saint Laurent and his partner, Pierre Bergé, both of whom I was meeting on my very first night in Paris, on my very first day in Europe. Still floating a few minutes later, Linda and I graced the minuscule dance floor with Irving watching us. A moment later, I heard, "Hey, Jeffrey! What are you doing here?"

It was my friend, the Broadway dancer Adam Grammis. I explained why I was in Paris, and then asked Adam why he was in town. "I am here with Shirley MacLaine's company," he said. "Would you like to meet her? She's just around the corner."

The next thing I knew I was shaking hands with Shirley MacLaine. Many years later, I asked Ms. MacLaine if she remembered that evening, and she said she did.

RIGHT The Broadway dancer Adam Grammis' life and career were cut short by AIDS.

OVERLEAF The late Lynn Kohlmann, a model who became a photographer, took these two very early portraits of me. They were done as a test as she was just starting out in her new career as a photographer, and both images were done within an hour of each other. Even today, they remain favorites of mine.

The next morning, as a light rain drizzled over Paris, Irving asked Linda and me what we wanted to do that day. I said, "Irving, you're gonna get a car and driver, and we are going to Versailles, because that's the only thing that might top last night!"

Irving's stellar reputation with retailers and his great track record with sales certainly paved the way for me as I started to make a name for myself in the menswear industry.

THE COTY AWARD FOR BEST MENSWEAR DESIGNER

As it turns out, the Holy Grail for me was to get the Coty Award for Best Menswear Designer. In 1982 I was nominated once again and found myself at FIT, the scene of my earlier triumph. The difference this time was that I really, really wanted it and, in fact, felt I really had earned it. The other difference was that this time we would not know who the winner was until the envelope was opened that very evening. I came with a large retinue of Jeffrey Banks and Merona Sport colleagues—so many that we took up about two whole rows in the auditorium.

Part of my wanting to win so badly was because of the hardworking young people who had come to believe in me and my abilities so passionately. I didn't want to let them down. I brought my mother as my date. She was resplendent in a gorgeous Bergdorf Goodman gown thanks to my friend, Betty Halbreich, the director of Solutions at the department store. My mind was racing as the other awards were announced. And then it happened, Brooke Shields and Ben Vereen, along with Geoffrey Beene standing nearby, announced my name. A deafening cheer rang out as my two rows of compatriots all rose to their feet.

All I could think about as I strode down the aisle was how nice it would have been to share that moment with a special someone in my life. But as I touched the silver trophy, I quickly banished those thoughts of romance from my mind. Plenty of time for that I thought. Time to bask in the moment, and bask I did.

Because nominees do not know if they are going to win or not, it's up to them to decide if they are going to have some sort of post-show after party, or not. I kind of thought it was bad luck to plan a party, but the Merona team would not hear of not having a celebration of some kind. The stately Union League Club was selected, and I had to remind my invited male friends on the invitation that jackets and ties, if not tuxedos, were required. The next day, on "Page Six" of the *New York Post,* it was reported that some staid members of the club were alarmed about the "funny-smelling" cigarette smoke emanating from the bathrooms at the party that night. I assure you, I had nothing to do with that. After the scheduled festivities were over, everyone wanted to know what was next in store. Since we were all dressed up and had a fleet of limos at our disposal to boot, I was asked, "Where shall we go now?" I cried, "There's only one place, Studio 54!" As we pulled up in front of the famous dance club, someone in my party, noting the huge throng already amassed in front, shouted, "How will we all get in?" As I held my award aloft, I answered, "Watch this," and the sea miraculously parted, and in we all went.

OPPOSITE Receiving my second Coty Award in 1982, as the Menswear Designer of the Year, was an extremely rewarding moment for me.

OVERLEAF LEFT The invitation for my after-Coty Awards party at the tony Union League Club was printed and sent out without knowing whether I would win or not!

OVERLEAF RIGHT The back of the invitation featured, *from left to right*, the models Chris Byars, Rick Hogue, and Jeff Aquilon in formal dress, photographed by Bruce Weber.

Please come celebrate

Jeffrey Banks'

Mens Coty Award Nomination

at The Union League Club

38 East 37th Street

Third Floor

Thursday, September 23, 1982

9:30 o'clock p.m.

R.S.V.P. 751-5027

Gentlemen are required to wear jacket and tie.

Please present this invitation at the door.

PREVIOUS PAGES LEFT Models who wore Jeffrey Banks at the 1982 Coty Awards Show included, *top row from the left*, Todd Irvin, Charles Williamson, Tony Sanchez, *bottom row from the left*, Denis La Marsh, Jeff Aquilon, and Renauld White.

PREVIOUS PAGES RIGHT The model Rick Hogue wore a Jeffrey Banks tanuki fur coat over a lamb-suede vest in the 1982 Coty Awards Show.

LEFT Brooke Shields and Ben Vereen presented me with my 1982 Coty Award.

OVERLEAF LEFT TOP I was photographed with the designer Geoffrey Beene, who seemed to have gotten over Edie Raymond Locke's 1977 Coty Awards slip of the tongue,and Brooke Shields at the 1982 Coty Awards.

OVERLEAF LEFT BOTTOM At the Coty Awards, I was photographed with the interior designers Charles Swerz and Jerry Van Deelen, who designed my home and showroom.

OVERLEAF RIGHT A very excited Eleanor M. Banks was next to me as I telephoned a friend about winning the award.

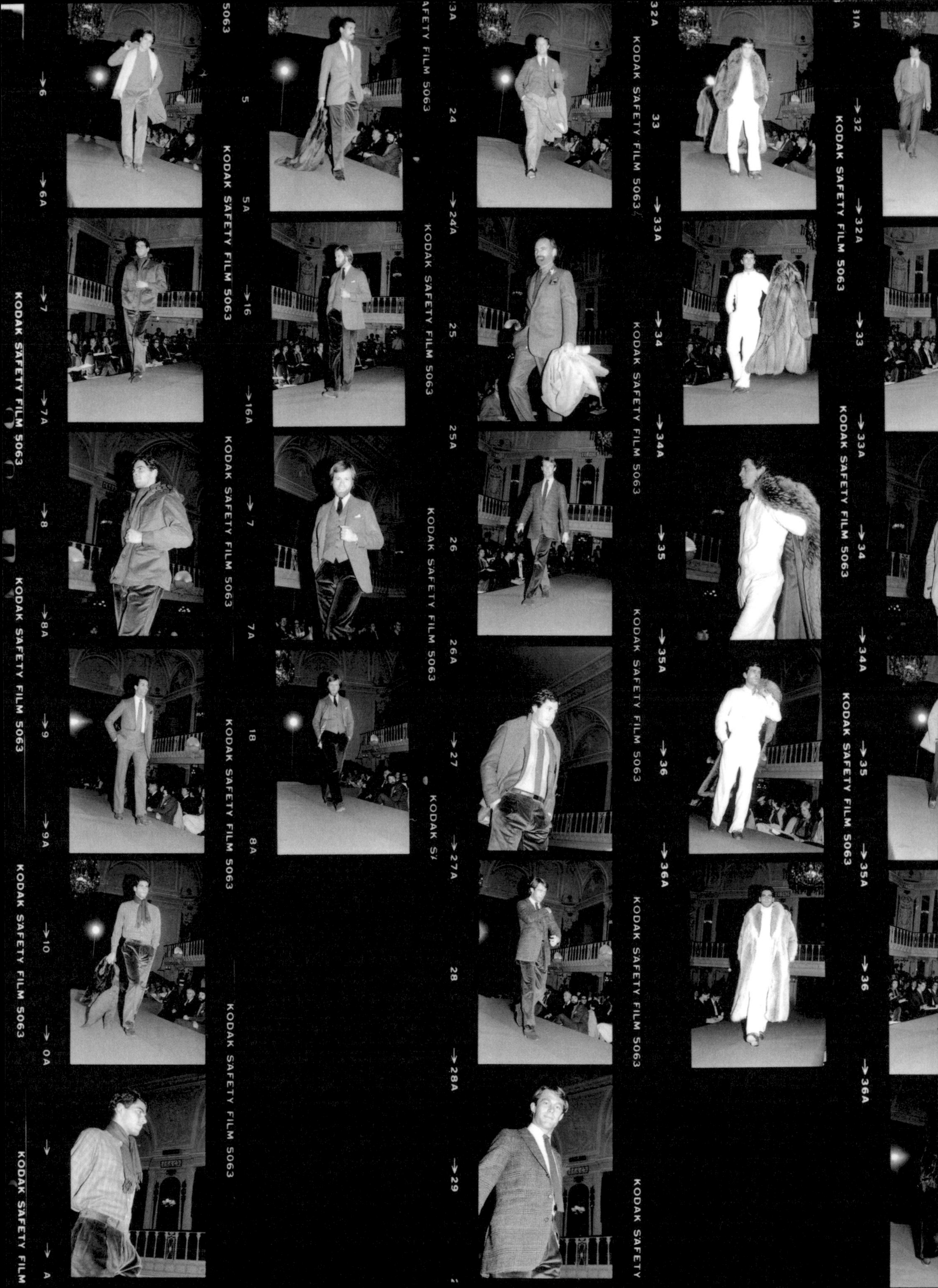
KODAK SAFETY FILM 5063

KODAK SAFETY FILM 5063

Perhaps it's my frustrated desire to be an art director that has driven my love of planning and executing fashion shoots. Of course I am sure my love of collecting photography, particularly fashion photography, has a hand in it too.

Working with brilliant and uber-talented photographers such as Bruce Weber, Thom Gilbert, and Horst P. Horst, was not too shabby either. Planning shoots is a lot like planning a film with the correct cast of models and actors, director, photographer, and important locations. Whether working in a studio, or at the beach, in Ireland or St. Barts, all those elements must combine to tell the right story for the clothes. I have had the good fortune to work with incredible models such as Hoyt Richards and Renauld White, to name just a couple, which only makes the job of showing off my designs in their best light that much easier. They act out the part without saying a word.

When designing a collection, sometimes I had a theme in mind that inspired me. One year it was the film *Chariots of Fire*. Another time, it was a book about Ernest Hemingway's connection to Key West, Florida. I had never been to Key West, but I imagined what the colors and clothing being worn there might look like. Of course, after designing and photographing the collection, I actually went to Key West, and it was nothing like I had imagined it would be, but that's just part of the fun.

Eventually, it became such a big part of what I did that my Japanese licensee asked me to cast, art direct, and produce the advertising campaigns for their house brand called New Yorker, giving me carte blanche to select the clothes and the themes for the shoots. It was thrilling to be entrusted with the public face of this other brand.

I also art directed a couple of advertisements for my friend, the photographer Thom Gilbert.

All in all, being directly involved in these shoots was the culmination of designing the clothes, as I was able to put them in the ideal context on perfect models and in exceptional settings.

PREVIOUS PAGES These contact sheets are from a fashion show that was given at the now-demolished historic Biltmore Hotel in New York in the early 1980s, where I introduced Jeffrey Banks Boyswear.

OPPOSITE A fashion shoot with a Hollywood theme, photographed on the beach in Santa Monica by Thom Gilbert, included models resembling Carole Lombard, Tyrone Power, and Maurice Chevalier. It is always fun to have a theme.

OVERLEAF In the shoot that literally started off his career, Hoyt Richards, who was still a student at Princeton and was introduced to me by Bruce Weber, instantly became associated with my brand. Here, he was photographed in a pastel striped cardigan, *left*, and a doeskin flannel double-breasted suit, *right*.

PAGE 136 A trio of worsted wool Fair Isle sweaters from the fall 1984 collection were worn by, *from left to right*, David Womack, Bruce Hulse, and Jeff Aquilon.

PAGE 137 The Olympic athlete John Skudin was photographed in a barleycorn tweed windowpane coat and Harris tweed sports jacket.

PROD. NO.
SCENE
TAKE
ROLL
DATE
SOUND
PROD. CO.
DIRECTOR
CAMERAMAN

JEFFREY BANKS

JEFFREY BANKS

CORN&CO

JEFFREY BANKS SUITS THE MOOD

'Name' designers have become increasingly important in American men's wear. And now — a new one who is young, black and talented.

By N. R. Kleinfield

Jeffrey Banks, men's clothing designer, sat in a threadbare office in the B. Glanzrock clothing factory on lower Fifth Avenue. He is a broad-shouldered young man (40 regular), with a bit of a paunch, a cherubic face and quizzical eyes. Despite the pressures of his work, he is ordinarily serene, with a good laugh.

Thumbing through his sketches, he looked at one and frowned. "As a designer," he said, "you're insecure all the time. I doubt every garment until I see it on someone's back on the street."

At 26, Jeffrey Banks often sees clothing he has designed on people's backs. Three years ago, he walked off with a Coty Award, sometimes called the Oscar of the fashion industry, for his men's fur designs. He was the first designer to collect a Coty for furs and the youngest Coty winner ever. Jeffrey is also the only black designer to reach this level of prominence in the men's wear field, though he believes he has neither been helped nor hurt by his skin color. His suits, sport jackets, slacks, outerwear, shirts and furs are in some 150 outlets across the country, including Bloomingdale's, Saks Fifth Avenue and Nieman-Marcus. Last fall, Macy's unveiled a Jeffrey Banks boutique at its Herald Square store. This being fashion show time for men's wear designers — when the fall 1980 collections are shown to the press and buyers — Jeffrey recently unveiled his latest and most extensive line of fall fashions.

With the increasing importance of "name" designers on the American men's wear scene, Jeffrey Banks is the best known of the young, new breed. Bill Blass, the first major designer to switch over to men's wear, said of him, "His clothes seem totally natural. He doesn't make any statement that is false. I can't see that this guy isn't the absolute limit."

"He does attractive looking things," observed John Weitz, today's best-known men's wear designer. "I think he has ambition and drive and I expect him to become quite well known."

□

Men's fashion designing here is a congested field. With America pressing Europe for the fashion lead, and with the rise of the designer-celebrity, there has been an explosion of interest in the field. Men's Wear magazine recently counted some 62 American designer labels stitched into the clothes that American men buy. And countless aspirants are sketching away at the Parsons School of Design or the Fashion Institute of Technology, or lugging fabrics around for one of the big designers.

"Fashion careers are very slow," John Weitz declared. "Good careers span 20 years. Reputations take longer to develop than, say, for actors. You're lucky if 200,000 people in all of the United States see your work."

N. R. Kleinfield, a reporter for The Times, is the author of "The Hidden Minority: America's Handicapped."

In his studio, Jeffrey Banks with a jacket made of the natural fabric he favors.

Young men's fashion designers are very busy people. When not actually designing, they are conferring with buyers, visiting mills in pursuit of fabrics, coordinating fashion shows, sizing up models or checking up on manufacturers. They must also cope with problems unique to the men's wear field.

For example, when a women's wear designer deals with a department store, usually one buyer is involved. In men's wear, a good-sized department store is likely to employ a dress-shirt buyer, a sport-shirt buyer, a dress-pants buyer, a sport-pants buyer, a sport-jacket buyer, a suit buyer, a sweater buyer, a necktie buyer, a pajama buyer, an overcoat buyer, a topcoat buyer, a shoe buyer and perhaps a couple more.

"They all have their own opinions," said Jeffrey. "It's very difficult. Say the sweater buyer has an allowance of $50,000. You come along with a line of cashmere sweaters in rainbow colors. He may already have $10,000 worth of cashmere sweaters in basic colors that he always sells and knows will sell. So he says he can't buy your sweaters. But you say the sport-coat buyer just bought your jackets that coordinate with your sweaters. 'Tough,' you're told."

Even so, Jeffrey believes the field of men's clothing is promising: "American men are dressing more. It's very rare to walk into a room and see a man with a white shirt on. I don't think men's wear will match the volume of women's clothing, but it has much faster growth potential."

□

Jeffrey Banks grew up in a middle-class household in Washington, D.C. His mother was an equal-opportunity employment officer for the General Services Administration and his father was a cartographer for the United States Navy Oceanographic Division. Clothes mattered little to his father. Yet Jeffrey's mother "had a fabulous eye and a great sense of style." Jeffrey's boyhood thoughts were drawn repeatedly to art: "I knew when I was 11 or 12 that I wanted to be a designer."

By the time he was 13, Jeffrey was going to stores alone to buy clothes. "I was," he recalled, "constantly giving my parents heartache by doing things like buying a $20 tie." He favored a Georgetown boutique called Britches, where many smartly dressed politicians shopped, and when Jeffrey turned 15, the owners gave him a part-time salesman's job.

Following high school, Jeffrey enrolled in Pratt Institute in New York and got a part-time job as an apprentice with Ralph Lauren, the most prestigious American men's wear designer and Jeffrey's favorite. After two years, he transferred to Parsons School of Design. He left Lauren to focus on school, though he shortly got a job with Calvin Klein. "It was," he said, "very helpful working for someone much more business-oriented, rather than just fashion-oriented like Ralph."

After he graduated from Parsons, Jeffrey remained with Klein until, in early 1976, a new clothing firm named Nik-Nik Clothing, financed by a Japanese trading company, persuaded him to design clothes for it. His first collection was nominated for a Coty and $4.5 million worth of his clothes were sold in a languid year for men's clothing. "I was all of 22 years of age," he said, "and already designing and having very few restrictions put on me. We were selling to some of the best stores in America. It seemed too good to be true, and it was."

In the winter of 1977, the Japanese parent company telexed Nik-Nik to close its doors. Jeffrey knew that he had to pair up swiftly with a good manufacturer and get out a line for fall, the most important season. He signed up with Glanzrock, a company in business since 1917, run by two energetic brothers, Stanley and Walter Glanzrock. Jeffrey said of the firm, "All of their clothing is handmade in today's world where so much clothing is fused and bonded." Said Stanley Glanzrock of Jeffrey: "I liked him because he was young and very talented and not hungry for money. He didn't want to become a millionaire in an hour like some of the other guys." Starting in early 1978, Jeffrey got together a fall line in half the normal time. Although it was one of the last lines to appear, The New York Times reviewer declared: "Well worth the wait. . . ."

Now Jeffrey designs furs for Alixandre and outerwear for Lakeland and re-

PAGES 138–139 In a spring Americana-themed collection, photographer Thom Gilbert lensed blond-haired Troy Hixson and the dark-haired Douglas Tjelmeland, who was the focus of the campaign.

Page 140 For fall 1989, I was thrilled to work with Horst, the legendary photographer. The vicuña-colored wool Balmacaan swing coat with a deep inverted back pleat has a timeless quality about that never dates.

PAGE 141 Horst also captured the diamond-quilted loden suede shearling hunting jacket that can look either very casual or elegant as worn here by Stephen Mabry.

OPPOSITE How lucky was I to be featured in a *New York Times Magazine* piece on March 2, 1980?

RIGHT Renauld White and Tony Spinelli were captured walking the runway at a Men's Fashion Association show wearing Jeffrey Banks.

OVERLEAF The November 1982 issue of *Essence* featured a spread in which I was flanked by the fur coats I designed, which were modeled by, *from left to right*, George Patterson in a sheared nutria trench coat, Renauld White in a tanuki shawl collar coat, and Ben Lawson in a natural beaver pea coat.

Jeffrey Banks

"I've always believed in hard work. It may sound funny, but the harder I work, the luckier I get."

In the few years designer Jeffrey Banks has been on the fashion scene, he's created quite a stir among his competitors as well as his followers. Born in Washington, D.C., Jeffrey came to New York City to study at Parsons School of Design, and since his graduation in 1977 he has put together sensational sportswear collections for men, women and children as well as several collections of men's furs. In 1977 Jeffrey won a special award from his men's fur collection.

Designs with a masculine flair by J Banks for Alixandre Furs. LEFT: Dou breasted beaver trench coat with notched collar and button closing, $7,000. CENTER: Finnish raccoon coat with shawl collar, cozy slit pockets, $9,500. RIGHT: Double-breasted three-quarter-length coat in sumptuous beaver, $4,500. For more information, see page 158.

My one and only trip to New Orleans for an MFA conference was accompanied by unrelenting rain, so much so that, save for a very few local restaurants, I never really got to see the city at all. One of the very few times I dared to venture out, as I was hanging up my drenched jacket in the coatroom, a gentleman reached out to me and said, "You're Jeffrey Banks!" I said, "Yes, I am."

He replied cheerily, "Hi, I am Steve Eisendrath." He then explained that he was the vice-president in charge of sales and merchandising for Merona Sport. Merona was a line of colorful sportswear created by my friend Don Polley. Originally conceived as a private label program for Bloomingdale's, the line was unfortunately late in being shipped to them and in short order, Bloomie's canceled the whole order. Stuck with this unbranded merchandise and the daily mounting customs bills for warehouse storage, Polley enlisted the help of his fellow Westport commuter pal Aubrey Fletcher, who offered to store the merchandise until Don could resell it. Aubrey was the head of a Swiss mineral and chemical company called the Merona Corporation, and thus the name Merona Sport was born.

Consisting of six basic styles—a knit polo shirt, a pouch-banded rugby shirt, a regular rugby shirt, a pull-on pant, a pull-on short, and a French terry cloth sweatshirt in six primary colors, the rebranded line quickly became a huge hit in local specialty stores and eventually Bloomingdale's came crawling back and they bought the line they had recently canceled. Merona Sport was a trailblazer in that it pioneered the concept of athleisure, decades before that became a clothing term. I was aware of all of this, since I was an acquaintance of Don's from the menswear design community. That's why I was shocked when Eisendrath blurted out right after he had just met me, "Would you like to come work for us?"

I said, "But you already have a designer and his name is Don Polley. He's a friend of mine! I don't even want to be having this discussion with you." Still, Steve tried to make me change my mind. "Listen, Steve, if you ever part ways with Don, then maybe we could talk, but until then, this discussion is over," I said testily, as I stormed out of the cloakroom.

A year later, I was taking a shower on a Sunday evening before joining friends for dinner when the telephone rang. Dripping water everywhere, I picked up the receiver, "Hello, Jeffrey," the voice on the other end said, "It's Steve!" My mind raced. "Steve who?" The voice answered, "It's Steve Eisendrath."

Suddenly, my memory jogged and I said, "Oh, hi, Steve."

He quickly countered, "Are you ready?"

OPPOSITE Dressed head-to-toe in Merona Sport for a cover story for United Airlines magazine, Steve Eisendrath and I had fun clowning around.

OVERLEAF Bruce Weber's lens captured this Merona Sport cardigan and seersucker short in *Gentleman's Quarterly*.

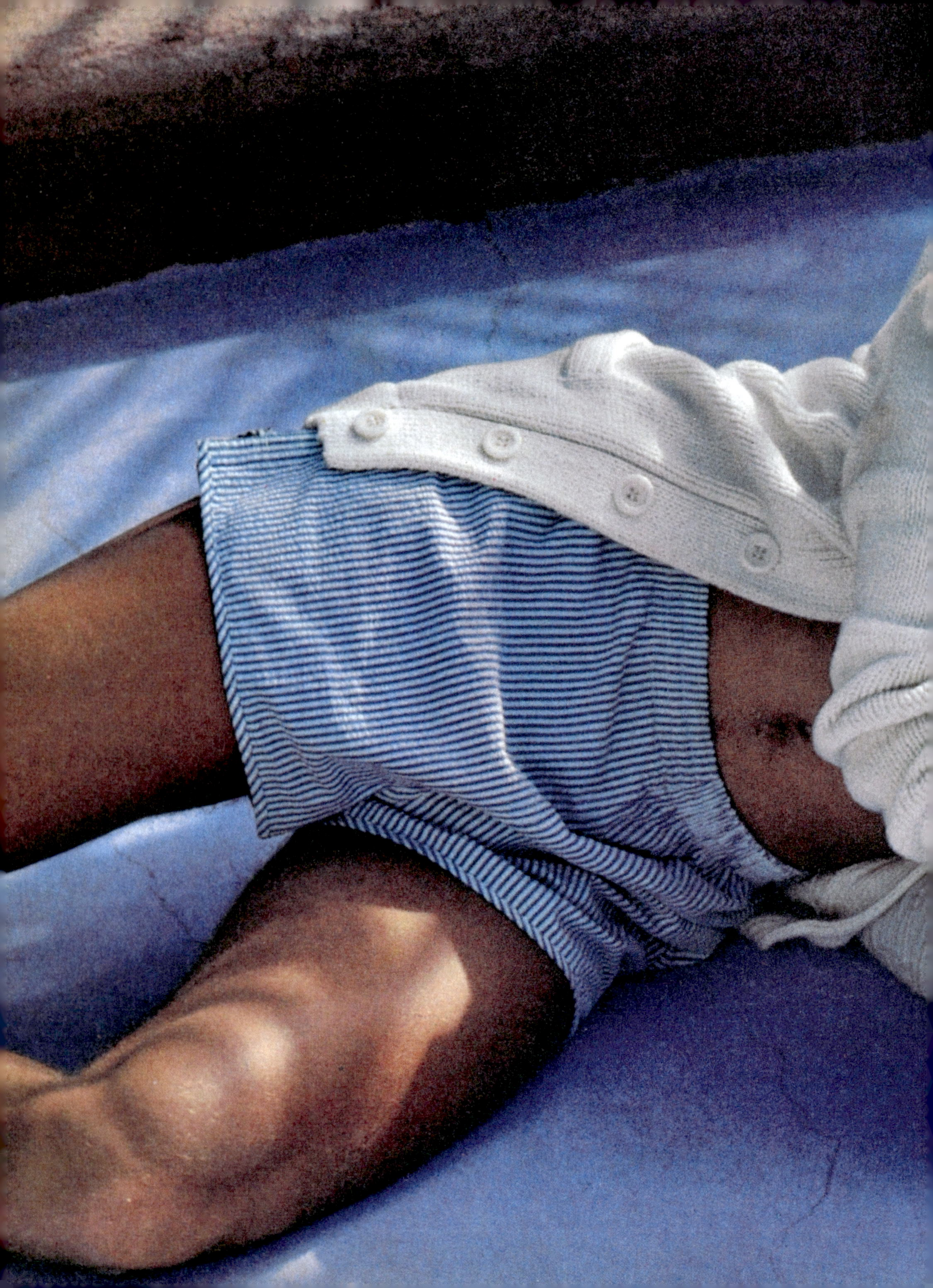

Bound for the shore. Find some reading room and warm up to a few leisurely lines. Continuing its study of the classics, swimwear embraces a traditional summer cooler: the breezy ease of cotton seersucker, about $30; its seaside companion is a seasonal lightweight champ, a cotton cardigan, about $74. Both by Merona Sport. (Towel: Descamps.)

OPPOSITE An ebullient Steve Eisendrath and I were photographed after my win at the Coty Awards in October 1982.

Totally stumped, I said, "Ready for what?"

Steve continued, "We fired Don on Friday. Can you start tomorrow?"

Totally at a loss for words—very rare for me—I finally said, "I can maybe come in and discuss this with you tomorrow." So, on Monday morning, off to 30 Rockefeller Plaza I went and, by the end of the day, we had hammered out a deal, and the adventure of a lifetime had begun.

Designing Merona Sport for men, women, and kids was a challenge, but one I really relished because of the incredible camaraderie of the United Nations group of young people on the team at Merona. We had kids from China, India, Israel, and South Africa. Everything was led by the high-energy, always-up ringleader Steve Eisendrath. From the beginning, Steve was my greatest cheerleader and supporter. It is so rare to have someone that you work with in business who always has your back and who unequivocally believes in you. Steve was my someone. Together we took Merona, which was pulling in about seven million dollars a year when I started, to over 70 million dollars in the first six months. Steve even championed that Oxford Industries should invest in my Jeffrey Banks menswear business, which allowed me to expand my offerings from just tailored clothing to sportswear and dress furnishings.

The work experience at the 30 Rockefeller headquarters was so collegial that many evenings after work were spent happily socializing with Steve and the staff. And the clothing easily fit that lifestyle. We used to say that Merona was the clothing you put on when you got home from work on Friday and did not take off until Monday morning, when you went back to work. Sometimes the party even continued on to Long Island at Steve's home in East Hampton. We worked and played hard equally. In short order, Merona's business surpassed 150 million dollars. Steve's relationships with retailers were golden, too. They trusted him, and he went out of his way to form lasting connections with them.

Steve lusted for life and all it had to offer, and his favorite phrase, uttered almost daily was, "I should have this, shouldn't I?" This was not meant to be a baby boomer's mantra of acquiring more things, but rather a positive state of being open to life itself. Taking Steve to Europe for the first time was such a wonderful experience of seeing the Milwaukee-born small-town boy exposed to the rich culture of Paris, London, Florence, and Venice.

Sadly, Steve Eisendrath's life was tragically cut short by AIDS. In a way, it was the end of our Camelot era as close friends and colleagues. I know that he truly touched so many lives and that my own life was forever changed by knowing and working with him.

I was loving designing for Merona Sport, and I especially loved working out of 30 Rockefeller Plaza, the magnificent Art Deco building designed by Raymond Hood. I loved it so much that I moved my office into the same building, three floors below the Merona Sport offices and showroom.

Every day I prided myself on personally doing every technical design scheme and answering every telex—this was in the days before emails. But there was only one problem. I was getting into work at 5:30am every morning to design Merona Sport, men's, women's, and kids, as well as Jeffrey Banks Men's, Jeffrey Banks Boys, Jeffrey Banks for Lakeland, Jeffrey Banks Furs for Alixandre, and Jeffrey Banks for Daidoh, my Japanese licensee.

Steve Eisendrath was afraid I was going to burn out, because I was working so hard. He very strongly suggested that I hire an assistant, and he said he had the perfect choice for me: Jeanne Shea, who had worked with the former Merona Sport designer. I was very reluctant to hire anybody, let alone Jeanne, as I was so used to doing every single thing myself. Steve taught me the best life lesson: "You need to hire someone better than you," he said. "It's the only way you'll have peace of mind, when you are out of office or out of the country." So I made the date to interview Jeanne, and we made the delicate dance around each other in the coffee shop at 30 Rockefeller,

LEFT BELOW I was photographed with Jeanne Shea at the Coty Awards after-party, just at the beginning of what became a lifelong friendship.

OPPOSITE Jeanne Shea and I had fun on a balcony at the Villa d'Este on Lake Como in Italy.

© 1983 Merona Sport
If only you could live your whole life in Merona Sport
available at fine stores or write Merona Sport 30 Rockefeller Plaza, New York 10112
Merona
SPORT

OPPOSITE The Archer family and their kids became stars as part of our Merona Sport campaigns.

OVERLEAF Customers who bought Merona Sport related to this very real family depicted in our advertisements. The Archers were truly the all-American family that is often talked about but seldom seen.

cautiously sizing up whether we thought we could get along and work together. In the end, I decided to hire the formidable redhead. And you know what? Steve was right, as it was the best decision ever. Not only did Jeanne end up working for me for decades, but she also became much more than a work colleague. She became and remains to this very day a trusted friend. I have traveled the world with Jeanne, been at her wedding and at the birth of her kids, and spent many holidays with her and her family.

Jeanne worked with me initially on menswear and when I ventured into womenswear, she pivoted along with Isaac Mizrahi to help design the womenswear, too.

Jeanne has always acted as a calming barometer for me, objectively giving counsel to my crazy ideas and reining me in, when called for. She has become the de facto sister I never had, and I love her for it.

Starting in 1980, the design of the Merona Sport collections was a real phenomenon for me. The line consisted of a men's, a women's, and a kid's lines, and eventually, accessories were included. Building on the six basic forms—the polo shirt, rugby shirt, pouch rugby shirt, pull-on pant, and French terry cloth sweatshirt, originally created by Don Polley—my mission was to expand the line and increase the sales of the sportswear brand. With the financial backing of Oxford Industries, we were able to greatly grow the brand long before the term "athleisure" was coined. Made initially of 100 percent cotton—wool was added sometime later—Merona's palette began with primary, secondary, and tertiary colors. One of the first things I did was greatly expand the color range, adding colors such as jade, loden, and lavender for all sexes, sometimes with contrasting color piping and trim. Next, I added cotton sweaters and signature stripes that came in a plethora of combinations. Eventually, I added woven fabrics such as seersucker and whimsical prints. I then added outerwear, baseball caps, blankets, and beach towels, canvas totes, and even footwear. This quickly made Merona blossom into an over $150-million-a-year juggernaut. At one point, our salesmen were more like order takers than true salesmen as the demand was so high. The greatest thing about Merona for me was when people told me how good they felt when wearing the comfortable and cozy clothes. I was particularly proud of the fact that the sales outlets ranged from Bloomingdale's to Bergdorf Goodman, and from Macy's to Robinson's. We were nearly in every major retailer and tony specialty store in the country. One of my favorite things to do at that time was

Available at fine stores
Merona Sport 30 Rockefeller Plaza New York 10112
© 1983 Merona Sport

Merona®
SPORT
you could live your
Merona Sport

to get to airports early to just sit and count the number of men, women, and children I saw wearing Merona before my flight took off. It did not matter which airport, or which city, the results were always the same—lots and lots of people.

The other amazing thing about the "Merona era" was the fact that our workforce at 30 Rockefeller Plaza was very diverse. We had employees from South Africa, Israel, Hong Kong, and India, as well as the United States. I was yet to turn 30 years old, and I was among the most senior people in the company. There were all these very young accomplished people running million-dollar divisions successfully and almost everyone was under 30. Best of all, we enjoyed each other's company so much that, at the end of the day, we would go out together socially. We lived the life of the brand.

The other amazing thing was to see how many celebrities embraced the Merona Sport aesthetic. There are countless episodes of *Cheers* with Ted Danson in our rugby shirts. The actor Judd Hirsch loved the brand a lot. The late Richard Simmons was a huge fan of the brand, and even once surprised us by bursting into a sales meeting at the Rainbow Room wearing our clothing. When the director John Schlesinger died, his *New York Times* obituary pictured him wearing a Merona shirt I had designed.

Merona changed the fashion landscape as to how men, especially, viewed color in casual fashion. Men who had never ventured beyond conservative greys and tans embraced the bright and cheerful colors, and the spillover began to infiltrate their business attire wardrobes, too. Suddenly news anchors began to sport pink and purple neckties, which was a real breakthrough in the 1980s.

I feel a large part of the success of the brand was due in part to the approachable advertising campaigns lensed by Bruce Weber, which featured the very real Archer family. Some stores even copied our scrapbooklike format when they produced their own advertisements. When Steve Eisendrath, the vice-president, decided to leave the company, shortly afterward, I decided to leave, too. Within a few months, the once gigantically successful brand was kaput. The Merona name was sold by Oxford Industries to Target to be used for their private label merchandise, although that product bore no relationship to the previous behemoth brand.

RIGHT BELOW Isaac Mizrahi and I—photographed backstage after one of his cabaret performances—have continued our friendship long past the time he worked for me.

When I finally made the decision to go into the women's designer collection business, there were a few firm parameters that I established in my mind. Firstly, although it was "designer," I wanted the collection to be affordable and accessible. Secondly, if a woman wanted a blouse or a skirt, I wanted her to be able to buy it in several colors and not break the bank. As a designer primarily known for menswear, I felt I had something to prove in that I could design clothes for women, feminine clothes, and dare I say it. . . pretty clothes.

In the process of defining what my collection should look like I called my friend Ellin Saltzman, who was then the fashion director of Saks Fifth Avenue. I said that I wanted to discuss something important with her and she invited me to come right over to her office. My office was at 30 Rockefeller Plaza, just opposite Saks, so it was less than a five-minute walk away. "What should I do that will be different from all the other designers?" I asked.

OPPOSITE My entry into the women's designer arena was marked by the fact that I wanted to create pretty feminine clothing, not menswear for women. The hand intarsia sweater and skirt combination sold thousands of pieces.

Without hesitation, Ellin said, "Prints! Women love them, but most top designers work only in solid colors." She added: "But they have to be the right prints, or you'll end up eating a lot of garments."

I thought that was easy as I loved prints, though I was still not convinced that should be my main message. Two weeks later, I found myself on business in London and, as I was at the hotel reception desk checking into Claridge's, I spied from behind a stylish woman in a man-tailored tweed jacket, grey flannel trousers, and a smart felt hat. As she turned in profile I realized it was Anne Ball, the fashion director of Neiman Marcus at that time. I went over to her and asked her if she might join me for tea as I wanted to discuss something with her. She agreed and, as we began to sip our Earl Grey tea, I disclosed my plan to go into the women's designer business. Posing the same question I had to Ellin about designer collections, I was surprised when she answered in the same way. "Prints," she said confidently. "There is a real dearth of them in the designer collections business." It was then that I knew precisely what I had to do.

Prints it would be. A passel full of florals in bold bouquets and small rosebuds on cotton. Snapdragons and peonies, trellises laden with flowers on linen and silk—all original prints beautifully rendered by the artist Doug Johnston just for me.

The next step was to hire an assistant to work only on the womenswear line. By now I had quite a few assistants working on the lines of Merona Sport, Jeffrey Banks Menswear, and Jeffrey Banks Boys. I decided I wanted someone young, from the talent pool at Parsons, and so I called my old teacher Frank Rizzo, who was now the chair of the fashion department, for some recommendations. He readily proffered the name of Isaac Mizrahi, who was just about to graduate. "He's perfect for you," he said. But there was just one problem. Isaac was working part-time for my good and close friend Perry Ellis, and I was adamant that I was not going to poach an assistant from a dear friend. "No, no," Frank said. "Isaac is going to leave anyway, as he is the third man on the totem pole after Perry's top two assistants, Patricia Pastor and Jed Krascella. "You must see him!" Frank insisted. I agreed, albeit reluctantly. Informed by Frank of my friendship with Perry, a somewhat wary Isaac agreed to meet with me but only someplace away from Seventh Avenue as he did not want Perry catching on that we were talking. His paranoia notwithstanding, we agreed to meet on a blustery cold Saturday morning in February by the ice-skating rink in front of Rockefeller Center.

As I surveyed the sketches in his portfolio, it was instantly apparent to me that this boy was not only immensely talented, but also that I did not need to look further. Isaac was the one. I tried to put on my very best poker face so as to conceal my utter satisfaction with him, as I told him that I would get back to him shortly. I also said to myself, if he comes with me, I will be lucky if he stays for two years. One cannot hold onto this kind of talent for long. You simply must nurture it, shape it, and then send it on its way.

I called Frank right away to discuss what I should pay Isaac, and he tried to reassure me once again that Perry would be understanding as Isaac was already determined to leave his employ. Isaac and I spoke by telephone and hammered out the details. Isaac disclosed that he was going to give Perry two-weeks' notice. He felt it was best to tell Perry he was leaving at the end of the day when almost everyone else had left. With only Perry and him in the design studio, Isaac expressed his desire to leave. "But where are you going?" Perry asked.

"I am not at liberty to say," Isaac demurred. "You'll read about it in *Women's Wear Daily* soon enough."

Perry said, "I insist on knowing," barricading the studio door with his back against it, arms folded sternly against his chest.

"Okay, okay, I am going to work for Jeffrey Banks," Isaac blurted out. And Perry, his wicked sense of humor on full display countered in mock indignation, "You're leaving me for a Black woman?"

Isaac did come and work for me, and he was sensational, reminding me a lot of myself when I was his age with terrific confidence and tremendous style. However, there was still a lot of education to be had. For instance, when he came to me, Isaac had never seen the film *Funny Face*, but he was a very fast learner. Shortly after Isaac started work with me his father died, and he inherited his father's very large convertible. One Friday morning, Isaac proclaimed that he was going to drive out to the beach solo in his boat of a car for the whole weekend. Both my other assistant, Jeanne, and I admonished him that he must slather his very pale skin with tons of sunscreen lotion before taking in the sun at the beach.

Monday morning, a very lobster-red Isaac turned up at the sample room in intense discomfort, every inch of his once-pasty skin was now a bright shade of vermilion, even the soles of his feet. He said that the wearing of clothes, even the light loose shirt and pants he had on, was painful as it touched his skin. Sympathetic to his plight but bemused nonetheless by the comic figure in front of us, we suggested that he try to find some article of clothing in the sample room that might be more comfortable to wear. A few minutes later, Isaac emerged in a teal-colored cotton sleeveless floor-length caftan whose roomy shape provided a modicum of comfort for his sun-bruised body. Jeanne and I were in hysterics when a shoeless Isaac answered the door and let in a visiting salesman, proceeding to view swatches as if nothing were out of the ordinary.

I have always felt that Isaac missed his true calling—Borscht Belt comedian. He, along with designer Michael Kors, are two of the

OPPOSITE This slouchy cotton/linen trellis-patterned pantsuit and crepe-pleated blouse from my first women's collection appeared on the cover of *Women's Wear Daily*.

OPPOSITE Part of my strategy with my first women's collection was to use humble fabrics such as cotton broadcloth and transform them by using original prints as in this floral halter dress.

OVERLEAF LEFT Daniela was swathed in a violet cashmere evening gown with a matching coat and opera-length gloves.

OVERLEAF RIGHT I did a new take on the skirt suit with an oversized easy jacket and slim pencil skirt.

funniest designers I know. As predicted, Isaac stayed with me for exactly two years and then briefly worked for Calvin Klein as his assistant before branching out on his own and starting his own label. I cannot begin to tell you the amount of pride I felt at his first and every subsequent fashion show, knowing that I had played a very small part in shaping the talent of Isaac Mizrahi.

As much as I wanted to do womenswear at some point, in the early 1980s I was riding high on the waves of success mostly in menswear, and womenswear was not foremost in my mind. But Oxford Industries and its chairman, Hicks Lanier, had other thoughts. I think they were very concerned that their cash cow might sign up to do womenswear with someone else. After all, I was doing men's outerwear with Lakeland, furs with Alixandre, Jeffrey Banks Boys, and was in talks to do much, much more.

So, I was aggressively approached about signing with Oxford to do a Jeffrey Banks women's collection. I do not think they realized the scope and investment needed to start a collection business. Unlike Merona Sport, which was sampled and produced entirely offshore, a women's collection business would require a New York sample room, a separate sales force, showroom space, a huge investment in women's media advertising, and the heady cost of semiannual fashion shows. I carefully explained to Hicks that, because of all of this, a return on investment would probably not happen for at least four or five years. Unlike Merona, we would probably be in the red until that time. Not swayed by my protestations, Hicks, on the contrary, insisted on going forward with the project and urged me to sign a three-year contract that amounted to several million dollars to license a Jeffrey Banks women's collection.

Upon signing, we immediately went to work creating a beautiful dual showroom for menswear and womenswear that looked like the interior of a 1930s ocean liner, nodding to the stately lines of 30 Rockefeller Plaza, the building where our offices were located. I engaged Charles Swerz and Jerry Van Deelen, who had designed my apartment, to craft the space using lush materials like linen velvet and herringbone linen and take their cues from Jean-Michel Frank, the famous French interior designer. I wanted the clothes to be the stand-out colors in a beige/taupe/cream world that resembled a residence, so I devised a system whereby the clothes were housed in custom-made oversized steamer trunks crafted from drill cloth, wood, and brass studs. We found an old maker of trunks in New Jersey who

could put Vuitton to shame. We hired away from Norma Kamali a crackerjack president named Shelley Moran to run the division and rented a penthouse sample room space on Sixth Avenue in the garment center. I hired the young Isaac Mizrahi to work alongside my longtime assistant, Jeanne Shea Russo. Various sample hands were hired, and sewing equipment was acquired. There was only one problem: All of these people were quickly in place by the early spring, but Oxford Industries wanted to delay launching the collection for almost a full year, so that we would only debut the following fall. I thought it was crazy and a waste of a tremendous amount of money to wait, while keeping all those people on the payroll. Fall collections do tend to be the biggest money-makers when it comes to sales, but I thought waiting almost a whole year was simply slothful.

Fortunately, I convinced the powers that be to launch in spring and not wait for the traditional fall market. My vision for the line was that it should be entirely feminine. There would be elements of tailoring which I always loved but my mantra was that these clothes had to be "pretty." Most importantly, although I wanted them to be considered "designer," I also wanted them to be desirable and affordable. Luckily, we were launching at the same time as Anne Klein II, a less expensive version of the mother collection whose price points coincided with ours, and a new segment of the market was born. It was coined "bridge" by buyers and editors alike. Using a lot of great, but reasonably priced base fabrics interspersed with some stunning European gems, we were able to price the print-laden floral-filled collection in a way that made them very appealing to retailers. Several cover stories in *Women's Wear Daily* and excellent media coverage greeted the new collection. I was ecstatic and tremendously pleased with all the retailers we sold to right off the bat, including Neiman Marcus, Saks Fifth Avenue, Bergdorf Goodman, Henri Bendel, and Lord & Taylor. I flew to Dallas, and Neiman's gave me a tremendous send-off, with lots and lots of sales and a great party afterward at the Stark Club, a newly opened hot spot. At the end of the day, we made four million dollars on a first collection that no one wanted to do initially.

Then, we were on to fall. Feeling my designer oats, I went for a more sophisticated look with Art Deco–inspired prints and elegant cashmere-knit evening pieces. What I should have done was just recolor the spring florals into fall colors, and we would have had another monster hit, but my designer ego got the best of me. Still, we booked a sizable business, and lessons learned, I was determined in the future to listen to our sales team a lot more closely.

To my great surprise, that was not to be. Hicks showed up unannounced in my office and said that a decision had been made not to continue with the women's line. When I asked why, he said, "Well, it's going to take a while until you reach $40 million."

I quickly countered, "But I said you weren't going to make *any* money until the fourth or fifth year."

Hicks added, "Nonetheless, I think you'll be happy with everything else you are doing with us, designing Merona Sport and Jeffrey Banks Men's." Well, boy was he wrong. He had signed a three-year multimillion-dollar agreement with me with both eyes wide open and I intended to make him honor it to the very last dollar. My resolve was strengthened the very next day, when *Women's Wear Daily* published a story, without ever talking to me, that stated, "Jeffrey Banks to close women's line." I was furious and mortified at the same time. I wanted to hide under the covers and never leave my apartment. When I did, I felt that every passerby was eyeing me and thinking . . . what a failure.

I hired a lawyer and decided to take on Oxford and its chair by suing in New York and not in the company's home base of Georgia. Our first bit of luck was finding out that the judge was a woman and that she was Black. Second, I decided to hire a sexy female process server to come into the Merona offices and embarrass one of their executives by serving him the papers in front of all his colleagues. I was also very vocal, vowing to vent my feelings about the closing of the line at the upcoming meeting with all the shareholders. Ultimately I prevailed and although we parted ways, I received a multimillion-dollar settlement and plowed that right back into the menswear business.

In July 1993 I was on vacation in Houston, visiting my friends John Conroy and Dr. Bob Parke. It was about 110 degrees, and I was in their swimming pool sniffling with a summer cold. Bob, who practiced as an otolaryngologist, or throat surgeon, questioned why I was experiencing a cold in such hot weather. "I get colds all the time," I replied.

"That's not normal," Bob said. "I think you may have a deviated septum, and I intend to fix that," he said firmly.

And just as firmly I replied, "I am here for 10 days on vacation, and you are not going to give me a nose job!"

"No, no, the way I do this surgery, if I operate on you at 9am, you will be out of surgery by 1pm, back here by 4 pm, and drinking margaritas by 6pm.

"Really?" I said.

"Yes," he countered. "I want you to call your ears, nose, and throat doctor in New York and have him FedEx overnight X-rays of your head to me so I can see exactly what I am working with."

I did as I was instructed, and my doctor did as I requested, but the next day when Bob received the X-rays, he was not happy. "These aren't very good, and if I am going to operate, I need something much clearer," he said. He decided to order a very early morning MRI for me at the sister hospital near Baylor where he had an office. In Houston, there are 21 hospitals in a 2.1-square-mile district. I had never even heard of an MRI before, but I was game. So, at 7am the next morning, I had my first full body MRI. If you have never had one, there is this intensely loud sound like jackhammering in a very close coffinlike chamber for at least 25 minutes. And you must stay perfectly still.

Fortunately, I am not claustrophobic, and I actually fell asleep.

Delivering the results to Bob in person using the skyway between the hospitals, I felt totally relaxed knowing that I was in his talented hands. You see, Bob had actually operated on the Shah of Iran's nephew whose throat was almost severed due to a serious car accident. Even though the accident happened in Iran, he was airlifted to Texas to be successfully operated on.

Bob took a brief few minutes to examine the MRI results and then said, "Will you excuse me for a few minutes? I will be right back."

I said, "Sure," not feeling the least bit worried.

About 25 minutes later, Bob returned with 10 doctors in white coats in tow and I began to get a bit concerned. "What's going on, Bob?" I asked.

"Well," he said, his Texas sense of humor coming to the fore, "the good news is that I canceled the septum operation." So, I asked him what the bad news was.

"You have a really big brain tumor," he answered. It seems that Bob spotted what he perceived to be a tumor on the MRI charts, and given that he was a throat surgeon, he consulted with the other doctors he had invited to accompany him to my room.

And thus began the grand inquisition. The doctors in the room bombarded me with a host of questions and a battery of tests. Did I get migraines? Any fainting? Any lapses of memory? As I said no to all of those questions, other symptoms did show up. The doctors discovered that I was starting to lose my peripheral vision and if this vision loss was not addressed, I would be blind. In addition, my pituitary gland, which is usually the size of a small walnut, had been eaten up by the tumor and was now only about the size of a fingernail. My hormones were so out of whack that they said if nothing was done my chest would soon start to lactate. Also, I had been gaining weight slowly for about 10 years, though I was seldom eating more than once a day. It turns out that my body was not—due to the undersized pituitary gland—producing an adequate amount of testosterone. Without it, all the exercise in the world would not reduce fat. The lack of testosterone also contributed to my complete lack of sex drive, for which I had been seeing a therapist.

All of the various tests took several hours to administer and finally, at about 3pm when completed, I said, "Okay, fellas, what do we do about this?"

The lead doctor said, "We recommend a regimen of drugs and chemicals to shrink the tumor."

I said, "You mean chemo?"

They answered; "Well, yes."

I countered with "For how long?"

They said, "Oh, probably once a month, every month, for the rest of your life."

I responded, "There's no way I am going to be tethered to a chemo drip every month for the rest of my life. You cut this thing out of me right now." But the doctors did not go along with my suggestion.

"That would be a very serious and possibly dangerous operation and we don't really recommend it. In fact, we recommend that you go back to New York and consult with your primary physician before doing anything," they said. I asked why I should do that when I had 11 doctors right here in this room with me now. And as insistent as I was, the doctors were equally insistent that I should speak with my doctor.

In the end, I did go back to New York and consulted with my doctor, Dr. Jeff Greene. I told him to recommend a neurosurgeon he personally knew to perform the surgery that I considered absolutely essential.

"I can't," he said. "All the surgeons I know personally are heads of hospitals in different states, and they no longer operate." And so, I lied to my insurance carrier, saying that it was imperative that I have this brain surgery, and they agreed to pay for round-trip first-class airfare back to Houston, where I had the scheduled nine-hour surgery on the Friday of Labor Day weekend.

Dr. Bob even assisted in the surgery since it was actually done (gasp!) through my nose. I awoke woozily from the surgery with a group of doctors asking me a battalion of questions.

"How many fingers am I holding up?"

I answered, "Three."

Next was: "Who is the President?"

I said "Clinton!" Then, they asked more questions to ascertain the level of my brain's function. The large tumor had been removed and the early tests came back as being noncancerous. That was usually the case with my type of tumor, though not always. When satisfied that my answers corresponded with a successfully completed operation, the doctors left, and I relaxed for a few minutes. That is until I realized that I had a very large, roughly 12-inch-by-12-inch bandage on my abdomen.

Alarmed, I rang the nurse to get Dr. Bob back quickly in my room. As he entered I shouted, "Why do I have a bandage on my stomach when I just had brain surgery?" Trying to calm me, he explained that after removing the tumor they realized that the empty cavity was so big that I would be plagued with a lifetime of migraines if it was not filled. Therefore, while I was under anesthesia, they filled the cavity with fatty tissue from my tummy. "You mean," I said, "that I have a fat head?"

Bob said, "In a manner of speaking, yes, you do." I bounced back in record time staying in the ICU only a couple of days and by the week's end, I was on a jet ski for hours on a lake outside of Houston.

A few months later at a black-tie affair at the New York State Theater, I spied Ralph Lauren, who had had a serious brain tumor several years prior. "I don't know if you are aware of this," I said, "but Ralph, I just had a brain tumor myself." Looking up at me very seriously Ralph said "Jeffrey. . . Are you copying me?" We then both roared with laughter.

One of the very first gay porn actors to achieve notoriety was Casey Donovan, who was born in New York as John Calvin Culver. The 1971 film *Boys in the Sand* cemented his status as a film icon. Although he acted in several mainstream productions, he was known primarily for his adult film work. His blond, blue-eyed good looks landed him a stint as a highly paid model at the Wilhelmina Models agency. He also acted in Broadway and off-Broadway plays.

When I rented a house in the Fire Island Pines in the 1970s I loved to go dancing with my friends in Cherry Grove on Saturday nights. At the end of one very warm Saturday evening, I walked back through the wooded area between the Grove and the Pines known as the Meat Rack. A sexual assignation was definitely not on my mind as I briskly walked through the trees, but I was keenly aware that for many men this was ground zero. I suddenly came upon a solitary figure tied to a tree with his back to me and his trousers puddled at his feet. In my naivete, I thought someone had played a cruel trick on him, whom I quickly recognized as Cal Culver. When I asked if he needed help, he smiled and tried to reassure me that his tied-up state was intentional. "I am fine," he said.

"Are you sure?" I asked, as he suddenly kissed me full-on. I must admit I kissed him back, but when he told me once again that he was okay, on my way I went.

The next day, while lounging on the beach with my friends in the late afternoon, who should stroll by but Cal, with a couple of his friends. He spotted me immediately, left his friends, came over to me, and proceeded to tell my friends what a great kisser he thought I was. I instantly achieved superstar status with my friends who made fun of me for the rest of the day about my kissing abilities.

A few months later, I called Cal when I found out that our birthdays were one day and ten years apart and asked him if I could take him out to dinner. Happily, he said yes, and I took him for prime rib to the One If by Land, Two if by Sea restaurant in Greenwich Village. What was so great about the dinner was that I found out what a smart, funny, and utterly charming man this former schoolteacher was. After dinner, I asked if he would like to come back to my apartment and, once again, he complimented me on my kissing skills. Although I asked him to stay the night, he politely declined and said his goodbyes as I went to bed still somewhat in disbelief, only to be awakened by a sharp knocking on my door. My neighbor said that there was a man trapped in the elevator who was calling my name. I glanced quickly at the clock and realized that poor Cal had been in the elevator for about 20 minutes, as I quickly ran down four flights

OPPOSITE Calvin Culver, a former schoolteacher, also known as Casey Donovan, was featured on the cover of one of my vintage *After Dark* magazines.

AFTER DARK
MAGAZINE OF ENTERTAINMENT
$1.00
DECEMBER 1972
BETTE DAVIS
BEN VEREEN
PLACIDO DOMINGO
CAL CULVER

OPPOSITE Cole Tucker, whose real name was Richard Allen Karp, became a porn actor at the age of 43.

of stairs to the firehouse next door for help. The firemen quickly dislodged the imposing steel doors only to reveal a smiling, utterly calm Cal who shrugged it off as though nothing had happened. Unfortunately, Calvin Culver died in 1987 of an AIDS-related pulmonary infection at the age of 43.

Richard Allen Karp was quite the anomaly in the world of gay porn, making his first film at the age of 43 under the name Cole Tucker. His macho, cigar-chomping looks, redolent of a grown-up G.I. Joe doll, were an instant hit and he developed a huge fan base. With his closely cropped dark blond hair and a massive tattoo on his left shoulder, he was handsome and forbidding.

I had decided to make one more foray to the Black Party, the infamous annual bacchanalian event held at Roseland, which was mostly full of black leather-clad men dancing all night. I wanted to go because of rumors that this might be the last one, as the ballroom was slated to close and possibly be demolished. Roseland got its start in 1919 and was famous as a "dime-a-dance" hall during the Depression. In the 1940s and 1950s, it was a popular big-band venue, moving to its current location in 1956. With its imminent closing, I felt it was like the end of Weimar Germany and a bit like John Van Druten or Christopher Isherwood trying to take in the whole scene before it was gone forever. As I stood on the balcony looking down at the hundreds of undulating bodies dancing below me, I happened to glance backward and there, along the back wall with a host of friends, was Cole. He was instantly recognizable even among the similar-looking musclemen surrounding him. I turned away quickly and began to lean over the balcony again when I suddenly realized there was someone standing mere inches away. I looked up to see Cole, standing right next to me. "I am really proud of you," I said, not even looking at him. You see, I had read that he had been embroiled in a scandal in Great Britain as he had been carrying on an affair with a prominent married politician and one of London's scandalous tabloids was on the verge of outing not only their liaison but Cole's HIV-positive status. Cole boldly got ahead of the story by announcing not only his health status, but that he was proudly romantically involved with the politician. "I think what you did was great, and I am proud of you," I reiterated. Suddenly, and with no warning, he kissed me passionately and then thanked me.

"I hope you'll stick around for the show later," he said. I surmised he meant one of the several live sex shows that were part and parcel of the Black Party. I didn't stick around and left, feeling totally satisfied. Cole Tucker died in 2015 of an AIDS-related illness.

IV. MENTORS

From the moment I learned about Ralph Lauren, years before the internet or his advertising campaigns, I was determined that I wanted to work for and learn from him. His attention to detail and uncompromising design integrity immediately appealed to me. I think what I loved was his innate ability to tell stories through his clothing. It was not just an article of clothing but the world in which that piece existed. Ralph dreamed big, and I wanted to dream big with him.

After being offered a part-time job while attending college, I was beyond thrilled. When I called him to tell him which days of the week I was available to work, he asked me if I would be attending my prom. I said yes. "What are you going to wear?" he asked.

I answered, "You know, I am having a real problem with that." As it was 1971, powder-blue tuxes with matching ruffled shirts and matching platform patent leather boots ruled. That was the antithesis of how I wanted to appear. I wanted to look like Fred Astaire in a sleek black tuxedo with peak lapels and a white wing-collar tuxedo shirt.

After I relayed my dilemma, Ralph said, "What size are you?"

I replied, "37 Regular."

He said, "So am I. And what size shirt?"

I replied, "14½, 33."

Ralph added, "So am I. And what size shoe?"

I said, "7½!"

Ralph said, "Me too! I am going to let you borrow my tuxedo for your prom."

Believe it or not, as this was in 1971, there was no FedEx, so Ralph had someone in his office take the shirt, tuxedo, shoes, and bow tie, packed in a small box to the Greyhound bus station where it was put in the undercarriage of the bus for me to retrieve several hours later in Washington, DC. After a little tailoring (I had to lengthen the pants a bit), I got to wear Ralph's personal tuxedo to my high school prom.

Working for Ralph at the age of 17, I have to say I was treated very well. If he was invited to an event, I was invited. I was constantly wearing my tuxedo—by now I had my very own—and I was always learning. I remember one Saturday, spending the day with him going to Brooks Brothers, where we each bought several pairs of the hand-turned cable wool socks, after the salesclerk informed us that Brooks Brothers was going to be discontinuing them. I remember they were a staggering $6.50 each! As we walked uptown, we stopped at Paul Stuart, where he introduced me to Clifford Grodd, the owner of the chic menswear haberdashery. We then landed at Bonwit Teller, where Ralph explained to me the finer points of the roll of a button-down collar using a Bill Blass men's shirt as an example. As we walked

OPPOSITE A denim-clad Ralph Lauren, around the time I met him, was supremely confident in his ability to conquer the world.

OVERLEAF In April 1973, Fred Astaire was the second person to be honored by the Film Society of Lincoln Center. In this photograph, I was standing directly behind Martin E. Segal, president of the Film Society, and of course, Fred Astaire. Also included, *from left to right*, were Ralph Lauren, Sal Cesarani, and Nancy Cesarani.

east, Ralph was gobsmacked as we caught sight of the actress and model Candice Bergen around the corner from Roland Meledandri's tailoring shop.

One very muggy day about a year later, I arrived at the office early to see that only Michael Bernstein, Ralph's head financial guy was already at his desk. As I said good morning, I noticed that Michael had a look on his face as though someone had just died. "What's wrong?" I asked.

"Sit down, Jeff," he said, motioning for me to sit on the chair opposite his desk. "I have some bad news, we cannot make payroll today."

My immediate thought, was, as the latest hire and the youngest person there, that this was liable to be my last day at work. Michael cautioned me not to say anything to anyone else. And so, as the other employees began to arrive, I was burdened with this horrible secret that the end might be near, and I could not say a thing.

By the time Ralph arrived at the office in a denim jacket and jeans, the muggy morning had turned into driving rain, and he was soaking wet. He immediately went into a closed-door meeting with Michael and others for what seemed an eternity. In the meantime, I learned that the Coty Award Committee had voted to give Ralph his second Menswear Award the day before, with the actual awards ceremony to take place in September. However, that almost seemed negligible as a furrowed-brow Ralph finally emerged from Michael's office.

"Jeffrey, I need you to go with me now." Ralph said, as he came into the office I shared with Buffy Birrittella.

As we went down the elevator in silence, I thought, "Okay, this is the end." Waiting in the pouring rain without an umbrella, Ralph explained that he wanted me to accompany him back to his apartment, as he needed to change his clothes. Finally, someone emerged from a cab nearby, and we grabbed it as the feeling of dread swept over me. As we departed, Ralph turned to me and I thought, here it comes . . . I am going to be fired right here in this taxi. "Jeffrey, what should we do for the Coty Awards show?" Ralph asked earnestly.

I couldn't believe it. He couldn't make the payroll today, but that was Ralph's focus? Well, my brain went into overdrive, and I blurted out, "It's got to be in black and white, like a 1930s film, very Gatsby-esque!" Ralph said excitedly, "I love it! As soon as you get back to the office, start to work on it." We had arrived at Ralph's apartment, and he quickly changed into a smart dark suit and asked me, as the rain had stopped, to drop him off at Bloomingdale's on my way back to the office. Little did I know that this was to have lunch with Marvin Traub, Bloomingdale's CEO, to ask him if he would advance him funds for the merchandise that had yet to be made or shipped for the fall. Miraculously, Marvin famously agreed, allowing Polo to go forward another day by being able to pay their employees, including me.

OPPOSITE This is Ralph as I always remember him nattily attired and limousine-ready.

OVERLEAF On the occasion of Ralph Lauren's 50th year in business, he received a special CFDA Award. That evening, I along with several others, was asked to speak about Ralph. Here, we paused for a moment before the proceedings.

My vision for the Coty Awards show was to have giant projections of male movie stars as a background to handsome male models clad in black cashmere turtlenecks, black satin trousers, and white alpaca Polo coats draped over the shoulders of white cashmere sweaters and white flannel trousers, equestrians in cream cavalry twill jodhpurs, and black-and-white tweed jackets. In the middle of the show, there would be a pastel interlude of womenswear with 1930s-style veiled hats by Don Kline and chic angora twinsets. I borrowed ivory cigarette holders and jewelry from Cartier, and it all looked very cinematic.

I was very happy to work on the men's and the women's collections, and my knowledge of womenswear from years of poring over *Vogue* and *Harper's Bazaar*, particularly when it came to fabrics, came in handy. If Ralph wanted wool jersey, I knew to call Jasco, and if we needed suede, I was off to Libra Leathers.

I have to say that from day one, I believed in Ralph Lauren's vision, and none of the things he ventured into, long after I left his employ, were a surprise to me. I knew he would be as big as he is today, and I never doubted for a moment that he wouldn't be.

On the occasion of his 50th Anniversary in business, Ralph was given a very special gold-plated CFDA award. Thom Browne, Tommy Hilfiger, Michael Kors, John Varvatos, Diane von Furstenberg, Marcus Wainwright, Alexander Wang, Vera Wang, Jason Wu, and I were asked to speak briefly about the impact Ralph had made on us and the America fashion industry as a whole. In his acceptance speech, Ralph stopped mid-speech and brought me over to the mic. He proceeded to use his time to applaud me as someone who had worked for him and whose success he was so very proud of. It was one of the greatest moments of my life.

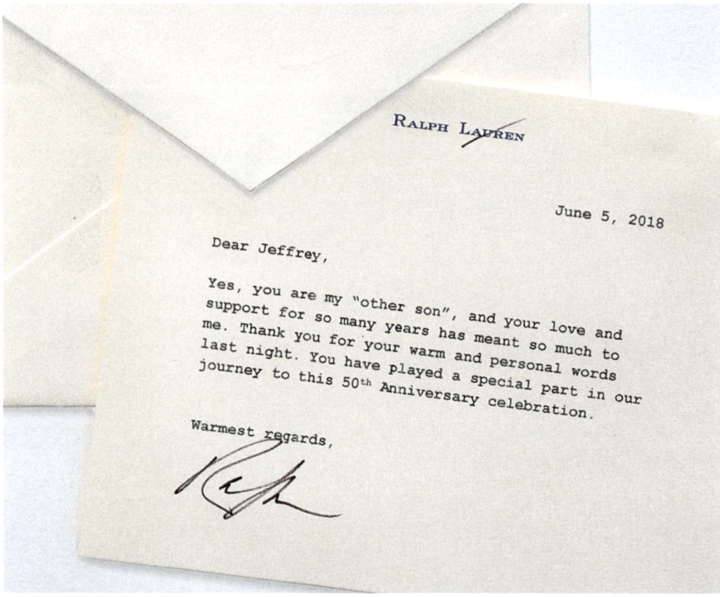

RALPH LAUREN

June 5, 2018

Dear Jeffrey,

Yes, you are my "other son", and your love and support for so many years has meant so much to me. Thank you for your warm and personal words last night. You have played a special part in our journey to this 50th Anniversary celebration.

Warmest regards,

LEFT BELOW I received this personal note from Ralph Lauren following his big CFDA evening.

OPPOSITE The invitation to Ralph Lauren's 50th anniversary show and the black-tie dinner that came after it is a memento from a special evening.

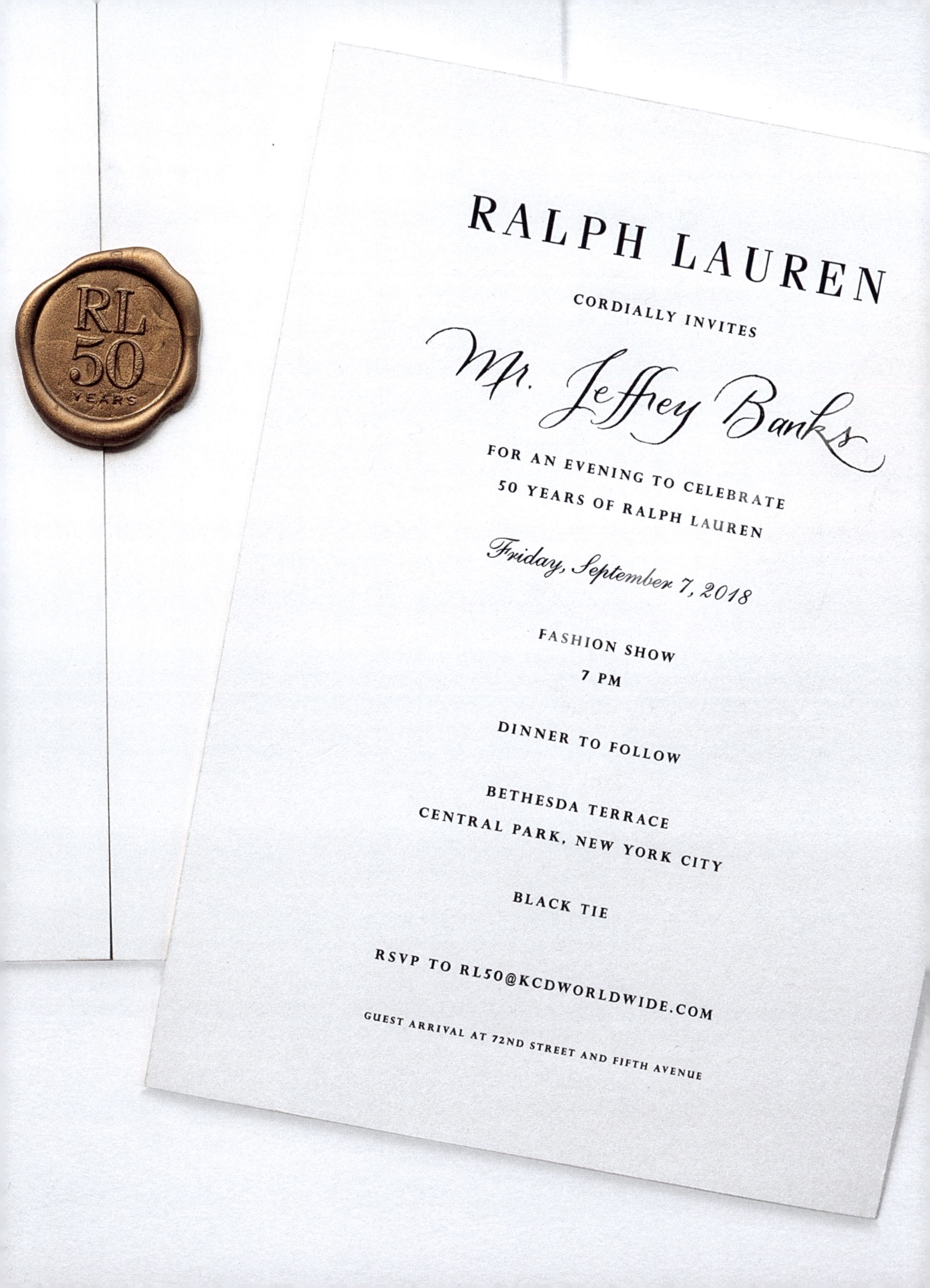

RALPH LAUREN

CORDIALLY INVITES

Mr. Jeffrey Banks

FOR AN EVENING TO CELEBRATE
50 YEARS OF RALPH LAUREN

Friday, September 7, 2018

FASHION SHOW
7 PM

DINNER TO FOLLOW

BETHESDA TERRACE
CENTRAL PARK, NEW YORK CITY

BLACK TIE

RSVP TO RL50@KCDWORLDWIDE.COM

GUEST ARRIVAL AT 72ND STREET AND FIFTH AVENUE

Derrill Radcliff Osborn was a combination of the entrepreneur and circus maestro P. T. Barnum and Anna Piaggi, the flamboyant Italian fashion journalist. When I first broke out on my own working with Irving Selbst, the uber-menswear maven, he arranged to have Mr. Osborn, the men's and boys' tailored clothing buyer at Saks Fifth Avenue, be the first buyer to see the line.

I had stolen the Anne Klein sportswear concept of mix-and-match tailored separates as a jumping-off point for the first spring collection. Utilizing fabrics like cotton poplin, seersucker, cotton gabardine, and linen, all of the pieces that included pants, sports coats, vests, and shorts came in red, pink, olive, navy, grey, yellow, white, and light blue, leaving the customer the freedom to combine their outfits at will. As we were waiting for our new showroom at 1290 Avenue of the Americas to be finished, we were working out of a suite at the nearby Warwick Hotel. Irving insisted that I present the collection to Derrill, and I was somewhat terrified when this P. G. Wodehouse–like character arrived sporting a straw boater and walking stick and speaking in a somewhat indiscernible accent that was in turns vaguely British and faintly Southern. He sat in silence as I laid out the swatches and described the clothing models. When I finished, there was nary a word or comment from him, and I thought, this man hated everything. Irving quickly spoke up. "So, Derrill, what did you think?" After what seemed an interminable silence, Derrill replied, "Mr. Selbst, we like it very much and would like to feature it in all of the Saks Fifth Avenue 49th Street windows for next Easter."

Irving was over the moon excited knowing that up to that time all the men's windows had never been devoted to just one designer. As he placed his hand on the doorknob to leave, Derrill turned back and said, "There's just one thing . . ." Irving quickly answered: "Anything." And gesturing toward me, he added, "We want his name on the label." And with that, he was gone.

A few weeks after that auspicious first meeting, I was speaking to my friend Vincent Petragnani, who was telling me about this nattily dressed man he had met and gone home with from an Upper East Side bar. "You would just love the way he was dressed!" he said, excitedly. "I think he works in retail." I asked what his name was. "Derrick Osborne!" he quipped.

"No, it's not," I shot back. "It's Derrill Radcliff Osborn, and he's my buyer from Saks Fifth Avenue!" Subsequently, I learned that Derrill was from Abilene, Texas, and the faux British accent, I guessed, was taken on to school the Texas drawl out of his syntax. In any event, despite our professional relationship, we became great friends, and

RIGHT I often likened the original style of my colleague and friend, the iconoclastic Derrill Radcliff Osborn, to a male version of the Italian fashion writer Anna Piaggi's persona to his right.

he was definitely one of the earliest supporters championing my line. By the second fall season, Saks was featuring my tartan Shetland sports coats not only in their windows but in a full-page advertisement in the *New York Times* that, in my naivete, I directed the art department not only in choosing the Central Park setting but also which horse and male model they should use.

When I went to London for the first time shortly after meeting Derrill, I went to Lock & Co. and purchased a chocolate brown derby bowler hat as a gift for him, which he thoroughly enjoyed and wore forever. Over time, Derrill became a trusted mentor as well as a valued friend. His beautiful hand-painted and calligraphed holiday cards were sent to me but also my mother. I saved them all.

Eventually, Derrill returned to Dallas and Neiman Marcus where he had started his retail career, as a vice-president. His death shortly after his retirement from Neiman's was a blow to the industry and his memorial—planned in every detail by Derrill years in advance—was choreographed like a royal state funeral as only he could have done.

OPPOSITE The photo-journalist Bill Cunningham started his career in fashion as a milliner using the name William J, so as not to embarrass his conservative Boston family.

On September 14, 1982, Bloomingdale's debuted another of their blockbuster-themed store-wide promotions. This time, instead of France or Spain, the theme was "America, the Beautiful." Throughout the store, products touting all things American were front and center. Midway through the evening, guests were asked to leave the store and reconvene at the Cinema 1 movie theater across Third Avenue for a special film celebrating the theme that was narrated by Bill Cunningham. As we crossed 59th Street on the way to the theater, passing the newsstand at the corner, my assistant, Jeanne Russo, spied a stack of newspapers with the glaring headline: "Princess Grace of Monaco Is Dead."

She pulled me back to the stand to see the unsettling news for myself as we dejectedly filed into the theater. I was morosely upset until the lights went down and I heard Bill's soothing New England voice describing the merits of the heartland of America. Though he was completely unseen, Bill's knowledge and humor came through loud and clear in the film about what made America great. I remember thinking at the film's end that I just wanted to lock him up in a room with a tape recorder and let him expound on whatever subject he wanted to for hours on end, knowing that regardless of subject, it would no doubt be brilliant.

I don't remember exactly when I met Bill for the first time, but I do know he was one of the very first visitors to our new 1290 Avenue of the Americas showroom in the early 1970s. He had called me and asked if he could come up and see the clothes, having heard that I was doing some interesting things.

It was at this first meeting that I received the official Cunningham sobriquet of "child." So many Bill fans will know what I mean as he bestowed that blessing on many (old and young). My immediate impression was that this man was perhaps the most knowledgeable person I had ever met when it came to fashion. His mind was like a fashion encyclopedia, with instant recall when it came to historical references and creative influences. Bill was the kindest human being, and I think the foulest thing to ever escape his lips might have been an "Oh, shoot!"

At one point, my office was in the old Henri Bendel building on 57th Street. I got to see Bill, sometimes on a daily basis, but was always careful not to interrupt him as he stalked his fashionable prey in front of Tiffany and Co. or Bergdorf Goodman. Although Bill was overwhelmed on a daily basis with hundreds of invitations to shows, galas, exhibits, and parties, often going to five or six in a single evening, he was extremely loyal and always seemed to attend

LEFT Nick Nicholson, along with me and several others, spearheaded a campaign to have the corner of 57th Street and Fifth Avenue in Manhattan named after Bill Cunningham. It happened, albeit briefly.

anything I invited him to, whether it was a book launch, charity gala, or birthday party.

One of the secrets I employed was knowing that Bill did not do email, so I would personally go to the *New York Times* mailroom entrance and drop off a printed invitation no sooner than a day or two before the event, ensuring it would be at the top or near the top of the plethora of mail he received on a daily basis.

Once, on the eve of the launch of my book on Perry Ellis, I had not heard back whether Bill would attend (which was not all that unusual). But as I was headed east on 40th Street, I saw the back of Bill's famous blue jacket in a deli. I screamed for the cab to stop, hurriedly paid the driver, and rushed into the deli, the Perry Ellis book in hand, to implore him to attend that night. He assured me he would be there and give the launch generous and glorious coverage. As a New Yorker, being photographed by Bill was a badge of honor, to be remembered and bragged about for years to come. Just ask anyone who was captured by his lens.

Unfailingly shy, Bill hated to be the center of attention and fought vigorously not to have that great documentary made about him. After seeing his documentary film early on, I ran into Bill on the street and breathlessly exclaimed how great I thought the film was.

RIGHT On a sweltering July 6 in 2016, workmen anointed the corner of 57th Street and Fifth Avenue by naming it after perhaps its most famous habitue, Bill Cunningham.

"Never saw it, never will," Bill said, cutting me off. He felt the film ruined his anonymity, which he understood to be so important for his reportage. What Bill would not acknowledge however, was that he was as famous a New York City icon as the mayor, Brooke Astor, or George Steinbrenner.

Not long after, Bill had a very untimely and unexpected death, and I, along with Nick Nicholson and several others mounted a grassroots social media campaign to have the corner of 57th Street and Fifth Avenue renamed in his honor as "Bill's Corner." Amassing hundreds of names on a petition, we surprised ourselves at how fast we got the city to agree, and in just over two weeks, a street sign with a grand unveiling by the mayor's wife, Chirlane McCray, was planned. The only caveat was that we were told the renaming would not be permanent as state legislation would have to be enacted for that to happen. But despite what we were told that sign was there for almost the next six months.

The spirit of Bill haunts me whenever I walk down Fifth or Madison Avenues, but in a very good way. Bill Cunningham represented everything good in New Yorkers and what we all hope to achieve someday as great citizens.

OPPOSITE I have loved tartan plaid since I was a child. Bruce Weber captured my horse-blanket-sized sports jackets in a myriad of tartans.

They say that one should never meet one's heroes as one is bound to be disappointed. I do not believe that for a single second. Always an ardent fan of the beautiful work of the photographer Bruce Weber, meeting him only increased the admiration I had for him, not only as an artist but also as someone who has become a close and loving friend.

When I first started designing the Merona Sport line, I was dismayed by the utterly dismal advertising they were doing: Quarter-page black-and-white advertisements in *Gentleman's Quarterly* for this very colorful line were shot on salespersons from the showroom. As I said to Steve Eisendrath, "If you are going to do advertisements, they should at least be a full-page or a double-page spread in color, shot by a professional top-notch photographer." Steve asked whom I would suggest. "It has to be Bruce Weber," I insisted. I was a fan of Bruce's naturalistic, wholesome style and of the gorgeous work he had done for both Calvin Klein and Ralph Lauren.

I cannot tell you how excited I was to meet him when he came to our offices at 30 Rockefeller Plaza. The meeting had been brokered by Don Wise, the head of our advertising agency at the time who happened to be in our showroom as I discussed my vision for Merona advertisements. "Bruce," I said, "I love what you do for Ralph but those model families always look so perfect and so pristine with nary a scuff on their white sneakers and a look of a certain distance between family members. There must be a real family out there that's good-looking and all-American, but not necessarily model-perfect." Bruce looked at me with a twinkle in his eye and reached into his back pocket for his thick wallet. He took out a Polaroid snapshot of a real family—mother, father, and children in a rowboat on the water. I knew at once this was it, that this was the family I had been searching for. They were the Archers: Bob Archer, a neckwear salesman for Christian Dior; his wife, Madolin, who was a schoolteacher; and their three children. What was unique about them was that they were not models. In fact, Madolin was slightly taller than Bob and was an athletic yet very attractive size 12.

The very first campaign was based on a family's full day at the beach. Unfortunately, Bruce only had half a day for the shoot. We shot it on the beach in Bellport, near Bruce's summer home on Long Island. During a brief break, Bruce, and I were discussing our mutual love of the work of photographer George Hoyningen-Huene and Michael Trask, the art director from Wise's office, interrupted us asking who he was. Incensed by his lack of historical knowledge of fashion photography, I ran off to a pay phone and called Trask's boss and asked that he be immediately called back to his office. I did not feel he was needed any longer, and it was at that moment that I felt Bruce and I truly bonded as friends. That first campaign was a huge hit with consumers—and especially with female customers who saw themselves in Madolin's less than model-sized figure, but also with the retail trade in general. The family snapshot layout of the campaigns worked so well that when the Archers eventually had a fourth child, the baby was written into the campaign and we created Merona Sport diaper covers as part of the line.

It was only natural, when I began to do advertisements for the first time that I used Bruce to shoot my campaigns, and I was thrilled with the results. Bruce had seen a young surfer by the name of Rick Hogue in California, with tremendously large shoulders, a small waist, and sun-bleached, almost white, long blond hair, whom he thought would be ideal for my first campaign. Again, seeing a single snapshot and Bruce's excellent judgment, I said, "Let's go with him." Shortly thereafter, Rick took a red-eye flight Friday night and arrived at 30 Rockefeller Center early Saturday morning. I had made a suit in advance in a size 44 long owing to Rick's broad shoulders, but the waist of the jacket was tremendous. When I asked Rick to try on the suit trousers, he hesitated briefly and then explained *sotto voce* that he wasn't wearing any underwear under his OP corduroy shorts. Amused, I gestured to my office as a place where he could change out of view of any prying eyes. When he emerged, I also informed him that we needed to cut his hair. He happily obliged to great results and, I must say, for years after, he maintained the haircut we had given him.

Every time we shot together thereafter, I was intensely in awe of Bruce's creativity, and his unerring eye for detail, and the quiet and commanding confidence of his work. I looked forward with the greatest of pleasure to every shoot and the magic that Bruce could make using his lens and the clothes that I had designed.

I was told that usually, when shooting a designer's collection, Bruce preferred that a designer not be present, but he really enjoyed it when I was there, paying me the ultimate compliment by saying I was the most organized designer he had worked with and that we had accomplished more shots in one day than he had ever done before.

What I love most about Bruce is that he is a true Renaissance man, with a curiosity about so many different things and a true calling that goes beyond photography. He is interested in the theater, literature, film, and music, and these interests color and inform everything he does. His many books speak to his fondness for so many things and especially his beloved dogs.

I worked with Bruce exclusively for about five years until I just could

OPPOSITE The surfer Rick Hogue cleaned up nicely in my subtle grey plaid suit.

OPPOSITE The moment I met Bruce Weber many years ago, I knew that we were kindred spirits. All these years later, I am still awed by his talent.

not afford him any longer, as I was not in the Klein/Lauren income league. Even though we were not working together, our friendship has only deepened over the years. Bruce and his partner, Nan Bush, are two of my dearest acquaintances and I feel blessed to have them in my close circle of friends.

What is there to say about the legendary editor Polly Mellen that has not been said already? We know all about the enormous talent, the unerring eye for beauty, and the pronouncements about fashion that have often veered into sartorial legend. But the Polly Mellen I know was a flesh-and-blood, hardworking aesthete, unable to compromise her discerning eye, be it in the collar of a coat or a prized flower in her garden.

I first met Polly when I was an assistant at Calvin Klein. She swept into our workroom to preview in sketch form the first samples of an exclusive summer collection we were creating for Bloomingdale's. Inspired by Audrey Hepburn, Calvin's assistant Zack Carr and I had put together all-American fabrics such as gingham checks, cool cotton seersucker, and lightweight cotton canvas into classic reversible dirndl skirts and sleek capri pants. I'll never forget Polly excitedly examining a pair of those canvas pants and shrieking in that wonderful voice of hers to Grace Mirabella, *Vogue*'s editor-in-chief, "Grace, look at these pants! They have a crotch! They have a crotch!" Not knowing at the time whether to be amused or alarmed, I soon learned that these occasional outbursts from Polly were indeed serious thoughts about the state of fashion and were never uttered merely for shock value. Listen and learn. After all, this was the woman who traveled to Japan for weeks with the photographer Richard Avedon, the model Veruschka, and a seven-foot Japanese giant to turn out a magical *Vogue* spread that, decades later, still resonates in my teenage memory.

Years later, when I used to visit my friends Vincent Petragnani and Larry Himelfarb for the weekend in Kent, Connecticut, I would run into Polly, sometimes in town, but more often in the local gardening store. You see, Polly adored gardening. It was a very serious occupation for her—so serious that during these brief encounters among the potting soil and new seedlings, conversation was always kept to a minimum. It was as though Polly was on an important mission and chitchat was deterring her from the mission at hand.

When I began to work on my book on Perry Ellis, I thought that I must reach out to Polly to get her take on one of fashion's most original designers. I contacted her and said that I was happy to come to Connecticut to speak with her about Perry. We agreed to meet at her modest but warm and cozy home on a Saturday morning, where the first thing I noticed was a beautiful patchwork needlepoint tartan rug. Polly explained to me that she used to do needlepoint at photo shoots as she waited for hair, makeup, and lighting setups to be finished. That was just another fascinating surprise about Polly. Probably the most wonderful surprise of all was to hear about and witness for myself the incredible love and affection between Polly and her husband Henry, who joined us briefly. They held hands like lovesick teenagers, the tenderness palpable. Polly told me that every single day, Henry brought her breakfast in bed. How very romantic is that? As it turns out, Polly was a great fan of Perry's original style, and she was very helpful to me, also urging me to speak with Grace Mirabella, which of course I did.

After speaking with Polly and returning to the city, I happened to mention to my friend Fern Mallis that we had chatted for several hours. Fern said that she would love to interview Polly as part of her "Fashion Icons with Fern Mallis" at the 92Y. I said that I would speak with the now-retired editor to inquire if she might be interested. When I called Polly, she said, "But Jeff (she had a way of stretching out my foreshortened, given name in a way that was almost aristocratic), who would want to come and hear me speak?"

I shot back, "Are you kidding? Every fashion student and professional in New York would love to hear you expound on your life and career. It will be a full house!"

Happily, she finally agreed, and in December 2012, to a full house and positively enthralled audience, Polly captivated us all with stories of her fantastic career in and out of *Vogue*. It was certainly one of the most successful and lauded interviews in the series.

As I started working on my book about the designer Norman Norell, Polly immediately came to mind to write the foreword. After all, she actually knew Norman, who had died some 40-odd years before. It took a while to get ahold of Polly, as by this time, her husband Henry had died, she had sold her house and moved to another town in Connecticut to be closer to her daughter. When I was finally able to reach her, our conversation had to be done over the telephone, unlike our previous in-person chat about Perry Ellis. Excitedly, I laid out my plans for a major biography of Norell with hopefully Polly penning the foreword. I was met with a deafening, seemingly endless silence, and then finally, she said, "Oh, Jeff, I really didn't like Norell. I thought he was very pompous and I thought his clothes were awfully stiff." My heart sank, I was completely deflated that the fashion god I so revered was not held by Polly in the same esteem.

I did know, however, that given Polly's tone of voice, there was

OPPOSITE Polly Mellen was the ultimate fashion editor–direct, confident, stylish and, above all, no-nonsense.

OPPOSITE Cher wore the much-discussed Norman Norell dolman-sleeve bugle-beaded gown styled by Polly Mellen and photographed by Richard Avedon.

absolutely no sense in arguing the merits of Norell's design genius, as Ms. Mellen was completely and definitively intransigent in her belief about his talent. I quickly decided to change the subject and asked Polly which young designers she was currently fond of. For the next 20 minutes or so, Polly exuberantly talked about her favorite new design talents, showing once and for all the lady was, and is, still very much with it. At this point, I guardedly decided to circle back to Norell.

"You know, Polly," I said," You say you were not fond of Norell, and yet, you photographed his bugle-beaded dolman-sleeved dazzler on Cher for *Vogue* in 1972."

She replied, "Oh, no, Jeff, that was Bob Mackie!"

Treading gingerly, I said, "Yes, Polly, you did photograph the Mackie dress with feathers at the hem, which also appeared on the cover of *Time* later, but you also photographed the Norell on Cher wearing the 1920s bob wig." Not acquiescing at all, and not wanting to anger her further, I offered to send the disputed photograph to Polly via her daughter.

"Yes, please do that," she said, a bit vexed. I did as told, subsequently got Ralph Rucci to write a beautiful foreword, and never heard back from Polly about the photograph.

As I write this, word has just arrived that Polly has died at the age of 100. She left a lasting legacy of an exacting standard of always seeking perfection and boundless enthusiasm for, not only fashion, but everything new and exciting. Fashion's greatest cheerleader is gone, but the example she set is one to always strive for.

My great friend Betty Halbreich recently passed away. Betty had been such a tremendous influence on so many lives, especially mine. She was always blunt and direct, so you always knew where you stood with her and what she thought. There was never a halfway point with her, and for me that was part of her great charm.

I met Betty in the early 1970s when she managed the World of Geoffrey Beene shop at Bergdorf Goodman. I had become enamored with his clothes as he changed directions midcareer—after a severe chastising by Kennedy Fraser, the *New Yorker*'s fashion critic—from 1960s stiff, paper-doll clothes, to lighter and more body-conscious dresses. Beene's clothes were beautifully made and finished. I would go to Bergdorf's on Thursday evenings to inspect the offerings, turning them inside out to examine the workmanship. After a few visits, Betty recognized me, and unbeknownst to me, had also noticed that security guards had been following me as I traipsed throughout the store perusing the racks of the designer clothes fearing, I guess, that I was a shoplifter. "You must be a student at one of the design schools," she said by way of a first introduction. "Bring the coat with you, and come into my office," she entreated. The coat in question was Beene's cloudlike mohair collarless confection with precise cartridge tucking that gave the coat shape and had been displayed in the window over a Jasco matte jersey speckled printed dress with a Dr. Zhivago fox-fur Cossack hat, pale grey hand-knitted cashmere tights, and tan gillie flat shoes. How Betty knew I was a fashion design student is still a mystery to me, but that was the very beginning of a long and fruitful friendship.

Those weekly visits became part of my fashion education. Betty was extremely generous with her knowledge about the industry in general and high fashion in particular. Having grown up in a very privileged home in Chicago, she had access from the very start to the best things, from clothing to fine surroundings. Marrying into a prosperous New York family, she moved to an expansive eight-room apartment on Park Avenue with a lot of household help and all the trimmings. Unfortunately, the marriage did not work out, even after two children—her son John dated one of my Parsons classmates. Betty, after meeting an executive of Chester Weinberg's at a cocktail party, decided to get a job for the very first time in her life. Quickly, she graduated to Geoffrey Beene's department at Bergdorf's, and eventually, Ira Neimark, the chairman of the store, suggested she leave Beene and help in the store as a personal shopper to all of Bergdorf's high-end customers—from Lauren Bacall to Babe Paley. Immediately successful, her clients, well-known or not, seemed to

RIGHT To say that I adored Betty Halbreich with her quick wit and sharper tongue is a gross understatement. I simply loved her to pieces.

appreciate her honest no-nonsense approach to clothing advice that she dispensed daily. You see, with Betty, it did not matter if you were Grace Kelly or Mary Jones, you were treated fairly by her, which was the quality about Betty that I adored. You could be wearing a $100,000 dress and if it did nothing for you, Betty would be the very first to say, "Take that off!"

Her sage advice was often offered, sometimes, without having been asked for. But in each and every instance, she was always right. Although she dressed a "Who's Who" of well-known women from soap-opera stars to Park Avenue matrons, Betty was not one to gossip or drop names, which is why women trusted her so much. Perhaps her most admirable quality was that she treated them all equally with respect and grace. Although my mother was not a regular customer, the few times that Betty helped her, she came away feeling like a queen.

Betty's books were all very successful, and the book launches at Bergdorf's became huge events like rock concerts with thousands of fans and clients showing up to pay homage and get their books signed by the lady herself. Her star status really rose when she became the breakout star of the documentary *Scatter My Ashes at Bergdorf's*. She was no longer just New York's treasure but the world's. Every year in November, I would drop by her office, often unannounced, to celebrate her birthday (during the pandemic, I called to serenade her with "Happy Birthday" on the telephone.) Last year, I brought her my friend Stan Herman's brand-new book as a birthday present. Betty always displayed my books in her office and would proudly introduce me to customers and salespersons alike if I visited unexpectedly. That last birthday, she read me parts of her newest book from her legal pads that were famously written in her expressive longhand and will now be published posthumously. Knowing and loving Betty was a tremendous honor and a special distinction I will treasure forever.

In, I believe it was 1980, I was out in San Francisco doing a trunk show at Macy's and talking to Ray Wills, the store's fashion director on the sales floor. Ray mentioned that Richard Avedon was in the store also doing a personal appearance for one of his books. I was almost hysterical in relating to him what an Avedon fan I was.

"Would you like to meet him?" he asked.

"Would I ever?" I said, almost levitating as we reached the other floor and I got to finally meet one of my heroes. As I gushed like a fanboy about how much I loved Avedon's work and especially his work on *Funny Face*, I was totally surprised when he asked me if I had plans for later that evening. "No, none at all," I said. "Why?"

Avedon said, "Well, we are showing the film to a class at Berkeley so would you like to join us and then have dinner afterward?"

Of course, the answer was a resounding "Yes!" He asked which hotel I was staying at and at the appointed hour, a limousine with Dick pulled up in front and into it I went.

"I hope you won't mind, but I have to make a brief stop on the way?" I replied, "No, not at all." The next thing I knew we were at an imposing home in the Bernal Heights neighborhood which belonged to Francis Ford Coppola for a cocktail party. The home even had a swimming pool in the basement.

Shortly after, we were off to Berkeley for a big-screen showing of *Funny Face,* followed by a great Q&A where I got to ask, along with the students, all the questions I had ever had about the making of the film. And then on to a late dinner with Dick to end the evening.

But this was only the beginning of my Avedon association. For my 30th birthday, my assistants arranged, as a surprise for me, a day with Richard Avedon at his Upper East Side studio. In the morning, I got to watch him shoot an editorial spread. We had lunch together, and, in the afternoon, I saw him film a commercial with a male model dressed in my designs. The cherry on the cake at the end of the

OPPOSITE This scene of Audrey Hepburn and Fred Astaire in *Funny Face* is emblematic of so many of Audrey Hepburn's films: The duckling, who was never really ugly to begin with, becomes a lovely swan.

OVERLEAF For my 30th birthday, my staff surprised me by specially commissioning Al Hirschfeld to create a scene from *Funny Face*. He chose to draw Fred Astaire dancing with Audrey Hepburn. It is one of my most prized possessions.

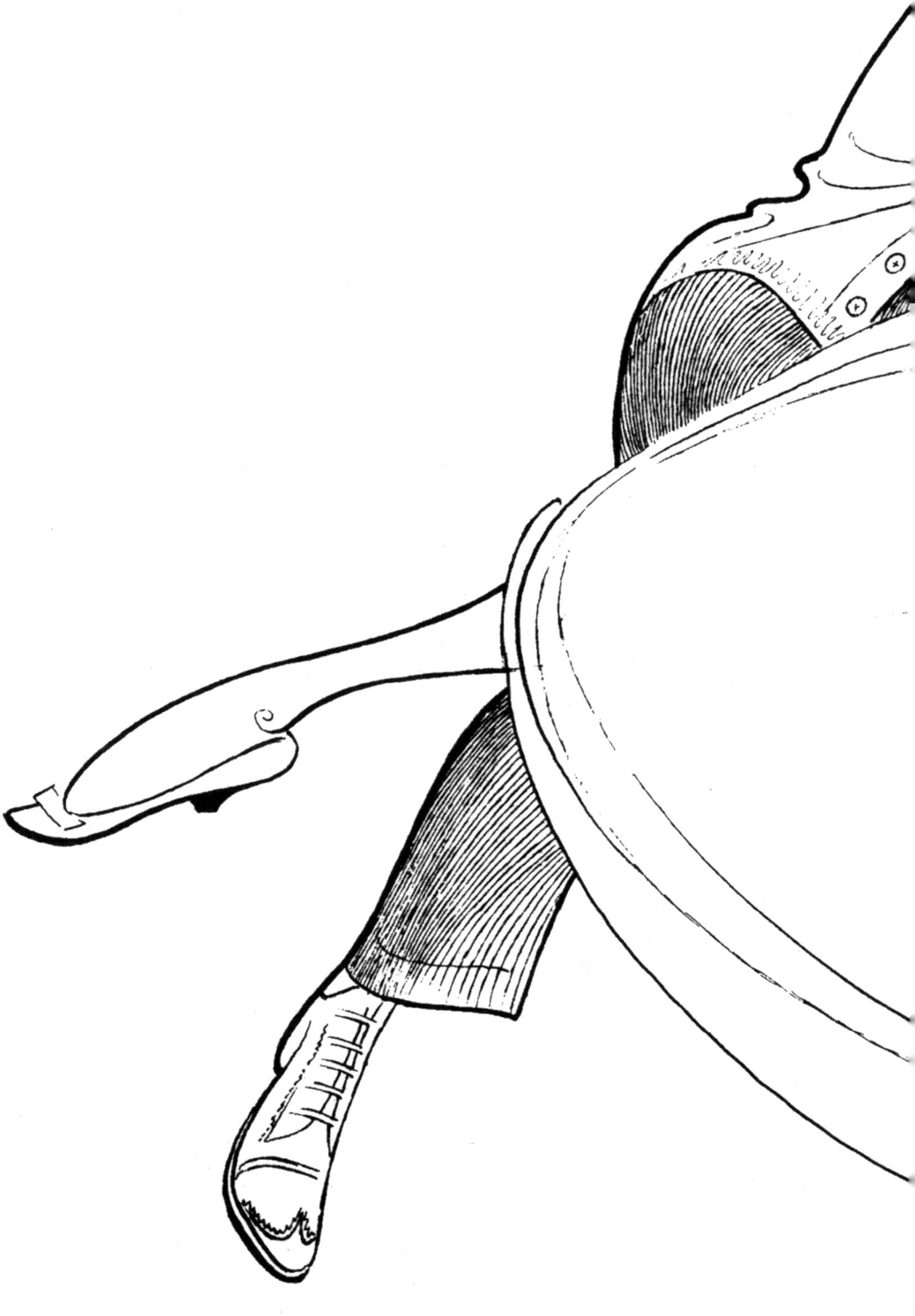

HIRSCHFELD

LEFT Audrey Hepburn—her eyes, brows, nose, and lips emerging like magic in the film—was truly Richard Avedon at his best.

day? I was allowed to pick out one print of his to add to my growing photography collection. I knew exactly which image I wanted. Early on in the film, there is a scene when Audrey Hepburn is lured to the headquarters and escapes into Fred Astaire's darkroom studio. Avedon took a portrait of Audrey's face and "burns" out the background so that the finished portrait looks as if Audrey's eyes, nose, and lips are emerging from white space. The finished image was used for the film's soundtrack album and for several film posters. The only problem was that Dick disavowed all knowledge of this image. Even when I acted out the scene from memory, he feigned not knowing what I was talking about. After a while, I gave up my pursuit of this photograph, especially when I realized that there were three images he had already preselected for me to choose from. I ended up choosing the double portrait of the Duke and Duchess of Windsor that has its own fascinating backstory.

My last time with Avedon before his death was spent as a guest at a luncheon years after he had received an honorary degree from the Parsons School of Design. I teased him all afternoon by calling him "Dr. Dick." But I was far from finished with my lifelong affection for *Funny Face*. One Friday evening, I came home from a dinner to find an email from an unknown sender. Usually skeptical about opening such things, I was somehow intrigued only to find out that the video company that was putting together the 50th Anniversary DVD wanted me, along with my friend Pamela Keogh, to do the fashion commentary on the film. Talk about your full-circle moment! My friends tease me all the time about the fact that they can never watch the film with me, because after literally hundreds of viewings I can recite almost every line of dialogue from memory.

I never had a brother and never longed for one until I met Ivan Bart. Charismatic to a fault, Ivan had that distinctive ability to make anyone he was talking to feel as though they were the only one in the world who existed at that moment. Funny in a devilishly delightful way, Ivan's true gift was his unique idea of beauty, which was prescient because he ended up heading IMG, one of the world's largest modeling agencies. It was at IMG that his all-inclusive concept of beauty was able to truly come to life. You see, in a world where homogenized beauty of all white, all blond, all too thin reigned supreme, Ivan almost single-handedly broke down the barriers of what we now consider beautiful. His forceful charge to his agency of diversity and inclusion led many other fashion firms to rethink their age-old paradigm of beauty. Models like Ashley Graham and Paloma Elsesser certainly owe their *Vogue* covers and outsized careers in large part to Ivan.

To say that Ivan was totally beloved by all who knew him is truly an understatement. From the seller at the farmstand to the budding designer seeking his help, all who knew him came to adore him. And no one loved Ivan more than his close family and friends, his brothers, his sister-in-law, his cousins, his Aunt Rhea, and his Big Fresh Pond family of friends, including Stan Herman, Brett Beldock, Carla Rich, and Fern Mallis.

I especially cherished my conversations with Ivan on a myriad of subjects—food, theater, film, books. The list goes on and on. Cooking with Ivan was great fun, and he always asked me to make my sautéed mushrooms and onions whenever we were together. But the core of Ivan's love was the love he shared with the talented filmmaker, his husband, Grant Greenberg. They had a symbiotic relationship, whereby thoughts, words, and actions were telegraphed by a mere glance, a gentle touch, or the softly intoned "Mr. B," a signal that it was time to retire for the evening.

After almost an entire career at IMG, Ivan's leave-taking was a shock to all of us in the industry, particularly to all the models he represented. An even greater shock was his sudden death a few months later, which seemed so unfathomable at the time and still does today. The incredibly beautiful and moving celebration of life service held

LEFT In Stan Herman's Southampton kitchen, Ivan Bart and I cooked some of the many meals we shared together. How I wish we had had more.

for Ivan was one of the most tremendous outpourings of love from the fashion industry that I have ever witnessed. Mourners came from every corner of the fashion business and traveled across oceans to be there. It was a true testament to the high regard in which Ivan was held by so many. He took care of so many people in his life and this was the time to take care of him.

I do not think there is a week that goes by when Ivan and his generous spirit are not on my mind and in my heart, and I know that this will continue forever.

Michael Vollbracht was indeed the proverbial Renaissance man. A painter, illustrator, artist, author, and designer, Michael had limitless talents. As an army brat, he moved to different towns many times as a child. As a result of what amounted to a not particularly happy childhood, his true refuge was the movies, where his mother would often leave him for hours on end. The glamor of Joan Crawford and Marlene Dietrich never left him and was a through line in both his art and his design. One of the highlights of Michael's later life was the friendship he developed with Joan Crawford after writing her a fan letter and receiving a response in return. His apartment on the Upper East Side of Manhattan had all of the blue-matted and framed letters he had received from Joan, hanging around his living room like a continuous molding.

Michael was an exceptional design student at Parsons School of Design, which he entered in 1965. He received the Norman Norell Gold Thimble Prize in his senior year. Shortly after graduation, he became part of Geoffrey Beene's design team along with a young Issey Miyake. After a couple of years, he went on to assist the designer Donald Brooks. In 1973 he became the in-house illustrator at Henri Bendel. And, for only one year, he taught design at Parsons out of his brownstone apartment on 58th Street. I was lucky enough to be in that singular class. I will never forget Michael opening the door, clad in blue jeans and bare feet, with "Love Unlimited" and Barry White blaring on the stereo. Mounted on the wall was a giant neon Mobil Pegasus sign he had stolen from a gas station on Long Island.

Michael's fanciful advertisements for Henri Bendel attracted the attention of Bloomingdale's, which stole him away. It was there that he created the first of a series of "Face" shopping bags. Legend has it that the printer forgot to add the Bloomingdale's name to the original version, but they became such an instant hit that subsequent versions had no store name on them either. The chic shopping bags simply dripped with sophistication and glamour, and definitely upped the status quotient of Bloomingdale's in the 1970s.

In 1979 he launched his own line, which was so well received that it earned him the coveted Coty Award the very next year. Michael was the ultimate showman, and his dramatic, thematic shows in exotic venues, which ranged from bank lobbies to the Circle in the Square Theater, were a hot ticket. His gigantic original printed-fabric gowns were prized by everyone from Elizabeth Taylor to Janet Jackson and Barbara Bush. Later, Michael published two versions of his book, *Nothing Sacred*, a compendium of illustrations and wicked musings

LEFT Michael Vollbracht was fashion's bad boy, as skillful as a designer and artist as he was a gossip. Talking on the telephone with Michael was like eating a six-course meal. You felt full and yet you still wanted more.

on the famous and infamous people he had come to know. In the 1990s Michael came back to fashion as the creative director of Bill Blass after Blass' retirement and death.

I could listen to Michael regale me for hours on end with stories about the golden age of fashion or film in enormous detail and with quite a bit of naughtiness, too. My telephone calls to him in Florida, while I researched my book on Norman Norell, to ask about a single name or date were never less than 20 minutes long and often went on ad infinitum. I have to say that I loved every minute. Michael was looking forward to coming back to New York from Florida for the launch of my book and exhibition on Norell, for which he had been so helpful. He was so disappointed that illness, which ended up being terminal esophageal cancer, kept him away. I miss our chats every single day but feel so privileged to have known and loved him.

I am so grateful that one of the truest friends and mentors I have had in my life is Joseph J. Barrato. Serving initially as Ralph Lauren's right-hand man and the head of sales of Polo when it was called Polo Fashions Inc., Joe was the interface with all the major stores as well as the crème de la crème of specialty stores during the nascence of Ralph Lauren's empire. The son of a mail carrier and a homemaker, Joe started out as a stock boy at Brooks Brothers in 1958 at the age of 17. That's where he met fellow employee Ralph Lauren, and a long friendship began.

The perfect embodiment of the Polo aesthetic, Joe is handsome, charismatic, intelligent, and equipped with the most beautiful manners. Men wanted to be him, and women wanted to be with him. I will never forget the second time I met Joe. I had been hired by Mr. Lauren and came to New York to finalize my part-time work hours. There was Joe in a chocolate-brown, chalk-stripe flannel suit with snuff-brown suede shoes, a brown-and-white glen plaid shirt with a white club collar, and a brown-and-white polka-dot silk tie.

Initially, after being hired by Ralph, I was assigned to be an assistant to Joe in the sales area. The first thing he taught me when I asked for his advice was how to create a dimple in my half-Windsor knot. I had noticed his and was envious of the fact that every day Joe's ties were perfectly knotted. The second thing he taught me was the double entendre meaning of the Yiddish word *putz*, which could mean a stupid person or, specifically, a small part of a man's anatomy. While it was thrilling to work and learn from Joe, the reverie lasted a mere two weeks. After that, Ralph came downstairs and said that he felt I was being wasted in sales, and I should join him upstairs in design. Despite no longer having that day-to-day interaction, the bond Joe and I had only grew stronger and remains so to this very day. Joe continued and continues to be a mentor and a good friend. I babysat one of his kids once, and according to Joe, the kids still talk about me as one of their favorite sitters. Like Ralph, Joe always treated me like an adult, and that treatment definitely helped me to mature quickly. His interest in music, particularly jazz, rubbed off on me.

After leaving Polo, Joe had several stints at other distinguished menswear companies. He became a vice-president of the tony Julius Garfinckel & Co. department store in my hometown of Washington, DC. He spent two notable decades as CEO and president of Brioni, the Italian menswear brand that dressed much of Old Hollywood including Clark Gable and Cary Grant, as well as today's celebrities, such as Daniel Craig, Kevin Costner, Hugh Grant, and Pierce Brosnan,

LEFT My enduring impression of my friend and colleague Joe Barrato is of someone who is always impeccably dressed. A serious jazz enthusiast, Joe has interests that go way beyond the fashion world.

with Joe personally working with many of them. Later, he was president of North American operations for the Italian brand Moncler, responsible for all sales and marketing in the United States. Moncler was a sleepy Italian company known primarily for its down jackets. Joe turned it into a behemoth fashion apparel company known for its innovative collaborations with designers such as Thom Browne, Rick Owens, Pierpaolo Piccioli, and Simone Rocha, among others. Moncler's volume today is over 3.1 billion euros.

I refer to him as JB1, and he refers to me as JB2, and he has always been my biggest cheerleader, referring to me often as his other child. He has five other ones, not to mention 12 grandchildren. Joe's kindness and integrity are legendary, and I learned so much from him. Although, admittedly, he was not always the best husband, he has always been an incredibly devoted father and a doting, loving, and involved grandfather.

When Ralph Lauren decided early on that he wanted to expand, and take his women's business very seriously, he reached out to Salvatore Cesarani. Sal was an accomplished tailor, designer, and window-display dresser who had worked extensively with Cliff Grodd on the dramatic and beautiful Paul Stuart windows. Sal knew all about proper fit and how to make Ralph's fledgling ladies line take off commercially.

Sal was a graduate of the High School of Fashion Industries and attended the State University of New York. He had also studied fashion design at the Fashion Institute of Technology. At the High School of Fashion Industries, Sal met fellow student Nancy Staluppi, who, in her senior year, received a scholarship from the Fontana Sisters to study in Rome. After his military service and his return to school at FIT, Sal married Nancy. Theirs was one of the happiest marriages I have ever had the pleasure to witness—a true partnership in terms of the personal and later in Sal's business.

Before Polo, Sal had worked as a designer for the phenomenally successful sportswear house Bobbie Brooks, which in 1959 was the very first women's garment-making company to be listed on the New York Stock Exchange. When I first came to New York, Sal and Nancy were the closest thing I had to a second set of parents. Many Sundays were spent at their apartment working on my school projects, both of them helping to develop my underwhelming sewing skills and then providing Sunday supper. To this day, Sal insists that I drank my weight in orange juice every time I was at his house. I learned so much about merchandising a line from Sal, as well as an incredible amount about the history of fashion and the garment trade. Sal also became an invaluable asset to Ralph, and not just in womenswear. His insights and taste level regarding menswear meant that he traveled with Ralph to Europe to look at fabrics and manufacturers for everything with the Polo label on it.

Sal and Nancy were so close to me that they were the ones I called at 3am when I had my first kidney stone, and it was Sal who came and got me and drove me to the hospital. They also helped me furnish my first studio apartment and helped me move into it.

When he left Polo, Sal designed menswear, first under the Country Britches label and eventually under his own label. Sal Cesarani menswear won him two Special Coty Awards for Menswear in 1974 and 1975, before winning the main Menswear Award in 1976. In 1982 he was awarded the Coty Menswear Return Award. He has also won the Fashion Group Award of Boston. He had the honor of designing the uniforms for the Olympic torchbearers and ceremonial

LEFT Sal and Nancy Cesarani were like my parents away from home. When I attended college, I spent virtually every Sunday at their home for dinner.

OPPOSITE Sal Cesarani is, to this very day, always immaculately put together, and looks as if he is in a Paul Stuart window.

officials at the 1980 Winter Olympics. Although she was no longer a designer, Nancy had business acumen that kicked in big-time when Sal started his own business. Nancy dealt with everything from fabric purchases to hiring salesmen, and she had a very close relationship with all of his buyers, who loved working with her. That perfect partnership sadly ended with Nancy's untimely death from cancer in 2011. Lisa and Christopher, their children, as well as so many of us, were devastated by her passing.

Sal's greatest gift is that he is an unbelievable teacher and mentor, not only to me, but also to the scores of kids he has taught over the years at FIT and Parsons. Beloved by the faculties at these institutions, he is as highly regarded by the world of academia as he is by the garment industry.

V. BEST FRIENDS FOREVER

OPPOSITE I am not particularly fond of having my picture taken but I do love this candid photograph by Bill Cunningham of Stan Herman and me. In fact I liked it so much that Bill made a print of it just for me.

RIGHT BELOW Stan Herman masterminded "Take Off," one of the first AIDS benefits on the East End of Long Island. Here we are at the event with his former assistant, Lorenzo Deras.

I met Stan Herman when I was 19 and a student at the Parsons School of Design. He was not my critic, as our class was divided into three sections, but he did critique my friend Susan Shacter's section and ultimately gave her a Gold Thimble Award. I was a big fan of Stan's work long before I had ever met him. His penchant for making young, stylish dresses and sportswear for women in the 1960s and 1970s, when fashion was rapidly changing, was no mean feat. Along with contemporaries such as Anne Klein, Gayle Kirkpatrick, Leo Narducci, and Don Simonelli, Stan had designs that became the go-to for everyone from Ali MacGraw to Amanda Burden. He made clothes for young women who wanted to look stylish and chic but did not want to dress like their mothers. His career shifted in the 1970s from sportswear to loungewear and uniforms. Stan has carved an almost impenetrable niche for himself as the uniform king of America. He has dressed hundreds of thousands of workers through his designs for McDonald's, JetBlue, TWA, and FedEx—to name just a few of his clients.

Stan and I became closer friends when, as the new president of the Council of Fashion Designers of America (CFDA), he asked me to join the board and in so doing broadened my understanding of the garment business and its myriad players. Stan's belief in me as a designer and, even more importantly, as a vital board member gave me tremendous confidence. His work at East End Gay Organization (EEGO) and his support of my work at the Hetrick-Martin Institute really brought us together as friends and activists. His family's embrace of me, particularly his brother Harvey, helped make me

feel grounded in a way that only real family can. Stan's no-filter stance can sometimes be taken the wrong way. Although he can be brutally honest, he never means to hurt or belittle anyone. When he says to me, "You need to lose some weight," it is truly constructive and spoken with great concern. In many ways he is a true Virgo and in others not at all. When doing a sketch, he is fastidious to a fault, but he hasn't made his bed since he was in the Army. He hates all forms of confrontation but will dig in his heels if he feels an injustice warrants it. Generous to a fault, his largesse in picking up dinner tabs is often taken advantage of.

Stan's 16-year-long reign as president of the CFDA was important for many reasons, but especially in that young, sometimes unknown, designers felt that they were "seen" by Stan. He visited their showrooms, went to their shows, encouraged them, and introduced them to scores of people who might be helpful to their careers.

Stan's intense love of opera helped me expand my exploration of this musical art form. He has and shares his vast knowledge of not only the various artists, but also the composers and the history of the entire genre. Sitting with Stan and Terrence McNally at a production of *Andre Chénier* at the Metropolitan Opera was like taking a master class. There's nothing like watching Stan listen to a favorite aria or a conductor directing a favorite piece, seeing the emotion swell over him as he dissolves into tears. He stated many times that he could not live without music.

Stan's passions for all the things he loves—music, art, writing, and fashion—illuminate his discussions about drawing people in, and make everyone whom he meets seek out and discover what is unknown to them. His personality is that forceful.

Stan is like a real-life Forrest Gump. His friendships, acquaintances, and lovers are like a "Who's Who" of the social zeitgeist of the 1950s, 1960s, and 1970s. Ask him about anyone from Jerry Robbins to Arthur Laurents to Chita Rivera. He knew them all. He and Gene Horowitz, his partner of over 40 years, welcomed people such as the New York City Ballet dancer Tanaquil Le Clercq to dinner at their home in Southampton, New York, as well as such Long Island artists as Jane Freilicher and Larry Rivers. Other notable friends such as Frank O'Hara, John Gruen, Jane Wilson, Edward Albee, Bill Flanagan, Gore Vidal, and his mother, Nina Gore, all intersected with Stan at one time or another. Listening to him tell the very personal and sometimes intimate stories of these notables has brought these often-outsized names to a human scale.

One of the greatest things that Stan did as president of the CFDA was to take the copious amounts of money raised at the 7th On Sale and have the New York City AIDS Fund distribute it to worthwhile AIDS-related organizations. I was vice-chair of the Hetrick-Martin Institute and brought him to a recital of school children's works written at the Public Theater. Having been helped by Stan's great friend, Terrence McNally the work was so impressive that as I looked over at Stan during the performance, he looked back at me with tears in his eyes and whispered that we must give Hetrick-Martin a good chunk of money. As it turns out, we gave them the largest single grant of our fund, which allowed them to move into a newer, larger, and safer place in which to operate. Over time, Stan has probably become my closest friend, one I can rely on for the best career advice and one whose investment in me is purely to help me succeed. His wisdom is always considered, if not always followed, and his long time on Earth has garnered great experience.

At the beginning of the pandemic, Stan was thinking of reviving his long-held idea of writing his memoir. Years before, he had made an attempt to write it accompanied by his hand-drawn illustrations. The book was to be called *Notes and Sketches*. Due to an unscrupulous literary agent, he abandoned the book. As he was COVID-bound in his weekend retreat in Southampton, I strongly pushed him to restart what I thought would not only be a great project for him but also one that would have great historical value. Fortunately, Stan took the bait, encouraged by daily cheerleading calls from me. The result was magnificent, a truly beautifully written story about his life, and the golden era of the garment industry. I was taken aback by how this first-time author wrote so well, almost poetically. When it was completed, I insisted that there should be art to accompany the book's terrific prose. Stan fought tooth and nail against art being included. "It's a serious memoir, not a coffee table book," he said.

However, I stood my ground and replied, "You write about Princess Diana and Elizabeth Taylor, and you have photographs of you with them to prove it. Readers will want to see that!" After much back and forth, and with the help of his new agent, Jane Lahr, we finally convinced him to include photographs and his lovely fine pen drawings.

Relenting, he said, "I don't know anything about that. You do it." And do it I did. I felt that I had been given a special task, to preserve and amplify Stan's treasured text and help his story visually come to life, which I must say was a tremendous experience. The most gratifying thing of all was to see how pleased with and proud he was of the finished result. My next challenge once the book—now titled *Uncross Your Legs*—was done was to try and see if I could get him a segment on *CBS Sunday Morning*. After all, I had gotten my first book on the show, and I wanted the very same thrill for Stan. And we did it, along with lots and lots of other positive press.

As an openly gay man, Stan has continually taught me and so many others what it's like to be an out, proud member of society. He is a terrific example of a modern citizen in today's world. Perhaps the greatest thing I have learned from my ongoing friendship with Stan is how noble it is to grow old gracefully, while still being an active, contributing, and valid member of society. He has always done that, setting a standard and high bar to which one can only aspire.

Since 1943 the Coty cosmetic and fragrance company had sponsored and awarded the Coty American Fashion Critics' Awards to promote and celebrate American fashion. It was considered the fashion world's Oscar and continued until September 1984, when the company and fashion designers alike felt there might be a conflict of interest because many fashion designers were getting into the beauty industry.

OPPOSITE Stan Herman did a marvelous job presenting me with my CFDA Award. He should take to the stage. Oh, wait, he has done that already.

After the Coty Awards were discontinued, the Council of Fashion Designers of America (CFDA) stepped in to present their own industry recognition award to fulfill a similar role. This quickly became the gold standard in the fashion industry and was awarded to established designers such as Perry Ellis, Donna Karan, and Ralph Lauren; emerging designers were added in 1997. Over time, top retailers, fashion journalists, and even international designers have also been honored. The CFDA Awards are voted on by a group of more than 1,500 members including fashion editors, retailers, and stylists and announced at an annual black-tie gala, which is the major fundraiser for the organization.

After the publication of my fifth book, *Norell: Master of American Fashion*, in 2018, I thought that I was at least qualified to be in the running for the Eugenia Sheppard Award, given for excellence in journalism. I felt that I was the only designer who had written several serious books about fashion and other fashion designers, which should count for something.

I was told that, much like the Oscars, serious politicking needed to be done in order to receive the award—merit or no merit. I found that idea extremely distasteful,feeling that either I had earned it or not. Nevertheless, as repugnant as I thought this process was, I sent out over 400 personalized letters extolling the reasons why I deserved to win. What truly surprised me was how many kind notes and emails I received from many CFDA members saying they thought I deserved the award. I actually heard later from someone who attended the closed-door board meeting, that, in fact, I did receive the overwhelming lion's share of votes in that category. However, I did not win it.

As a former board member, I was aware of the kind of machinations that go on behind closed doors at those explosive board meetings. Although ballots are sent in and counted, the board has the final say over which awards are announced and which are eventually handed out. As with almost any strong organization, there are passionate factions that have been campaigning for their choice for weeks, if not days beforehand. Those discussions can become very heated

CFDA
SHION
ARDS

and often it is the loudest or the funniest voice that sways the group in a completely different direction from where it started.

I remember one such meeting when Elizabeth Taylor was brought up as a candidate for "Fashion Icon." Michael Kors campaigned vigorously that she should receive the award. Although I am a big Taylor fan myself, I was fully aware that she had recently had brain surgery and was not in good shape physically. I had visions of her standing at the podium, not looking her best with 30-foot-high projections of her at her peak beauty being shown behind her—an awkward, if not totally embarrassing, situation at best. I railed against her selection, and once again, I lost.

Memorably, the night of the awards, a very frail Taylor, her white hair shorn from her recent brain surgery, reached the podium supported by the elbows by two strong men, and while stating that she had been cited often on many worst-dressed lists during her long career, graciously thanked the CFDA board for the honor and hoisting her award aloft triumphantly shouted, "Take that, Mr. Blackwell!" As it turns out, the reason I was axed was that Carolina Herrera was stepping down from her eponymous label, and quickly the powers that be decided that she should receive a special CFDA award.

When I heard about it I was disappointed, not so much because the award did not come to me, but because I had compromised my integrity by proselytizing to get it in the first place. Imagine my surprise when, some four years later, I got an email saying that the board of the CFDA had bestowed upon me, on the occasion of their 60th anniversary, a special award for being an exemplary model member. This was a one-time-only award, never to be repeated, and best of all, I heard it was voted on unanimously by the board. I guess, as the saying goes, good things do come to those who wait.

RIGHT BELOW Many of the dreams Vincent Petragnani and I had for ourselves were shared for so long, along with many things that did not pan out.

Vincent Petragnani is one of my oldest friends, and like most great friendships, ours has had its ups and downs and has been through the mill and back, but thankfully has endured to this day. When I first met Vincent in the early 1970s, he was gainfully employed as an illustrator. His heroes were the legendary artists and illustrators Bob Peak and Richard Amsel. In 1975 he was chosen to create the movie poster and soundtrack artwork for Barbra Streisand's film *Funny Lady*. We were all so thrilled for him, but timing-wise, it signaled the beginning of the end of the golden age of movie poster art. With the advent of computer illustration, hand-drawn illustration started to become more and more scarce and Vincent began to see the proverbial handwriting on the wall for his profession.

I remember Vincent being almost as excited as I was when I went to Europe for the very first time, carefully selecting items from Sonia Rykiel's home collection from her boutique at 6 rue de Grenelle in Paris as presents for him. And I was thrilled several years later when, on his first trip to London, I could take him to see the home of Nancy Lancaster of Colefax & Fowler. For Vincent, it was the equivalent of

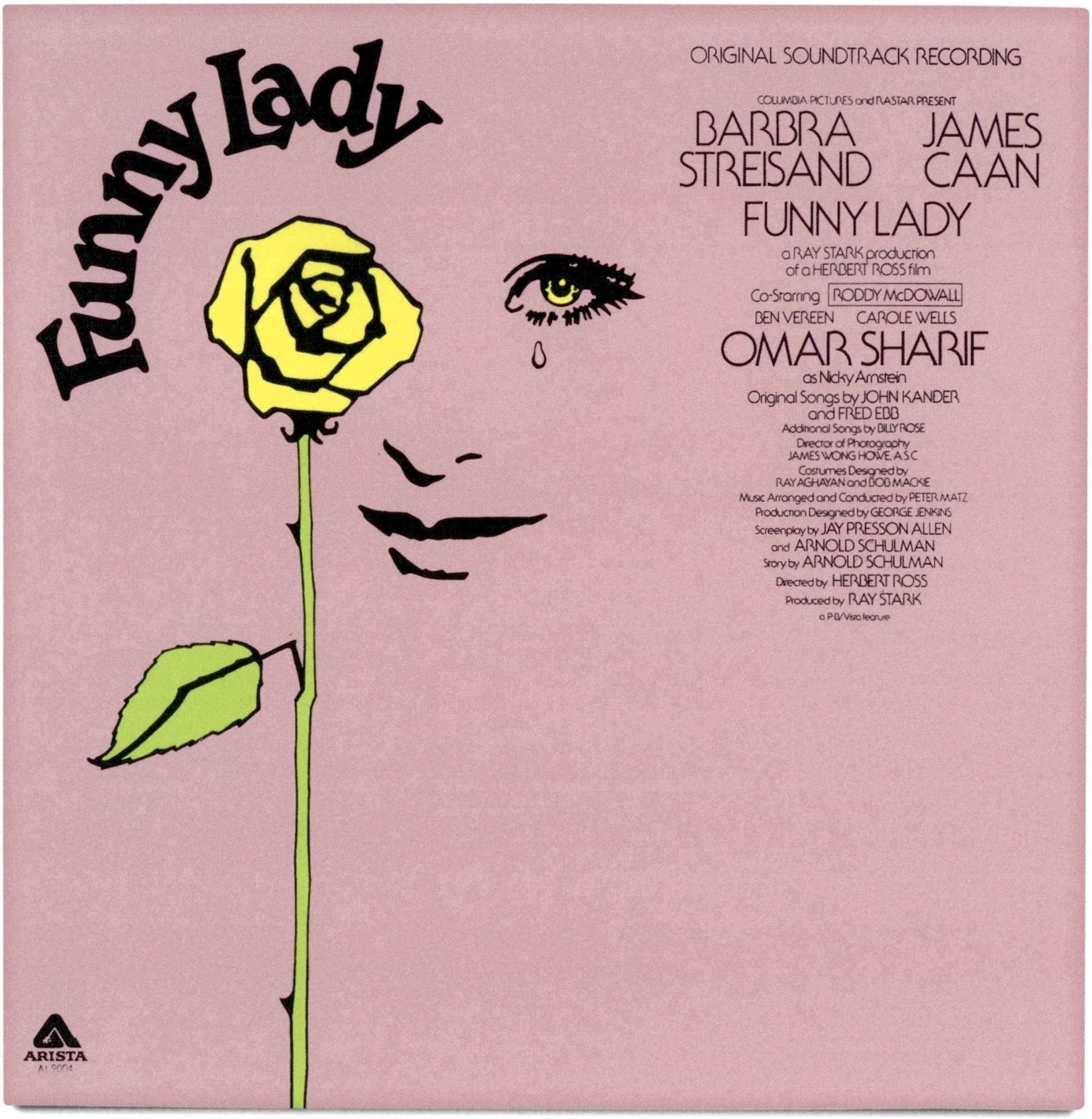
Funny Lady
ORIGINAL SOUNDTRACK RECORDING
COLUMBIA PICTURES and RASTAR PRESENT
BARBRA STREISAND JAMES CAAN
FUNNY LADY
a RAY STARK production
of a HERBERT ROSS film
Co-Starring RODDY McDOWALL
BEN VEREEN CAROLE WELLS
OMAR SHARIF
as Nicky Arnstein
Original Songs by JOHN KANDER and FRED EBB
Additional Songs by BILLY ROSE
Director of Photography JAMES WONG HOWE, A.S.C.
Costumes Designed by RAY AGHAYAN and BOB MACKIE
Music Arranged and Conducted by PETER MATZ
Production Designed by GEORGE JENKINS
Screenplay by JAY PRESSON ALLEN and ARNOLD SCHULMAN
Story by ARNOLD SCHULMAN
Directed by HERBERT ROSS
Produced by RAY STARK
a P.B./Vista feature
ARISTA

OPPOSITE I cannot describe the joy I felt for Vincent Petragnani when his artwork became the movie poster for *Funny Lady* and the art for the cover of the compact disc.

a pilgrimage to Lourdes in southwestern France. With his partner and my dentist, Larry Himelfarb, we spent many weekends antiquing in Connecticut at shows such as the legendary Brimfield Antique Flea Market.

No one was happier for me than Vincent as my professional star began to rise with the success of Jeffrey Banks Menswear, Boyswear, Womenswear, and Merona Sport, but I think that he also felt a bit left out and lost because his career was not progressing the way he had envisioned. He desperately wanted to work alongside me as one of my design assistants, but having no fashion design training, I was getting tremendous pushback from my design staff regarding hiring him. Not wanting to jeopardize the established working arrangement I had with my staff, I had to make the very difficult decision to rescind my work offer. This caused a terrible rift between us that was almost impossible to mend. For years, we did not speak to each other, and I felt tremendously guilty. However, sometime later when I was planning the guest list for the launch of my first book, I decided that I needed to invite Vincent and, if he came, so be it, and if he didn't, at least I had been the one to offer the olive branch.

The night of the launch at Saks Fifth Avenue, I sat with Doria de La Chapelle, my coauthor, furiously signing books for the hundreds of people patiently waiting between the velvet rope stanchions. I saw Vincent quietly standing in line, his head above the crowd. When he finally got to the front, I stood up and hugged him tightly, both of us saying, "We'll talk later."

And talk we did. The friendship resumed almost as if it had never left off. Vincent had experienced many difficulties over time, including changing professions from being an illustrator to becoming a senior designer at Ethan Allen. Unfortunately, he also had to cope with Larry's increasingly erratic and often violent bouts of alcoholism and other serious medical problems. Even though we do not see each other as often as we once did, the friendship has aged like a wonderful rich bourbon, with top notes of convivial fraternity and a strong accord of solidarity.

I am grateful that our friendship has continued and grown, despite its numerous trials and tribulations throughout the many decades we have shared.

OPPOSITE Reed Evins, photographed in Paris in his dark green velvet Saint Laurent jacket and top hat, at roughly the time I first met him, was so knowledgeable and fashion-aware even at a very young age.

I feel as though I have known the uber-talented Reed Evins my whole life. And practically, I have. Meeting as teenagers during my time at Calvin Klein, we forged a friendship that endures to this very day. Reed is the nephew of the late, great American shoe designer David Evins, who practically invented the designer shoe business in this country. In addition to his having his eponymous collection of ladies' footwear that was sold to stores including Neiman Marcus and Bergdorf Goodman, David Evins also served many Hollywood films, making shoes for Elizabeth Taylor in *Cleopatra*, as well as for other stars such as Grace Kelly. Most importantly, before the era of designer shoe licensees, Evins was the go-to guy for all the Seventh Avenue designers from Calvin Klein to Bill Blass to Norman Norell, to complete their collections.

Today, when designers work on their collections, shoes are usually the first thing they work on due to the long lead time it takes to produce them, especially if they are coming from Italy. But long before this was the practice, David Evins crafted his shoes in America, his nephew Reed often at his side learning from the master. As a teenage footwear prodigy he was assigned, often with his sister Melissa, the job of working directly with designers to develop footwear to accompany their runway shows. That is how Reed and I first met, as he delivered a wedge-heeled canvas espadrille that we immediately began hand-coloring in the bright lemons, limes, fuchsias, and turquoise shades of the Calvin Klein resort collection. An immediate connection was made, and Reed and I bonded over a love of the history of American fashion and our shared friends in the business such as André Leon Talley and Michael Vollbracht.

Reed has a raconteur's sensibility for society gossip and fashion lore that has served him well over the years. When our friend Michael Vollbracht died tragically of esophageal cancer in 2018, I chose Reed as one of the speakers at his memorial service that I planned with Michael's Parsons classmate Kay Unger. I really pressed Reed to speak about their longtime professional relationship as well as being neighbors in New York. He finally relented, and everyone who witnessed his speech was, in turn, captivated and enthralled. Even if you had never met Michael, by the time Reed ended his speech, you felt you knew him. Reed and Melissa had their own careers, with a successful youthful shoe collection called Two City Kids. Reed, an artist at heart and having studied at the Rhode Island School of Design, has also created pet portraits and women's accessories. The thing I love most about Reed is that he is essentially the same kid I met long ago and has not changed one damn bit.

In my new apartment on 16th Street—thank you, Mr. Bobby Short—I finally started to feel like a grown-up. Only three blocks away and a few minutes walk from the Parsons School of Design campus on lower Fifth Avenue, it was on a quiet tree-lined street. I felt the location was a good luck omen because across the street from the apartment building was a center that Audrey Hepburn had trained at for her role as a blind person in the film *Wait until Dark*. The apartment was a studio but had a couple of doormen who were polite and friendly, especially the Spanish-speaking David. Toward the end of the block at Sixth Avenue was a diner on the corner and a small newsstand that surprisingly carried *Women's Wear Daily*. Five days a week, I walked down the block and crossed over to the opposite side of the street to pick up my *WWD* on the way to school. Soon, as I left number 16 and strolled down the block, I used to see a very handsome man emerge from number 23. I had learned that this was also the brownstone where Lorne Michaels, the creator of the legendary television show *Saturday Night Live,* lived. Number 23 had very broad shoulders and horn-rimmed glasses and was always attired in a dark, dressy suit and tie. He got the *Wall Street Journal* and I got my *WWD* then he descended into the subway, presumably on his way to work. I nicknamed him Clark Kent as I fantasized about him changing into the Caped Crusader in a telephone booth. I assumed by his attire that he was either a stockbroker on Wall Street or a lawyer, a straight arrow if there ever was one. Many mornings, it was my secret obsession just to watch the back of Clark Kent and his broad shoulders on my daily walk to school.

Months later on a Sunday evening, I decided to walk to Greenwich Village and ended up at the Ninth Circle, a well-known steakhouse and bar on 10th Street. The upstairs restaurant catered to a straight and gay crowd of West Village patrons—people like Mary Travers of the Peter, Paul, and Mary band fame. The bar downstairs was definitely gay and on this particular night was almost empty. Sitting on my solitary stool, I ordered my drink and looked down the long expanse of the well-worn bar surface and saw a man that looked like my Clark Kent. I wasn't sure at first though, because he wasn't wearing a suit, but the eyeglasses gave him away. Then I did something I had never done before or since: I commandeered the bartender to send the man sitting at the bar another drink of whatever he was having, with my compliments. As the bartender set the drink down in front of him gesturing as to who the sender was, Clark smiled broadly, got up, came over, sat next to me, thanked me, and introduced himself. "Hi, I am Tom Crane," he said warmly. His next words surprised me. "Would you like to get out of here?"

I immediately said, "Sure." As we headed toward Sixth Avenue he said, "I live on 16th Street between Fifth and Sixth Avenues."

I replied, "I know, at number 23. Somewhat bemused by my admission, he listened intensely as I explained that I lived across the street and had seen—

stalked?—him many mornings at the newsstand.

I don't really remember what the sex was like that night, but what I do remember was how easy and comfortable he was in his skin and how tremendously satisfying it was to sleep with him. Ten years older than I was, my hunch about his occupation was correct. Not only was he a lawyer, but he worked at 1 Wall Street. Seeing Tom opened a whole new world of sophisticated, talented friends to me including people like Seymour Avigdor, the designer of the fabric collection "Vice Versa for Donghia," the writer Dave King, and the artist Franklin Tartaglione. Tom loved the ballet so we went numerous times to see the New York City Ballet. Our time together ended when he canceled a Friday night date, saying he needed to be with his ailing parents in New Jersey. Somewhat disappointed, I accepted it and decided to go to the movies by myself. Slowly walking home afterward, I spied Tom, about a block-and-a-half away with his arm around a young guy. Careful to not let him see me, I walked behind him all the way to our block, and then watched as he ascended the stairs with this number. I was not angry, just maybe pissed off at the lie he had told me. I knew then it was over, and I guess that was okay.

After a few years, Tom's firm moved into 30 Rockefeller Plaza, where I ran into him all the time. And although we were no longer seeing each other, we were still good friends. Tom's parents left him reasonably well-off after their deaths. Although he did not have to work, he loved the law and eventually went to work for Corporation Counsel, which paid him very little. Tom just loved working for the government.

Funnily enough, while I was on the board of the Fashion Institute of Technology, there was a union dispute and all the board members had to be deposed. I went down to the Corporation Counsel offices and was asked to wait a few minutes. Who should emerge to depose me but Tom Crane. We both laughed at the circumstances of our meeting on a professional basis after all that time.

It is a bit surreal when you meet two guys in an elevator and 40-plus years later they are still two of your closest friends. That is exactly what happened when I met Peter Stamberg and Paul Aferiat. The prodigious architects live and work on lower Fifth Avenue in Manhattan in a spacious and color-filled 13th-floor loft.

On the ninth floor of that same building, for several years, the brothers Stanley and Walter Glanzrock manufactured tailored clothing for me at their firm, B. Glanzrock. Started by their father and in operation for many decades, the company made beautiful garments with lots of hand tailoring. For many, many years, the district of New York from Fifth Avenue to 12th Avenue and from 14th Street to 23rd Street had some 500 manufacturers of men's and boys' tailored clothing. By 1980 less than 10 of them remained. B. Glanzrock, watched over by these affable brothers, was one of the last of its kind. Sharing the same office building as my then tailored-clothing manufacturers, I met Peter and Paul in the elevator shortly after I began working in the building in which they lived.

For architects, Peter and Paul have a very keen sense of sartorial style. We definitely bonded over discussions of clothing as we would see each other in the elevator or zipping in and out of the building. We also discovered that we had a great love of the theater, especially anything Stephen Sondheim. Because we have seen so many different and varied Sondheim productions, we have jokingly dubbed ourselves "The Sondheim-olics."

Peter and Paul became great early fans and shoppers of my designs, and the clothing they saved is a great archival repository of my past collections. In addition, they are a terrific sounding board for any and all of my various projects—my designs or prose.

Having had only two apartments in my many years in Manhattan, within two blocks of each other, in 1979 my accountant advised me to buy something for tax purposes. I looked everywhere in my current favorite neighborhood as well as in other neighborhoods I did not care for, such as the Upper West Side and the Upper East Side. After looking for a year and finding nothing that I liked, I happened to confide in the elevator to Peter and Paul about my frustration. "What about the building across the street?" asked Peter.

"It's a Barnes & Noble bookstore downstairs and the After Six tuxedos alterations and warehouse upstairs," I replied.

"No, no," said Paul. "They are converting the spaces above the store to apartments."

Excited, I ran over at lunchtime and offered the workmen 100 bucks to see every apartment under construction over the next week. Six

RIGHT What can you say about neighbors who just happen to be the closest of friends? The constant cheering squad that is Peter Stamberg and Paul Aferiat are the kinds of friends everyone wishes they had.

OVERLEAF Just days after the apartment was finished being decorated by the New York designers Charles Swerz and Jerry Van Deelen, I got a call from Jacqueline Gonnet at *House & Garden* asking if she could come and see it. So I spent hours preparing and her one remark was that she wanted the exact same flowers to be there when they came back to photograph it. Black-and-white photographs add graphic accents to the calm, all-white living room.

PAGE 240 The dining area has a custom-designed pedestal column dining table with the California designer John Dickinson's signature animal-leg chairs.

PAGE 241 The vintage quilt from America Hurrah on the bed provides a bit of color, and the pine faux-armoire door leads into a large walk-in closet.

months later, when the prospectus came out, I was in Long Island City at the developer's office at 8:30am with a certified check for a down payment. It was all thanks to Peter and Paul that I bought my apartment across the street from them all those years ago. And it is through Peter and Paul that I have many other longtime friends such as the restaurateur Phil Suarez and his wife Lucy, as well as the former Macy's executive Robin Hall and his wife, Betsy Jablow.

The three of us have gone through so much together—birthdays, holidays, and family deaths. I consider it a privilege to call them my close friends.

The first thing I remember was the rust-colored fur coat with its unique hand-tooled metal buttons all in different shapes. Funny how one's memory selects certain things and completely obliterates others. I recall what she was wearing, but I do not remember the exact date. And neither does Fern Mallis. We both think it was at a party at the Abitare Italian furniture store on the Upper East Side, where I had had a fashion show early on. What we do remember quite clearly was that it was an instant friendship that has only deepened and burnished with the passing of time. We were bonded, aided, and abetted by our mutual friends Scott Bromley and Robin Jacobsen and fueled by lazy days and fun-filled Fire Island Pines party nights. Fern was, and is, a dynamo, part of that rare breed of super-smart women who, if gender-swapped, would be labeled ambitious, bold, decisive, assertive, fierce, energetic, and enterprising. But because she is a woman, she has been called pushy, aggressive, in-your-face, pugnacious, discordant, and overambitious. I beg to disagree. Fern

LEFT BELOW Fern Mallis and her forever friend, the architect Scott Bromley. One seldom thinks of one without the other.

OPPOSITE Fern Mallis in the role in which she shines: "Boss Lady." Here, she is seen corralling the troops at New York Fashion Week.

gets the job done. She is one of only two women I know whose mind works like a computer, rapidly channeling ways to solve problems in short order.

Those extraordinary traits have come in very handy from her early days as a guest editor at *Mademoiselle* magazine, to one of her first jobs as head of public relations for the ill-fated Gimbel's East department store. Fern parlayed that experience into opening her own public relations firm and eventually masterminded the advertising and marketing for the interior design industry's Long Island City's outpost called IDCNY.

It was in that capacity that I thought of her while I was on the CFDA search committee for a new executive director. Fern Mallis is a friend of mine, but she was also, I was sure, perfect for the job. We had already seen a score of candidates, and I suggested her name as someone who could surely get the job done. And boy did she! She insisted that the CFDA have its own office, instead of sharing space in a designer's showroom, and hired Michael Bierut of Pentagram to design a corporate logo that still resonates to this very day. Most importantly she, along with Stan Herman, organized the American Fashion Industry, whose haphazard habit of fashion viewings had become not only untenable but also dangerous. Bringing the fashion shows to a centralized venue galvanized the industry and made America a world-class competitor with Europe.

Fern and I have shared many travels together, particularly one trip to St. Barts with our friend Jane Hertzmark Hudis that was almost derailed by a snowed-in New York. When we finally did get there, we laughed nonstop and had a memorable pig-out one day on assorted cheeses.

There have also been the sad and heartbreaking moments, too. I remember swimming in my friends' pool in Houston and feeling this sudden physical need to get out of the pool and call Fern and ask about her ailing mother. A distraught Fern answered to tell me that her mother had passed away moments before. Fern's younger sister, Joanne, was, to all who knew her, a spitfire of vivacity, and when this mother of three beautiful girls was stricken with cancer, a pall was cast over us all. I remember spending eight hours at Memorial Sloan Kettering Cancer Center alone with Joanne as she received treatment and was in agonizing pain. This is the kind of deep friendship that we have as our careers and lives have careened and crested and soared and crashed—always there for each other, no matter what.

Fern is not an easy person. She is complicated and complex, but ultimately a true and loyal friend, which at the end of the day, is what really counts.

I had resisted all attempts by my friend Fern Mallis to engage with her massage therapist Peter Warren. Although she touted him as virtually the Second Coming of Christ, I just didn't believe anyone could be that good. I had had a few massages before, but none were particularly Nirvanalike or justified repeating.

Fern had been urging many in her close circle to see Peter, with lackluster responses and, suddenly that summer, she took matters in hand and decided to book him for continuous sessions for an entire weekend. She then charted out those sessions in her calendar and informed each of us of what slot had been allotted to us, and that we were also expected to pay Peter directly afterward. My time slot was Saturday afternoon at 4:30pm in her garage studio before we were to attend a 6:30pm cocktail party and subsequent dinner.

As I lay face down on the massage table, I asked Peter to be extra careful with my left arm as after a fall, a fracture, and a later surgical break, my arm was in what my physical therapist termed "a permanent carrying angle"—meaning the arm was no longer able, even after extensive physical therapy, to fully extend. Peter took hold of my wrist, placed his ear next to my elbow and said, "Nothing about the body is permanent," as he began to tightly twist my wrist counter-clockwise. What ensued for the next ten minutes was the most excruciating pain that I have ever endured.

But when he was done, my arm could fully extend for the first time since before the accident and has remained so all these years later. As the hour-plus session ended, I rushed to shower and change to accompany Fern to the first of our two evening events. As we pulled out of the driveway, we saw the next friend, James Haigney, arrive for his scheduled session. James suffered from chronic debilitating neuropathy in his extremities, particularly his feet. He could not sleep for more than 20 minutes at a stretch, and he was taking enormous amounts of Advil to relieve the pain. I noticed it was 6pm as we left somewhat late for our cocktail party.

When we returned that night after midnight, we noticed that James' car was still in the driveway. Odd, we thought, as we assumed he had been long gone. Fifteen minutes later, James and Peter emerged. Peter had been working on James for over six hours, especially to relieve the neuropathy. Peter said James had been asleep for over four hours of that session.

What I learned in many subsequent sessions with Peter is that he is a healer and much more than a massage therapist. His intuitive sense of what ailed your body has been honed by years of rigorous training with Indigenous masters, in India, Tibet, and many other places. One does not see Peter for a relaxing massage, but for a physical and spiritual alignment of one's mind and body in which one is a very active participant and becomes healed in a holistic way.

To say that Peter is a character is to barely scratch the surface of this individual.

PEGGY TAGLIARINO

As a neighbor, Margaret Tagliarino was right out of central casting—jovial, outgoing, and bigger than life. It was beyond lucky that I came to live next door to her.

It did not exactly start out that way though. Peggy, fresh from a divorce, living on the Upper West Side, this single lady had moved into our brand new co-op mere weeks before me. Because she was a night owl, I used to hear her nocturnal movements, seemingly all night long. In fact, due to my lack of furniture in those early days, I initially thought someone was in my apartment when I heard those floorboards creak. Eventually, I figured out it was Peggy and I was able to sleep more soundly.

Peggy, gave new meaning to the phrase "open-door policy" as her front door was seldom locked. She presided always at the wall that comprised her kitchen opening, which was catty-corner to her apartment entrance. From her all-seeing perch behind the counter, Peggy dispensed not only her wisdom but also her culinary delicacies. You see, food was her passion and her business. Peggy had her own public relations firm specializing in restaurants, chefs, and almost anything else in the gourmet world. Originally she had an office on Broadway a few blocks away, but eventually she set up shop at home —more on that later. Along with the flotsam and jetsam of mail, keys, and flowers, her counter always contained a bounty of food of all kinds. In fact, one would never go hungry living next door to Peggy. Breads, cheeses, candies, and her latest epicurean obsessions all seemed to reside on that counter from which she held court. In addition, Peggy, who loved chocolate above all else, had a refrigerator crisper devoted to all sorts of chocolates, from high-end Italian, French, and Swiss varieties to the plebeian Nestlé Crunch. She insisted that the best Crunch bars absolutely had to come from Switzerland via France, and anyone traveling there had to promise to bring her some back.

Peggy's big personality was perfectly suited to the world of public relations. She loved people of all kinds, shapes, and sizes. She was genuinely interested in so many things, and we bonded particularly over theater and film. Most importantly, Peggy and I loved to laugh together. Peggy reigned supreme over the fourth floor and our neighbors, Robert and Carol Boghosian, Peter Keyloun and his wife, and Maxine and Mike Sheaber. Eventually, the floor seemed like my idea of a fraternity house. Such kinship and collegial vibes reigned that Robert was known to saunter down the hallway in his tighty whities, announcing for all to hear," What do you have to eat, Tags?" That was one of Margaret "Peggy" Tagliarino's myriad nicknames.

OVERLEAF Surrounded by a host of loving friends, Peggy Tagliarino, in a white jacket, celebrated her big 6-0 in the South of France. Her mother, Blanche Levine, is to her left.

She called me Beauregarde, and I dubbed her Cyrene Montgomery of the esteemed Southern Montgomerys, although she was not Southern at all, but a nice Jewish girl from New Jersey. Her first and only husband had been an Italian American, hence the Tagliarino moniker. A Francophile through and through, Peggy also answered to Madame de Fourcy (4-C, get it?). I used to say that she would readily board a plane to Paris just to have a morning cup of coffee at Le Comptoir. When, for a very brief moment, there was a Fauchon outpost on Park Avenue, Peggy would get up early—actually the only time she would get up early—throw her grey plastic raincoat over her Eileen West nightgown and corral me to go in her car with her. She ran inside as she kept the engine running to get the still-warm croissants.

Peggy was truly brilliant at her job, and the "Who's Who" of the gastronomy world all knew her. She came up with not only the concept of Terrence Brennan's Bar Bistro Fromagerie "Artisanal" but its name, too. She also had the excellent idea of taking all the small craft cheese makers that Brennan had found and wholesaling the cheeses to high-end retailers including Neiman Marcus. She also sold them in the restaurant's cheese cave, thereby monetizing all the time, money, and effort it took to find these small-batch wonders.

Peggy and I grew ever closer when she got Lily, a beautiful English Springer Spaniel. Although I had never owned a dog, I knew that they needed to be taken out early and walked daily. Getting up early was definitely not one of Peggy's strong suits. She loved to sleep and hated to go to bed. I explained to her that the dog needed to be walked early in the morning. Because I was an early riser, Peggy suggested that I walk Lily every morning. She left her apartment door unlocked every night and, at approximately 5:30am every morning I walked into Peggy's bedroom, collected Lily, and took her out for her morning constitutional.

Peggy Tagliarino loved fashion, but she loved a bargain even more. As a designer, I am always on the side of the hard-working designer, be he or she large or small. I spent several years working with the CFDA and their brilliant attorney, the late Alain Coblence, trying to get a design copyright bill passed in Congress. I say all this because I was chagrined and very disapproving of Peggy's bargain hunting, which often ran to buying fakes. We now know that buying copies and fakes can, in many cases, be supporting terrorism, which is often the method used to launder money for illicit efforts.

But back in 2002, we did not know such things. Peggy's defense was always, "Even if I wanted to pay full price, the waiting lists are interminable." Another thing you should know about Peggy is that when she wanted something, she wanted it *now*. Still I looked down on her illegal purchases as something beneath her, as after all, she made a nice living and could afford the real thing. And she had plenty of the real things, especially by Louis Vuitton. But the thrill of the hunt in pursuit of the unattainable had much more allure for her.

And then it happened, Marc Jacobs debuted his collaboration with Murakami for Louis Vuitton. Had there ever been a more desired and less available handbag than those first multicolored Murakami bags? The long-waiting lists! The lines around the world! It became a cultural phenomenon. Peggy just had to have one, and could not last another day without scoring one. Knowing how I felt about trafficking in copies, she tricked me into going in her car with her down to Canal Street with some ruse or another. However, as soon as we walked into the small little shop, I knew something was up. True, the few dozen bags on display were nondescript black or brown no-name, boring handbags. But as soon as Peggy said the word "Murakami," the owner's eyes lit up, and it was as if we had walked into a speakeasy and the password had just been uttered. He quickly ushered us to the shiny metal back wall and just as quickly raised that wall to reveal a narrow room the size of a very small closet, filled with Murakamis of every style and color—navy, white, Speedy bags, Sologne and Trouville shapes. They were all there, and Peggy was in heaven. I was horrified. Suddenly, the shop assistant yelled out something in Chinese, and the owner shoved us inside and pulled the metal wall down seemingly in one swift move. Apparently, the shop was being raided by the police. Peggy and I, in the airless sardine can of a metal closet, knew enough not to say a word. Eventually, a tiny ceiling fan was turned on and, though pouring sweat from every orifice, we were finally able to breathe a little.

Although, it seemed like an eternity among the faux-leather baggagerie, it was probably only about six or seven minutes in hell before the gate of a wall came up, and we were released from captivity. "Really Peggy," I said, "Were these bags really worth going to jail over?"

She smiled sweetly, looked up at me, and said, "Absolutely!"

After several trips to Paris with Peggy, we thought it might be fun to take our mothers on the next one. Deciding that a long Thanksgiving weekend trip might be just the thing, we made our reservations at the Hotel Relais Saint-Germain, a charming auberge on the Left Bank. Peggy asked her mother, Blanche Levine, who was then 85, and I asked my mother, Eleanor Banks, who was 87. Mom and I arrived Wednesday morning and Peggy and Blanche came the evening of Thanksgiving.

My good friend Connie Uzzo, upon hearing that my mom and I would be in Paris, promptly invited us to her famous expat Thanksgiving dinner held at her spacious apartment near the Place de la Bastille. Brooklyn-born Connie—who retained her distinctive accent her whole life—was hired very early on by Yves Saint Laurent to be his most trusted confidante in North America and was beloved by both Saint Laurent and his partner, Pierre Bergé. Connie handled everything from licensees to press for Saint Laurent. With about 25 guests, most of whom were Americans, including the designer Reem Acra, Connie made us feel more than at home with a sumptuous feast of several turkeys, two or three kinds of stuffing, cranberry sauce, both jellied and homemade, and all the rest of the traditional trimmings—cooked by Connie herself. When I asked Connie which item had been the most difficult to procure for dinner, thinking she would say the turkey, she surprised me by immediately blurting out, the sweet potatoes. It seems that the French do not really cultivate them and, according to Connie, there was only one market that carried them, which would only get about four or five a day. To have enough for her guests, she went back every day for a week.

It was a dazzling first evening for Mom's second visit to the City of Light. The day started earlier with a stroll around our new Left Bank neighborhood, and of course, some shopping. Wandering into a ladies' shoe store, Mom scored a pair of brown boots, but really coveted the Venetian high-heeled green suede boots she saw in the window. I was off the hook as they did not have her size.But that was only until the store owner offered to have the boots made for her and shipped to the United States when they were ready. As my mother batted her eyes at me, I caved right away and paid for the second pair.

Peggy was, of course, in charge of all restaurant reservations, most of which had been made before we left New York. I was in charge of everything else.

As the two older women excitedly discussed what they wanted to do, Peggy and I were amazed that these two women, who had only met previously on the telephone, seemed to be instantly joined at the hip. Blanche, the New Jersey Jewish doyenne whose visits to Paris had been an annual event during her second marriage, and my Baptist mother who was only in Europe for the second time. Adding to the mix was Peggy's iconic love of Paris. I was overwhelmed by all of this feminine energy. As they excitedly discussed all the shopping they hoped to achieve over the next few days, I realized I needed to have a plan of attack, as there were a few things I wanted to do during our short stay besides going into stores. I quickly hatched a scheme, asking the ladies to retire to their rooms for half an hour and make a list of every store they hoped to visit. We were all meant to regroup in the lobby in an hour, lists in hand. Meanwhile, I conferred with the hotel's concierge, asking him to engage an English-speaking driver with a van. When I reconvened with the ladies in the lobby, I took their lists, added up all the names of the shops, and divided the lists into Left and Right Bank locations. I am happy to say that on that Saturday, while visiting Left Bank stores in the morning and Right Bank stores in the afternoon, with a stop at Fauchon for lunch in between, we managed to get to 31 stores.

The greatest thing about the trip was to see the loving relationship that grew between the two mature women with their very different backgrounds, who bonded as if they were sisters. They became inseparable, and it truly was joyous to behold. The Friday afternoon of our first day together, Connie arranged a private tour of the Yves Saint Laurent Haute Couture Archive. For over three hours, the four of us were ensconced at 5, avenue Marceau with the most charming and handsome guide, who took us through the wonders of Saint Laurent's storied career, opening the vast hydraulically sealed room that housed the crème de la crème of the archive. We had to wear white cotton gloves to handle Catherine Deneuve's famous Mondrian-inspired sheath from the movie *Belle de Jour* as well as the legendary Lesage-embroidered jackets and capes depicting artists such as Van Gogh and Picasso, each of which took more than 600 hours to embroider. None of this was lost on Blanche, whose late husband, a commercial real estate developer, had taken her to Paris on frequent buying trips to the couture shows.

Besides dining sublimely every day—thank you, Peggy—I also took the ladies to see the Balenciaga retrospective at the Musée des Arts Décoratifs. It was a dazzling exploration of the fabled designer's œuvre, and we all enjoyed it immensely. At the end of the five days, friendships were forged that continued until Blanche's death a few years later. How strangely wonderful that these two such different women could get along and find such common bonds. If they could become soul sisters in such a short time and so far away from their homeland, why can't the rest of the world get along as well?

OPPOSITE When your friendship is so attuned to each other for so many years, it's no wonder that you start to dress alike.

It is really crazy how sometimes, such a small moment in one's life can have such a tremendous lifelong impact. In my early twenties, one of my earliest licensing deals was with a company called Enro Shirts. I had gone to their showroom to have a meeting with the firm's president, but he was delayed by a meeting that was running late. The curly-haired receptionist asked if I would please have a seat in the reception area to wait for him. I watched intensely as she calmly navigated the chaos of the reception area of the bustling shirt company, as salesmen and buyers rushed by while fielding calls from an irate regional salesman demanding to get two dozen cream broadcloth shirts delivered immediately.

"I am checking my inventory stock, and I don't have cream, but I can ship your ivory right away, if you like," she said, at the same time signing a messenger's delivery receipt.

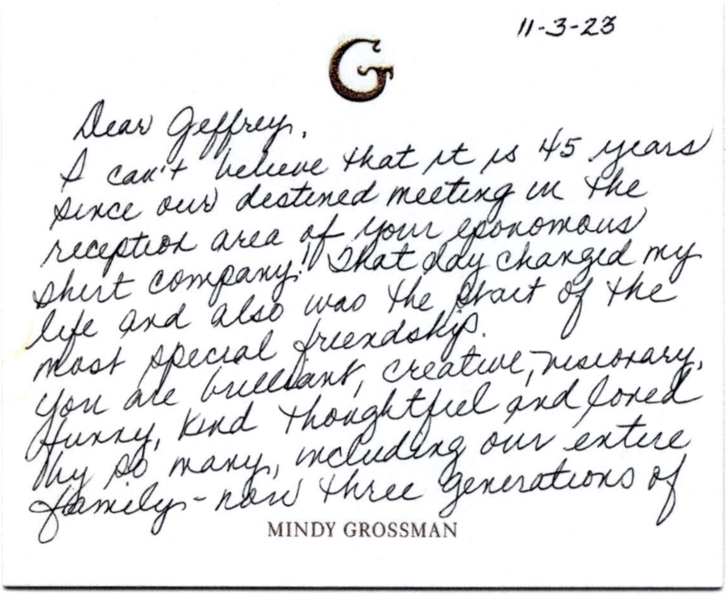

11-3-23

G

Dear Jeffrey,
I can't believe that it is 45 years since our destined meeting in the reception area of your enormous shirt company! That day changed my life and also was the start of the most special friendship.
You are brilliant, creative, visionary, funny, kind thoughtful and loved by so many, including our entire family - now three generations of

MINDY GROSSMAN

LEFT A lovely note from Mindy Grossman speaks to our timeless friendship.

OVERLEAF Don Witkowski, Mindy Grossman, and I were photographed at one of our famous Regent Hotel "bathrobes and room service" dinner parties, where you can see that fun was the antidote for a hard day's work in Hong Kong.

I marveled at her serenity in coping with all the craziness around that front desk—not knowing that Mindy Waldman was, in fact, filling in that day for a receptionist who was at lunch. She was, in fact, a 21-year-old sales associate. Eventually, I went into my meeting and, bowled over by what I had seen in the last 20 minutes, demanded that she work on the burgeoning Jeffrey Banks shirt division.

I will let Mindy continue here, "That was the most pivotal moment in my career. There I was, with a rolling bag of dress and sport shirts, traveling by plane, train, and automobile to meet with men's specialty stores all over the United States. Jeffrey was my mentor, my friend and, right at the start, we developed a special relationship."

A short while later, Enro pivoted out of the better designer business, but two years later, I had just begun as design director at Merona Sport and, of course, I wanted Mindy to join me; and she did. "It was a rocket ship and the world of spectator activewear was born," said Mindy.

Mindy was the perfect pilot, along with Andy Carter to propel Merona's sales into the stratosphere. Shortly after, Oxford Industries decided to bankroll Jeffrey Banks Menswear and to create Jeffrey Banks Womenswear.

Here's Mindy in her own words: "My next adventure was being made the vice-president of sales of the menswear business. It was an amazing team, an incredible fashion moment in menswear, and an unparalleled opportunity for a woman in the menswear industry. Little known was that my first hire as the Midwest sales representative was a young man named John Varvatos! Also, something else happened during that time—you see, I had a dating ritual. If I was thinking of getting serious with someone, they had to meet Jeffrey and get his approval. Fortunately, the first one did *not* get his approval, or I would never have met my husband, Neil Grossman, who *did* get his approval and now also considers Jeffrey a special friend. Jeffrey and I have celebrated many birthdays together. I so remember having to keep him away from his apartment making up stories as to why, so he could be surprised with a serious teddy bear party on his 30th birthday; he was with me for so many of mine. We both then launched new creative voyages, but our friendship only deepened. Jeffrey then became an author and it was fate that his book *Tartan: Romancing the Plaid* ultimately became the inspiration for Tartan House, an entire stone building on our property in Millbrook that is truly an homage to him. I have memories of waiting in line at Saks Fifth Avenue in New York to get my copy signed and loved seeing the entire industry come out in honor of him and his book. But we were bound to have even *more* new adventures. In 2007 at a fun Friday night dinner in an Italian restaurant, I told him I needed a Fabulous Fun and New Home collection. Within 24 hours—I am sure he never slept the entire time—he presented me with the most incredible portfolio of designs and concepts that became one of the number-one home decor brands on HSN. Utilizing all things tartan, we created Scottie dogs, crystal, plush bedding, and cashmere soft throws—our women loved everything he did and they loved Jeffrey. I was also lucky that my best friend ended up spending a lot of time in St. Petersburg, Florida. That's when he really got to know my daughter Lizzy, who truly adores him, and loves that he now also adores her daughters, our granddaughters, Emma and Hannah. We have had many fun weekends at our home in Millbrook, Connecticut, decorating with tartan everywhere and shopping for vintage bronze Scottie dogs. Jeffrey always surprised me with a special gift that was antique and unique, and they all have a special place in our home."

Being best friends with a woman I admire so much has been a real blessing for me. I am so very proud of her many accomplishments. Since I first met her Mindy went on to become vice-president of Menswear at WilliWear prior to joining the Ralph Lauren Corporation, where she launched the Polo Jeans Company. In 2000 Mindy joined Nike, Inc., overseeing its climb to becoming a worldwide multibillion-dollar apparel business. Mindy then joined Barry Diller to take over IAC's retail portfolio, which she then took public as HSN in 2008. As of 2014 Mindy was one of only 51 women who led a Fortune 1000 company. Oprah Winfrey picked her to become the CEO of Weight Watchers in 2017, and she is now the vice-chair of Consello.

I truly believe there is nothing Mindy cannot do, and I am so happy to have been one of the earliest people to discover just how talented she is.

Don Witkowski had the unique ability to put you at ease, almost from the first time you met him. His nearly fundamental need for laughter and fun filled every day and every conversation, whether you were a work colleague or friend. It is no wonder that decades after moving on, or even moving away, people still relish the time they spent with him as special. Growing up in Ohio, it was almost predestined that Don should land in the bright lights and big city that was New York. Although he was no actor, New York was certainly his stage, and he loved all the energy that radiated from the concrete surroundings that made up Gotham. The fashion business was only one of the drugs that fueled his enthusiasm for the Big Apple.

Don loved New York and the menswear industry equally, and we first became acquainted when Steve Eisendrath suggested that he should merchandise the Jeffrey Banks Menswear collection. We got along famously with Don's infectious sense of humor—the glue that bonded us forever. Also, it did not hurt that my design assistant Suzanna Ward and Don bonded quickly. They were inseparable, almost like sister and brother, and spent hours together after work. Don's innate skill to think like a retailer and his other skill as a super salesman were instrumental in merchandising and in helping the

LEFT BELOW It had been relentlessly raining for days on end in Donegal, Ireland, before my assistant Suzanna Ward's wedding to Rob Weldon.

salability of my designs. Don's love of Madonna was legendary and earned him the sobriquet of "MA-DON."

One of my fondest memories of Don was our trip to Ireland for Suzanna's wedding to Rob Weldon. The two had first met at an Irish sweater mill when Suzanna was working for me, and Rob was designing sweaters on his own. They fell in love and decided to get married in Ireland, where they first met. Don and I decided to fly to Donegal for the wedding. It had been raining nonstop for several days but, an hour before the ceremony, the sun magically came out. I was thrilled to introduce the married couple as they emerged from the ancient church.

Don went on to become president of Michael Kors Menswear, and we remained close until his untimely demise from glioblastoma. The outpouring of sympathy and remembrance when he passed was tremendous and truly showed how much Don was loved.

I have been obsessed with Audrey Hepburn since I was a small child. To me, she epitomized the ultimate in attractive feminine chic and beauty. On my weekly forays to the public library, I focused on anything I could get my hands on about her, particularly magazine stories. *The Readers Guide to Periodical Literature* became my best friend, introducing me to sometimes decades-old articles in *Life*, *Look*, *Time*, *Vogue*, *Harper's Bazaar*, *Good Housekeeping*, and *Ladies Home Journal* written about Audrey. In the years before VCRs, revival movie houses were my refuge to catch up on the film canon of her work that came out before I was born.

Of course, my indulgent mother escorted me to one such theater when I was about 11 or 12 to see *Funny Face*. The seminal film is ground zero for anyone interested in the fashion industry. And for me, even more so, as it had everything I loved in the world: Audrey Hepburn, Fred Astaire, Richard Avedon, George Gershwin, Hubert de Givenchy, and Paris. The film was playing on a double bill with *Lili* starring Leslie Caron, which played first. When *Funny Face* finally did come on, I made my mother sit through *Lili* a second time, just so I could see *Funny Face* again.

Any articles about Audrey I could not track down at the library I would make lists of and take those lists to a vintage magazine and bookstore downtown that had tons of old issues, which were not particularly well-organized. The shop owners allowed me to sort through their stock until I found what I was looking for. Because of all my research, I was convinced that I was the foremost authority on

Audrey Hepburn by the tender age of 13. My overall dream was to someday be lucky enough to be in the same room with her and possibly breathe the same air she was breathing.

In the early 1980s my friends and I often saw a man at the beach who we dubbed "the Italian Prince." Beautifully bronzed he looked like a Renaissance page or a Florentine duke, we decided. Suddenly, one Saturday afternoon, I found myself standing next to him at a bar. He introduced himself as John Rizzuto and asked what I did for a living.

"Oh, I'm in the fashion business," I replied. " How about you?"

He said, matter-of-factly: "I'm in the fashion business, too."

I countered: "Who do you work for?"

He replied, "Oh, a European designer you probably wouldn't know."

I shot back, "Try me."

He said: "I am the president of Givenchy North America."

I then blurted out, excitedly: "Do you know Audrey Hepburn?"

He said: "Well, as a matter of fact I do." Breathlessly, I recounted that one of my life goals was to meet the actress and fashion icon. "Well," he said, "The next time she is in New York, I will arrange to have you meet her!"

I guess I was so bowled over by the mere suggestion that my dream might be realized that I neglected to exchange numbers with John, and shortly thereafter we went our separate ways.

A few weeks later, I received an early morning call at home as I was dressing for work. "Is this Jeffrey Banks?" the voice on the end of the receiver asked. "This is John Rizzuto; I don't know if you . . ."

I quickly cut him off with, "Of course I remember you!"

He said, "Well, I wanted to let you know that Audrey is coming in the fall to celebrate the 35th Anniversary of the House of Givenchy accompanying Hubert at FIT."

I almost shouted to John, who took my excitement in stride: "I will buy the whole table next to her."

Somewhat bemused by my response, he said, "Okay, if that's what you want."

I thanked him profusely, hung up, and immediately called my friend Renny Reynolds, who, at the time, was the king of New York party planners. "Renny," I said. "I am going to need two dozen red roses for a dinner with Audrey Hepburn. No, make it four dozen. No, maybe six dozen." I don't remember how many we ended up with, but suffice it to say it was like a very large bush when he finished—so large, in fact, that on the evening of the event I went to FIT 45 minutes early to hide the roses under the skirt of my table, which indeed was right next to Audrey's.

That night, between the first and second courses, John came over so I could meet Audrey. I reached under my table to retrieve my impossibly large bouquet of red roses as I was led over to Audrey's

RIGHT AND BELOW A sweet remembrance from Hubert de Givenchy to Tom Fallon upon the death of Audrey Hepburn, which was written on the back of a postcard that depicts their friendship.

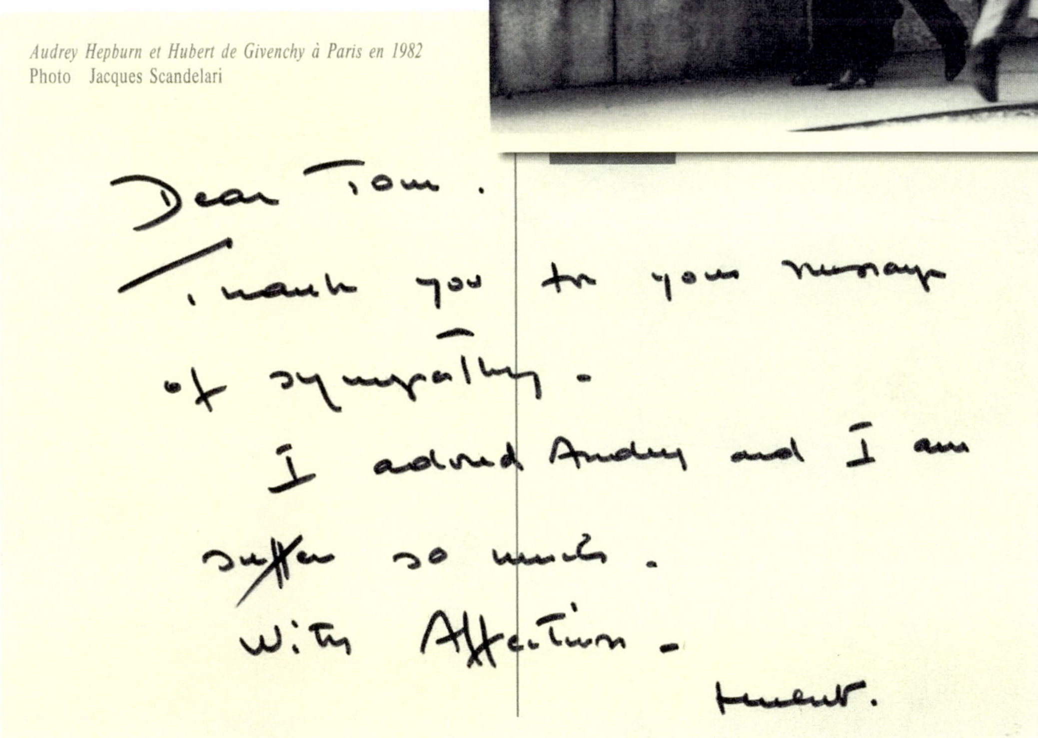

Audrey Hepburn et Hubert de Givenchy à Paris en 1982
Photo Jacques Scandelari

Dear Tom.
Thank you for your message of sympathy.
I adored Audrey and I am suffer so much.
With Affection.
Hubert.

OPPOSITE One other thing Ralph Lauren and I shared was our undying love for Audrey Hepburn. She even wore Ralph Lauren in her documentary television series *Gardens of the World* and the book that accompanied it. Also, Audrey had, of course, presented Ralph with the first CFDA Lifetime Achievement Award in 1992.

table. She was somewhat startled—wouldn't you be?—but she graciously accepted them, as pleasantries were exchanged.

I was, however, devastated. I guess I had built up in my head for years what this auspicious meeting would be like, and somehow it just missed the mark. There was a distracted quality to Audrey that night. I just could not put my finger on it, and I went back to my table somewhat disappointed. My friends who, of course, knew all about my fascination with Audrey, could tell I was not as elated as I had hoped to be and so at the end of the evening, with a couple of limousines at our disposal, decided to whisk me up to the Café Carlyle to catch Bobby Short to cheer me up. We were all dressed to the nines, and Bobby was in rare form, but it just didn't work.

The next morning, shortly after 8am the telephone rang. It was John. "Jeffrey, I could tell last night that you were disappointed."

I replied a bit sheepishly: "Was it that obvious?"

John continued, "Let me explain, Audrey was not herself at all last night. You see her mother fell in Switzerland a few days ago and broke her hip and Audrey was very ambivalent about leaving her. However, she knew that many people had bought tickets only to see her accompany Hubert and so she took the overnight train from Switzerland to Paris and then the Concorde from Paris to New York to be here. Then she did the reverse this morning to return to her mother. In addition, she called her mother from the event several times to check up on her." It was as though a cloud had lifted and the sun began to break through. "I promise you," he added, "the next time you meet her, it will be a totally different experience."

And you know what? He was right.

Dreams do come true. There were many more meetings with Audrey Hepburn over the years and John Rizzuto was right, they were all wonderful.

There was the time my friend, the producer Brad Siegel, invited me for a taping at the studio for AMC during a week of Audrey's films. Of course, I readily said yes, thinking that I was to be part of the studio audience, only to arrive early to find there was no studio audience at all, just Audrey, the director, the producers, the camera crew, and me. Brad showed me the list of questions the interviewer, Richard Brown, was planning to ask, and I was horrified. He had Audrey's birth date as well as her half-brother's name wrong, along with a host of other so-called "facts." I told Brad and he suggested that I make corrections with a highlighter on the script.

I did just that and, lo and behold, the interviewer went on air and asked the corrected questions that, in my total knowledge of Hepburn lore, I had provided. It was a glorious day with Audrey and Rob Wolders and I was so very appreciative that Brad had thought of me. I also attended the CFDA Awards at the Metropolitan Museum of Art in New York when Audrey presented an award to Richard Avedon. Then there was the time, thanks to my friend, Tony Impavido, that I attended the New York Film Society of Lincoln Center event at Avery Fisher Hall honoring Audrey in April 1991.

In the early 1990s, Audrey agreed to present Ralph Lauren with the first CFDA Lifetime Achievement Award. The week before the awards, I asked my friend Fern Mallis, at the time the executive director of the CFDA, if they needed anyone to pick up Audrey from the airport when she came into town, saying that I would make myself available. I received a swift and resounding "no." And so, licking my wounds, I retreated to Kent, Connecticut, to visit friends Vincent Petragnani and Larry Himelfarb for the weekend. These friends refused to pick up the telephone on the weekend since they did not want to speak to their respective families. At the time, I did not possess a cell phone, vowing to be the last man in New York to have one. So, on Sunday morning, as I sat reading the *New York Times*, I was annoyed as the telephone continued to ring nonstop.

Eventually, I yelled out, "Will somebody pick up that damn phone?" Bringing me the telephone, Larry said, "It's for you!"

It turned out that Fern had been calling all over town to try to find me, and my neighbors in New York had given her my friends' number in Connecticut. It seems that Peter Fonda, another presenter at the

LEFT BELOW I was photographed at the Home Shopping Network Studio in St. Petersburg, Florida, with Sean Ferrer, Audrey's older son, whom I have known for quite a while.

OPPOSITE BELOW Luca Dotti, Audrey's younger son, insisted that we take this selfie several times until he was satisfied that we both looked great.

awards, had arrived from Los Angeles on Friday night, there was no one to greet him, and he was mighty pissed. So Fern decided, in her infinite wisdom, that it might be best to have someone greet Audrey and Rob Wolders at the airport. And who better than me?

The problem was there were only about 20 minutes left to get me to a bus back into the city in time to meet Audrey's flight. I rushed my friends to start up the car as I threw my clothes in a bag. As we got to the bus stop just in the nick of time, we had to block the front of the bus with the car to keep the bus from taking off.

Returning to the city, I called my neighbors, Peter Stamberg and Paul Aferiat, to thank them for getting the Connecticut telephone number to Fern. As I described what I was going to do, Peter asked if I had ever had my picture taken with Audrey. I said I had not, and then he said that he had just gotten a new long-range camera lens and perhaps he should go with me to the airport. "Absolutely not!" I said. "No paparazzi!"

But as I quickly got dressed, I thought this might be my only chance. I called Peter and Paul back right away, and told them they could ride with me in the town car, but to dress as tourists and hide in baggage claim to surreptitiously snap us as I retrieved their luggage. We had arranged for a separate waiting limousine to take Rob and Audrey back to the Hôtel Plaza Athénée in the city. Peter, Paul, and I would return in the town car. Peter snapped away without my acknowledging his existence in any way. As I helped to load up the limousine with Rob and Audrey's suitcases, I bid them farewell, saying that I would see them at Lincoln Center the following evening.

"Aren't you coming with us?" Audrey asked.

LEFT Peter Stamberg took this picture surreptitiously of Audrey Hepburn and me with a telephoto lens. I am so glad he did, as it's the only picture I have of the two of us together.

I said, "No, I am sure you are tired and just want to rest."
Audrey added, "Well, if you have something better to do."
Thinking quickly, I said, "No, no. Nothing better to do at all. Give me just a minute." I walked in the direction of Peter and Paul, who were standing next to the town car, and without addressing them directly, said, sotto voce, "Take the town car. You are on your own."
The next thing I knew, I was in the limousine on the way back to the city and their hotel. They had a suite, and Rob immediately retreated to the bedroom behind closed doors. There I was, sitting on the sofa next to Audrey and chatting as if we were two old friends. Audrey ordered drinks from room service—Scotch for her, ginger ale for me. She told me a charming story about being in New York a few years before to attend a gala of some sort. She jumped in a taxi and realized that she had forgotten her lipstick. Speeding down Lexington Avenue, she spied a drugstore and asked the cab driver to pull over and wait. She quickly picked out a $3.99 Maybelline lipstick and went to the checkout to pay. As Audrey approached, the salesgirl's eyes widened in recognition of the movie star. When she tried to pay, the checkout girl shrieked, "But Miss Hepburn, we do have Chanel lipsticks!"

Audrey laughed at the retelling of this story, and we continued our cozy chat until I suddenly glanced at my watch and realized that we had been speaking for over an hour I had not let this woman take off her makeup, go to the bathroom, or get out of her clothes. I quickly excused myself saying, "I am so sorry, Audrey, I will see you tomorrow night at Lincoln Center." As I was leaving the suite, I noticed on a breakfront a small white nosegay of flowers and a note thanking Audrey from Ralph Lauren. As I left, the size of this very small floral offering somewhat upset me. When I got home, I immediately called my old pal Renny Reynolds at home.

"Renny, I need lilies of the valley—Audrey's favorite flower—peonies, roses, etc., etc., in an arrangement for Audrey at her hotel by 10am tomorrow morning."

Renny said, "Jeffrey, you are telling me what you want to have in the arrangement, but you are not telling me what you want to spend on it."

I answered, "Renny, it's for Audrey Hepburn! Money is no object!" That was clearly not the right thing to say to that man.

The next evening, we were at the New York State Theater, and I watched Audrey from across the room at Ralph's table, unable to eat her dinner because of all the well-wishers who wanted her autograph, picture, or just to chat. I was determined not to go over and interrupt her meal. Eventually, we were called into the auditorium for the awards presentation. As I started to enter, I heard a woman call my name. I turned and saw Audrey, her hands outstretched, running toward me. She took my face into her hands, kissed me seven times on each cheek, and told me that they were, "the most beautiful flowers I've ever received." She then began to name every species of flower in the arrangement and, I swear if you had shot me in the back at that moment, I would have died a very happy man.

From that day on, I vowed that whenever she came to the city and at whatever hotel she was staying, there would be flowers waiting for her from me. In 1991 Audrey was in New York to receive the Variety Club's International Humanitarian Award. Audrey asked me to join her and Rob Wolders for the dinner along with Connie Wald, who had introduced her to Rob several years before.

As I sat next to her, Audrey leaned over and said quietly, "Jeffrey, the flowers are lovely, but they are too much, they have to stop."

I replied, "There can never be too many flowers for you." And I meant it.

If one were to use the term "hard-hitting journalist" to describe Teri Agins, I would also have to add "fiercely loyal friend." As a longtime fashion business writer for the *Wall Street Journal*, Teri had the unenviable job of rooting out the real stories of fashion's biggest businesses and their successes and major failings. Despite this brief, she gained the trust and the ear of many of fashion's biggest players who knew that she would always be fair in her reporting.

I met Teri in the early 1980s and was astonished at her knowledge of the big companies as well as her awareness of the up-and-coming young designers, many of whom she championed in her reporting. "The best stuff is when you follow the money," she said. And follow it she has, for over 30 years, becoming one of the most trusted journalists covering the business of fashion.

She explained: "We didn't have a dedicated fashion section then. Like every other reporter, I had to figure out how to get on Page One. We had a lot of male readers, so I had to write stories about the fashion industry in which men would be interested. I had to come up with my own stories; get to know bankers and retailers, and get people to like me and tell me things I could develop into stories. I didn't care what the clothes looked like, and my opinion had nothing to do with it."

Teri's first book, *The End of Fashion: How Marketing Changed the Clothing Business Forever*, with its provocative title, pulled back the curtain on just how much the fashion world had changed over the years. Her next book, *Hijacking the Runway: How Celebrities Are Stealing the Spotlight from Fashion Designers,* shed even more light on America's cult of celebrity and its impact on how clothing is sold.

Teri was an early champion of my designs and the breakthrough a commercially successful Black designer could have on the garment business. Even more so, she was a tremendously vocal fan of how I pivoted as a designer into the home area with stylish, affordable, and highly covetable items geared to the public at large.

Teri insisted that my career should be included in the ultimate oral history known as *The HistoryMakers* by Julieanna Richardson. The groundbreaking digital repository covers the personal histories of politicians, civil rights activists, entertainers, and artists. The results reside at the Library of Congress. *The HistoryMakers* has recorded more than 3,300 videotaped interviews, all of which have been digitized. This represents nearly 11,000 hours of conversation. Not only did Teri want me to be included, she also interviewed me herself for six hours straight to get the job done.

Our frequent, spirited telephone and text chats are not just limited to

RIGHT I am so happy that Teri Agins found her person in Paul Hands. He is smart, kind, and funny and, best of all, he's a Scotsman. Our annual visit to the Tartan Day parade has become a tradition with us, along with going to hear the *Pipes of Christmas* holiday concert.

fashion, but encompass politics, the arts, and our love of cooking. Gatherings at the home she shares with her Scottish-born husband, Paul Hands, are always a delightful mix of intelligent, inspiring guests along with great food, and, if you are very lucky, a slice of Teri's famously delicious rustic apple pie.

Terrence McNally quickly became one of my heroes and a friend after I made his acquaintance through another of my great friends, Stan Herman. I systematically began to search out every stage production or screenplay he had ever had a hand in and was blown away by the sheer volume and diversity of his numerous works. From *The Lisbon Traviata* to *Ragtime*, to *Mothers and Sons*, to *A Perfect Ganesh*, there was a very real and human quality to his œuvre. There is something very noble about the way that Terrence led his life, especially given the many roadblocks he had faced along the way. Growing up gay in Corpus Christi, Texas, with a difficult mother and an unresponsive, alcoholic father, he relied on very sympathetic teachers who nourished his aptitude for writing and his love of the theater, which eventually led to his coming to New York and trying his hand in the big leagues. After a failed early romance with the already established playwright Edward Albee, he began to question his abilities. To bolster his confidence, especially in social situations, he began to drink heavily. Fortuitously, at a party where Terrence's drinking demons were on full display, Angela Lansbury took him aside and spoke to him sternly, saying that he was wasting his talents and that it would not end well for him unless he sought help and stopped drinking. This was just the jolt he needed to straighten out his life and become the giant talent for which he was destined.

Speaking to Terrence early on, shortly after his triumphant play *Love, Valour and Compassion* had opened, I asked him if the characters of the identical twins John and James Jeckyll had been inspired by Stan Herman's real-life friends, the identical twins John and James Haigney. A puzzled look came across his face. "You know I never really thought about it," he said, "but maybe, subliminally, I was thinking of them."

Terrence and I also shared the same birthday—along with Anna Wintour—and on November 5, 1995, a couple of days after our birthday, he gifted me house seats to the premiere of *Master Class*, his pioneering play about Maria Callas, starring the amazing Zoe Caldwell. Later, we attended the very crowded cast party, which was held at Maxim's on Madison Avenue. While Terrence and Stan tried to secure a table, I went up to the bar, which was at least three or four people deep, to try to wrangle drinks for us. Suddenly, I felt a slight presence standing next to me and heard a little voice utter, "How I would love to have white wine!" I looked at where the voice had emanated from and realized it was Zoe Caldwell. This tiny bird-like figure who seemed six feet tall on the stage was in desperate need of a drink, and she had certainly earned it with that stellar performance.

OPPOSITE Terrence McNally, *right*, and Tom Kirdahy were devoted to each other. I know that Terrence would be so very proud of the successful producer that Tom has become.

"Don't worry Ms. Caldwell," I shouted, "I'll get you that drink," as I began to elbow aside anyone in my way to complete my mission. After securing a drink and delivering it to the star, I got the drinks for our table and a discussion of the rave reviews from the attendant friends and family ensued. Terrence seemed happy but he expressed a bit of worry as to who should follow Ms. Caldwell on Broadway given that he thought the play would be long-running and her tenure as star short-lived. "The obvious one to me would be Anne Bancroft," I blurted out, somewhat sheepishly.

Terrence visibly brightened at the suggestion and immediately took out his cell phone among the noisy revelers and began dialing Ms. Bancroft. Amazingly, she picked up and, although she was quite flattered, Terrence relayed to us, she felt she could not follow Caldwell on Broadway. She would be up for it, however, if a national tour should happen. Although it never happened, and Anne died a few short years later from uterine cancer, I am still pleased that my casting suggestion to Terrence was at least seriously considered.

Terrence died of the effects of COVID in 2020 after having survived several horrific bouts of cancer. His shining legacy, however, besides his tremendous archive of work, is the love he shared with his husband, Tom Kirdahy, who has become, in the last few years, an outstanding and award-winning theatrical producer.

I met Lewis Esson on a warm Saturday night as we both grabbed a copy of the early edition of the Sunday *New York Times* from the long-lamented lost hole-in-the-wall newsstand on Sixth Avenue near Eighth Street. Our eyes locked and when he spoke, his accent, a softly blurred mixture of his native Scotland and his former home in London, combined to make a soothing and very alluring international vocal thirst trap.

As we walked back the short distance to his apartment on Ninth Street, just west of Fifth Avenue, Lewis told me how he came to live in New York. As a book editor in London, he had been sent to Manhattan to head up a new division of Penguin Books. A very proficient cook, he later published several cookbooks, including the international bestseller *Fast Food for Friends, How the British Fell in Love With Food*, as well as successfully translating the French *Larousse Pratique* into British measurements. Other books in his extensive canon of culinary tomes include *Keep Calm and Cook On, A Mediterranean Table,* and *Cowboys and Cookouts: Recipes.*

Lewis and I were not to be a couple, but as friends, the bond was

RIGHT Lewis Esson was a man of many talents: writer, editor, chef, and successful cookbook author, although you would never know it from his modest demeanor.

OVERLEAF Our version of the Algonquin Round Table, though set in Manhattan's West Village, included from the left Joel Dratler, Wallace Colvard, me, Lewis Esson, and Vincent Petragnani.

Pages 276–277 Wallace Colvard and I continued the conversation, or was it a debate?

instant and permanent. Less than two years after meeting, Lewis was called back to London and I was bereft at my friend's leave-taking. A couple of years later, on my very first trip to Europe, I stayed with him in his home in Courtfield Gardens in London. It was splendid in spite of a summer heat wave because Lewis acted as my personal guide.
It was Lewis who first introduced me to Paul Smith, the famed designer, who had his shop a few blocks away from Lewis' house. Paul and his wife, Pauline, actually went with us to see a film, *Chanel Solitaire*, which purported to tell the early life of Mademoiselle Coco from convent girl to shopkeeper in Deauville. The film's poor continuity left the four of us laughing so hard the manager told us that if we did not stop carrying on, he would throw us out of the theater. This was long before Paul became Sir Paul Smith.
When I decided to write my first book, *Tartan: Romancing the Plaid*, Lewis was perhaps my biggest cheerleader. He encouraged me, offering suggestions, and actually helped with some of the research. It was Lewis who found out that King George IV's long-lost highland jacket had been discovered days before the book needed to be

turned over to the printer and secured a last-minute photograph of the embroidered piece.

I was so happy that Lewis finally found his someone in Terry Shaw several years ago. The two married and moved to Kent, England. Sadly, a short time later, Lewis was diagnosed with early-onset dementia. The dementia, along with a myriad of other health problems, unfortunately hastened his demise in 2023.

I have a saying that there are not "Six Degrees of Separation," only two. My friend Richard Streiter is living proof of that. When I attended the Pratt Institute, although we never met, Richard was the dean of students. Exactly when I left Pratt to attend Parsons, Richard left Pratt to become the dean of students at FIT. He eventually became vice president of development, vice-president of international affairs, and subsequently, the executive director of the foundation at the college, in addition to opening satellite schools in both India and Italy.

The other lucky aspect about knowing Richard was that he is married to Vikki Barbero. The two met while they both worked at FIT, and their romance, like our friendship, blossomed quickly. Both having separated from their respective spouses when they met, they turned an office romance into a long-term love affair.

With Richard's background, his senior position in higher education was probably the least likely outcome. After leaving home at the age of 16, he played in mambo bands, rode a motorcycle across America, and taught English to Russians during the Cold War—not exactly the Harvard/Yale pathway to the ivory tower. Somehow along the way, the street smarts he acquired transformed him into an empathetic dean, who helped so many college students find their way to success.

During her time at FIT, my assistant Jeanne Russo had her dean's list signed by Richard. When I was asked by Marvin Feldman, the president of FIT, to join the board of trustees, I was met in the boardroom by Vikki, who was the secretary of the college. "Come, sit next to me," she beckoned.

An everlasting friendship was forged. Vikki and I laugh at the same things, love most of the same films, and truly enjoy cooking together. With her abundant and ridiculously well-stocked pantry at the couple's weekend home in New Jersey, I used to joke for years that when the apocalypse occurred, somehow, I would find my way to her house, because while I might die, I would not starve. And wouldn't you know, that is almost what happened. During one of my frequent long-weekend visits to New Jersey on Friday, March 13, 2020, the

RIGHT Richard Streiter and his wife Vikki Barbero, two of my "ride or die" friends for many decades, were photographed recently at a mutual friend's wedding.

pandemic lockdown started, and Vikki and Richard insisted that I must stay with them. I thought my stay would be a few more days. It ended up being the next three months.

Vikki and I filled those days deciding what we would cook together. Would it be French, Italian, or Greek? My caramelized risotto was a favorite. Despite it being only the three of us in our little pod, Vikki's love of entertaining meant that our dinners had unique, detailed tablescapes every time. Recording our efforts and posting them on social media not only became a diversion in those dark days, but sparked pangs of jealousy in some quarters.

Several years ago, we took an amazing month-long trip to Italy together, traveling to Florence, Tuscany, Venice, and Verona. In Florence, I made reservations on Vikki's birthday for an exquisite dinner at a restaurant I had dined at before. That afternoon on the Ponte Vecchio, Vikki had spied a cocktail ring whose contemporary lines she admired. Forced by me to try it on, she quickly removed it, stating without checking that it was just too expensive. We left the store, and Vikki went to take a nap before dinner, as Richard and I continued to walk around. Ultimately, we decided to double back to the jewelry store and, as Richard successfully negotiated the price down, we decided to share the purchase as a birthday surprise. Presenting it to Vikki that evening at dinner, disguised in an M&M shopping bag, was one of the high moments of our trip. For a woman who hates surprises, she was delighted. I count Richard and Vikki as two of my closest friends, whom I can always turn to for advice, solace, and constant emotional nourishment.

LEFT BELOW AND OPPOSITE
As my caramelized onion, blue cheese, and fig risotto is the most requested dish I make for friends, I am happy that it now has a written recipe.

Jeffrey's Caramelized Onion, Blue Cheese, and Fig Risotto

Prep Time: 1 hour, 10 minutes
Total Time: 1 hour, 30 minutes
Serves: 4

Caramelized Onions
Use a 12-inch or larger skillet, preferably a cast iron

- 2 tablespoons olive oil
- 3 large white onions, halved through the root and thinly sliced into half moons
- ½ teaspoon sea salt
- Freshly ground black pepper
- 1 teaspoon sugar

Drizzle of balsamic vinegar glaze

Risotto
Use a large stockpot (for stock) and a medium saucepan or Dutch oven for risotto

- 5 cups chicken stock, plus more if needed
- 5 tablespoons unsalted butter, softened
- 2 cloves garlic, finely chopped
- 1½ cups arborio or carnaroli rice
- 1 cup dry white wine
- 1 teaspoon salt, plus more to taste
- Freshly ground black pepper, to taste
- 1 ounce mild blue cheese, crumbled (such as Point Reyes)
- 1 pound fresh figs, halved and stems removed
- ⅔ cup freshly grated Parmesan cheese (optional, to be added at the end)
- Balsamic glaze (optional)

For the caramelized onions:
Heat the olive oil in a large, heavy-bottomed cast iron sauté pan over medium-high heat until the pan is shimmering. Add the onions and stir to coat. Spread the onions evenly over the pan, reduce the heat to medium-low, cover and cook it, stirring once, until it begins to brown, 6 to 10 minutes. Uncover, add salt, a few rounds of cracked pepper, and sugar. Increase the heat to medium and cook uncovered until the onions are rich, brown, and caramelized, 15 to 30 minutes, adding water occasionally if the onions start to dry out and scraping up the browned bits from the bottom of the pan with a wooden spoon. If using, add a splash of balsamic vinegar glaze and stir until it is cooked off. Set aside.

For the risotto:
Heat the chicken stock in a medium saucepan over high heat until it boils. Reduce the heat to low to keep warm throughout cooking. Melt 4 tablespoons of butter in a second medium saucepan or Dutch oven, over high heat until foaming. Add the garlic and stir until softened, about 1 minute. Do not let it brown. Add the rice and cook, stirring constantly, until golden and translucent, 2 to 3 minutes. Add the wine and stir, scraping up any bits from the bottom of the pan. Reduce the heat to low and simmer until the liquid is mostly reduced.

Add a ladleful of the warm stock, along with the salt and pepper. Stir gently and let it cook until the liquid is fully absorbed. Continue cooking by adding stock in small increments, stirring constantly, and allowing each addition to absorb before adding more. Repeat this process until all the stock is used and absorbed. After 20 to 25 minutes, the risotto should be golden and creamy and the rice tender.

Add the blue cheese, caramelized onions, and remaining tablespoon of butter. Stir gently until the butter is melted. Remove from heat. Stir in half of the figs. Taste and adjust seasoning as desired. Divide the risotto between serving bowls. Top with the Parmesan cheese, garnish with the rest of the fig halves, and drizzle with balsamic glaze, if using.

Note: The caramelized onions can be made up to 3 days in advance and refrigerated in an airtight container.

Patricia Underwood is a marvel, an artist, whose medium includes felt, straw, and horsehair. Creating three-dimensional sculpture for the head is how she describes the exquisite millinery confections she designs. Her career path was not a direct line: secretarial pool at Buckingham, expert car mechanic, an early marriage and move to America, and, eventually, an evening student at FIT taking millinery classes, just at the moment hats were going out of fashion. But she would not be dissuaded based on all the obstacles in front of her, and not only did she persevere, she triumphed, becoming the milliner of choice for Seventh Avenue, Hollywood, and Broadway to boot.

In her long career, Patricia has created hats for designers Ralph Lauren, Bill Blass, Oscar de la Renta, Cynthia Steffe, Isaac Mizrahi, Michael Kors, Marc Jacobs, Jill Stuart, and Rebecca Moses—among many others. Her hats have also been featured in films such as *Four Weddings and a Funeral* and *Sex and the City*. Her hats have been used in leading advertising campaigns, most notably in a worldwide Lancôme advertisement featuring Isabella Rossellini.

I met Patricia when she started making hats for Perry Ellis, and we clicked immediately, her wise yet easygoing manner and quiet humor charmed along with her stylish skills. When I ventured into womenswear, there was no choice but that Patricia would create hats for me. Her encyclopedic knowledge of hat shapes throughout history has always been so helpful in choosing the headwear to accompany clothing. From wool jersey turbans to straw cartwheel shapes, every hat she created for me was exquisite. I was particularly impressed when I staged an impromptu Perry Ellis retrospective to launch my book about him, and Patricia recreated from memory several missing hats virtually overnight. Patricia saved every note, thank-you note, and letter Perry Ellis ever sent her. In a huge Bonwit Teller clothing box, these invaluable missives from Perry to Patricia really helped Perry come alive in my book.

I have been lucky enough to spend time with Patricia and her husband, Jon Moynihan, in their homes in New York, Connecticut, and even London. One memorable visit to their London townhouse in Chelsea was to celebrate the 200th anniversary of the British victory at the Battle of Waterloo, replete with spirits from that era and historians describing the event between dinner courses.

Patricia and Jon honored me by asking that Doria de La Chapelle and I commit the story of her decades-long millinery career to print. We launched *Patricia Underwood: The Way You Wear Your Hat* at Ralph Lauren's Madison Avenue women's store in Manhattan, and

RIGHT I was enchanted with Patricia Underwood from our very first meeting. Her talent, wit, and grace are boundless and a good time is always had in her presence.

the next day at his Rodeo Drive store in Los Angeles. The very well received book is a testament to Patricia's well-regarded career and the many fashion industry friends she has made over time. Recently, her husband was named a lord in the House of Lords—he was already an Officer of the British Empire (OBE)—so they are now, Lord and Lady Moynihan of Chelsea.

I must say, that nothing beats perusing vintage markets with Patricia, something I have had the distinct pleasure of doing. Her discerning eye can ferret out the most unique and special gems that others might overlook. I feel blessed to call her a colleague and a friend.

OPPOSITE At our holiday get-togethers at Peter Luger Steak House, the famous Brooklyn institution, each of the participants always brings tons of gifts, prompting nearby diners to ask if they can be included.

OVERLEAF Several times a year, our group gets together for a great meal and tons of laughter at Peter Luger's. *From the left*: Dr. Clifford Hudis, Scott Bromley, the late Michelle (Mickey) Ateyeh, me, Fern Mallis, Jane Hertzmark Hudis, Steve Gold, Cindy Lewis, Tony Impavido, and Ron Roberts.

This very close-knit group of friends whom I have been privileged to know for decades are among my nearest and dearest. The group started as a collection of type-A New York women who were all very accomplished in their respective fields. The publisher Cynthia Lewis, known as Cindy, the jewelry executive, Michele Ateyeh, known as Mickey, cosmetics executive Jane Hertzmark Hudis, and the fashion executive Fern Mallis. Meeting for dinner at the Peter Luger Steak House in Brooklyn several times a year, the team labeled themselves the "Power Girls" and were very protective of their closed circle and rarely, if ever, invited other women to join them.

Eventually, Fern's longtime friend Scott Bromley, the architect who designed Studio 54, became the first man added to the group. He hit it off with the ladies so well that he became a perennial. Soon, Scott's partner, the Lincoln Center Film Society executive Tony Impavido, joined along with the marketing wiz Steve Gold, who was from Fern's original Brooklyn neighborhood. Then, I was asked to join this group of achievers. At one point, Jane married her handsome doctor boyfriend, Clifford Hudis, and he joined us, too.

Our visits to Peter Luger usually took place several times a year, always as a finite group and usually with a revolving member of the group picking up the tab. We also timed a visit during the holidays, with gifts for everyone. One year, as I was hosting the holiday edition, I got a call from Steve asking if he could bring a new boyfriend. Knowing what a tough crowd the group could be, I said yes, but only if the new boyfriend had the potential of being long-term. I did not want to have to revisit this situation with someone different in six months time. Steve assured me that that would not be the case, and he and the engineer Ron Roberts have happily been together ever since. For many years, until his recent retirement, Tommy Hobby, the maître d', served us well and was our gateway to securing our reservations every time.

This collegial group has weathered life's ups and downs with lots of love, laughter, and plenty of steak. Marriages and deaths have only brought us closer together. Our get-togethers have become legendary with many others wanting to horn in, and occasionally, we would invite a singular guest or two to join us. Of course, all the group members had to approve in advance.

Last year was a very difficult one for the group as we lost our beloved Mickey to cancer. I fear that our future outings will never be quite the same, but oh, the great memories we will have forever!

VI. AUTHOR! AUTHOR!

I do not know what possessed me to think that I could write a book, but I guess the same obsessive drive that led me to become a designer had something to do with it. I also think, especially with my first book, *Tartan: Romancing the Plaid*, it was a certain anger that I could not find the book that I wanted to read. All the books I read were virtually the same: how to find your family's clan or tartan. Where was the real history of tartan, the political ramifications of wearing it, and the romance that Scotland's own fabric implied? I wanted answers, and I finally thought the only way to get them was to write my own book.

Enlisting the help of my friend Doria de La Chapelle was the first and smartest move on my literary journey. I loved doing the research and planning the artwork. Doria's background was in copywriting and public relations, but she had never written a book. We were both novices, which maybe was advantageous for us in the end. After five years and three editors, our book was published to great acclaim. Our launch party at Saks Fifth Avenue in Manhattan had 750 revelers—and book buyers. The next day, Ron Frasch, the store's vice president, called me. "Jeffrey, you need to run for mayor!" he said. "The turnout last night was fantastic!"

I remember thinking wearily at the end that I would never, ever do that again. Boy, was I ever wrong. Barely two years after launching *Tartan*, I was asked by Steven Kolb of the CFDA to take a look at a book they were doing as part of a series on the history of American designer menswear. The book was being written by Robert Bryant, the longtime menswear editor at the *New York Times*.

"Do you really want my opinion?" I asked Steven after perusing the work so far.

"Of course I do," he said.

"Well, it looks like shit," I said, not holding back. "Where are John Weitz and Bill Blass? How can you do a true history without including them and others?"

"Do you think you could do better?" was Steven's retort.

"I know I could!" I said boldly.

"Okay, well do it!" he chimed.

And so Robert and I set out to finish the book, working out of his apartment on the Lower East Side. After a couple of days, I phoned Steven to inquire when the book was due. "In a month," he announced brightly. I winced, but for the next 30 days, working seven days a week and 12 hours a day, we got it finished, a far cry from my five-year timeline for my first book.

Shortly thereafter, my publisher suggested that I do a book about

OPPOSITE AND OVERLEAF
For a guy who said he would never write another book after the first one–*Tartan: Romancing the Plaid*–was done, I seemed to have gotten a severe case of author amnesia. Witness to this are the numerous books I have written.

TARTAN

Romancing the Plaid

JEFFREY BANKS AND DORIA DE LA CHAPELLE

FOREWORD BY ROSE MARIE BRAVO

RIZZOLI NEW YORK

patricia underwood
THE WAY
YOU WEAR
YOUR HAT
JEFFREY BANKS
DORIA DE LA CHAPELLE
NORELL
MASTER OF AMERICAN FASHION
NORELL
BANKS
Electa
AM
IVY STYLE
DORIA DE LA CHAPELLE
PULITZER

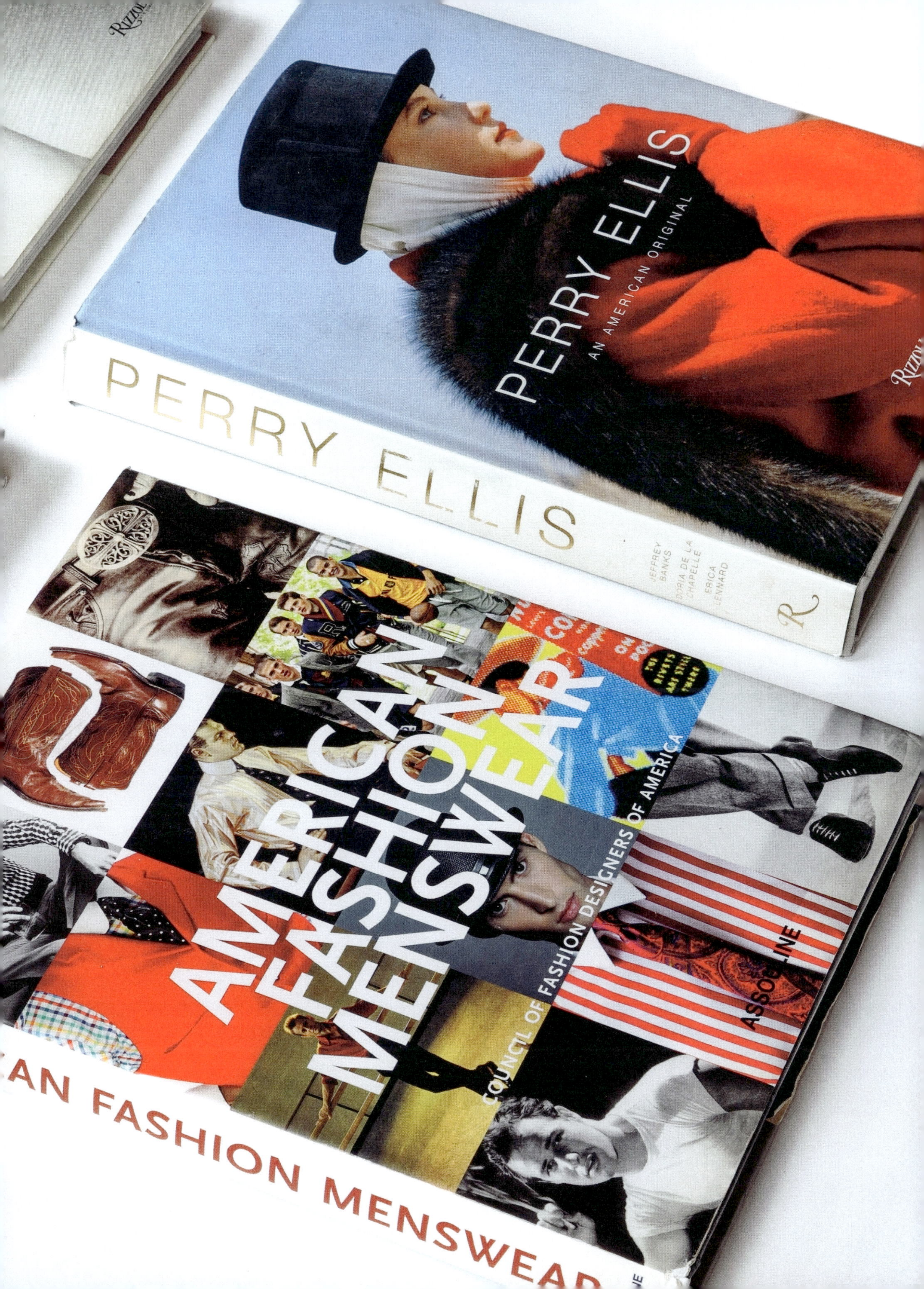
PERRY ELLIS
AN AMERICAN ORIGINAL
PERRY ELLIS
JEFFREY BANKS
DORIA DE LA CHAPELLE
ERICA LENNARD
AMERICAN FASHION MENSWEAR
COUNCIL OF FASHION DESIGNERS OF AMERICA
ASSOULINE
AN FASHION MENSWEAR

the history of preppy dressing. I was very aware that a revamp of the very successful satirical book *The Preppy Handbook* was in the works to celebrate the 25th anniversary of its original publication. "Nevermind," said my publisher, who wanted an elegant, serious, historical tome portraying the origins and continued popularity of the preppy aesthetic. And so, *Preppy: Cultivating Ivy Style* was born. I am so happy that we got Lilly Pulitzer to write the foreword shortly before she passed away. And Brooks Brothers was so thrilled that I picked a 1940 advertising poster for the cover that they recreated the tie and the blazer and bankrolled a tour for the book.

My next book was a passion project to honor my dear friend, the designer Perry Ellis. Shortly after his death in 1986, a small, poorly done book had come out that did nothing to burnish Perry's creative reputation. I was determined to right that wrong, and Doria and I, joining up with the photographer Erica Lennard, who lensed most of Perry's campaigns, produced a book that I think would have made Perry proud.

Taking the first copy of our *Perry Ellis* book to show my friend, the milliner Patricia Underwood, led to our very next book assignment. To celebrate her 40th anniversary as a preeminent hat designer, her husband Jon Moynihan commissioned us to write a book about her prestigious career. Working with a living and present creative was challenging, but I think we were all happy with the finished result. At the book launch after-party, my publisher said I could now do anything I wanted, and so my next project would become my most ardently devoted subject matter: the American couturier, Norman Norell.

Norell, with his chic, timeless fashions, inspired me early on to become a fashion designer. I wanted to study at the Parsons School of Design because he was a critic there. And some 30-odd years after his death, I was shocked that no one had ever written a true biography about him. Despite an initial reluctance and eventual green-lighting of the book project, the original print run was quite small. But the public's immediate reaction to the book and the retrospective Norell show I curated at FIT to coincide with the book's launch necessitated a book reprint in less than a month. Having located Norell's former CEO, who was retired in Florida, I FedExed one of the first copies to Max Bernegger. Upon reading the book, Max proclaimed: "You have brought Norman back to life."

I could not have asked for a greater compliment. I have tried to make each book the end-all, be-all document of that particular subject matter, so that they will live on, way beyond my existence.

RIGHT BELOW My British cousins: Sarah Turner and her husband, David Hunt, keep me in gales of laughter whenever we get together.

The United Kingdom, and London especially, has always seemed like a second home to me. Having spent so much time sourcing fabrics over the years in Britain, Ireland, and Scotland, it is no wonder that my consistent love of tartan has intensified over time. After years of living together, my London friends, Sarah Turner and David Hunt, whom I had met through my longtime friend Lewis Esson, decided to tie the knot on November 3, my birthday, shortly after 9/11. I had been mulling over the idea of doing a definitive book about the humble and aristocratic fabric known as tartan for years and, as I crossed the Atlantic, I was thinking about it more than ever. One great thing that came from attending Sarah and David's wedding was the solidification of the idea that I should write that book, once and for all. Arriving in London, and encouraged by Sarah and David, I took the opportunity to ring up my old friend Rose Marie Bravo, who was the CEO of Burberry, to discuss the book idea with her. She asked me to come to the corporate offices in Haymarket the next day. And so I went along with a handwritten single-page outline of my proposed book, planning to ask Rose Marie to write the foreword. Without hesitation, she said yes. I was now committed and I had to follow through.

Sarah and David, or Lord and Lady Muppington, as I sometimes

fondly refer to them, were very enthusiastic about the project and proved to be very helpful over the course of the book's five-year gestation period. Sarah's marketing acumen and various business contacts throughout the United Kingdom were an invaluable help in bringing my first literary effort to life, and their encouragement, along with Lewis Esson's, helped to make *Tartan* a reality.

As our friendship has deepened over the years, we have striven to celebrate their wedding anniversary and my birthday together whenever possible, on one side or the other of the pond. I look at them both as though they are my long-lost British cousins, separated somehow by a mistake of birth or adoption.

As I write this, news has just come in that Terron Schaefer, my wonderful friend has passed away. Terry was an indefatigable ball of creative energy with buckets of charisma to spare. Close friends with Mort Kaplan, my licensing agent, he had an accomplished background in both advertising and retail marketing that allowed him to work with Federated Department Stores, Harrods in London, and Saks Fifth Avenue as their executive vice president and chief creative officer. In that job, he did everything from redesigning Saks' logo to creating their now-iconic holiday facade lighting extravaganza that is as much a part of New York's Christmas display as the tree at Rockefeller Center. Terry devised, in a genius coup of marketing, to give the ladies' shoe floor at Saks its own zip code, thus engendering not only tremendous press but also hordes of shoe-buying fanatics. He was an otherworldly impresario who blended all of his knowledge, creativity, and friends from all walks of life together as if he were conducting a world-class orchestra.

Always impeccably dressed and usually in some form of Savile Row bespoke tailoring, Terry gleaned his knowledge of the world from his love of travel, especially to exotic locales like Bali. Born in Brazil, his travels, both for work and pleasure, took him around the globe.

Terry even appeared for a time as a judge on the television show *Fashion Star*, sharing his knowledge and vision with aspiring young designers. As the rise of the designer website began, Terry envisioned the ultimate luxury site STYLE365 that would blend art, fashion, and home with portals to other luxury brands such as Gucci and Yves Saint Laurent. Beautifully lensed by the photographer Bruce Weber and launched at an over-the-top party that took over the whole of Manhattan's famed Four Seasons restaurant, STYLE365 became a legendary, yet beautiful failure only because it was ahead of its time.

RIGHT A true Renaissance man, the late Terron Schaefer was the perfect combination of charm, tact, and consummate elegance.

In 2007 planning the publication of my first book, I had hoped to have its launch at Bergdorf Goodman. Catching wind of my plans, Terry would hear nothing of it and promised to break both my knees if I didn't present my book at Saks Fifth Avenue. The truth is, I was not sure if Terry was joking or not, and so I joined my friend and the whole Saks Fifth Avenue marketing and public relations team for a very serious meeting at their executive office across the street from the store. Trying to get a handle on the possible number of guests that might attend, it was suggested that perhaps we should plan on 75 to 100 people. "Oh no," I protested. "You don't know my friends. There will be at least 200 to 300 people coming."

Terry took it all in stride, suggesting that an RSVP hotline should be created to keep accurate tabs on responses. He also contacted Burberry to cohost the event, so that drinks, hors d'œuvres, staffing, and even a DJ would be on board. That evening, 750 or so people showed up, and I sat for over three hours signing books.

The next morning Ron Frasch, the vice-president of Saks at the time, called me and said, "Jeffrey, you need to run for mayor!" "What do you mean?" I exclaimed. "We've never had that many people show up for an event, let alone for a book signing, and they all bought books," Ron said. I owe it all, and so much more, to Terry Schaefer.

One of the best things in life is the ability to make great friends unexpectedly, even when one is older. Nena Ivon is one such friend I never expected to have and now I cannot imagine not ever having. In 2019 shortly after my book on Norman Norell was published, I was invited to speak about the designer and sign books at the Service Club of Chicago. Arranged by my friend Peter Martino, the event was to be staged in two parts, a welcome cocktail evening at the Harry Winston jewelry store, and the next morning, a breakfast at the Ralph Lauren restaurant, with Nena interviewing me. This was a special honor as the restaurant is normally only open for lunch and dinner.

I do not remember who told me, but I was warned that Nena was a formidable fixture on the Chicago society scene and the longtime but newly retired fashion director of Saks Fifth Avenue Chicago. I have to admit I was a little intimidated prior to meeting her. I need not have been. Nena was smart, chic, and wickedly funny, and I found myself falling under her spell almost immediately. Most impressively, she knew her stuff. Nena was no fashion neophyte. She could go head-to-head with any esteemed fashion historian, and I would place my bet solely on her. All of the women I met in Chicago, from Paula Borg to Julie Barrish to Sherry Lea Fox, were all accomplished, beautiful, and fascinating. But it was Nena with whom I formed an instant bond. Her knowledge of Chicago and its place in fashion history was remarkable. When she invited me on a private tour of the Chicago History Museum and its treasure trove of fashion-history items, she could easily have been mistaken for a curator, as she explained their holdings in detail. I truly could have listened to her for hours on end.

Until that trip, I hadn't been to Chicago since 1983, and I must admit that after my whirlwind three days, I didn't want to leave, but the departure was softened as I had made the acquaintance of Nena and the roots of friendship had already started to sprout. Shortly thereafter, Nena contacted me about the Fashion Book Club, an organization she founded whose members discuss and celebrate books about fashion and its creators. Their monthly meetings were initially in-person with drinks and nibbles. During the pandemic all the meetings had to be conducted via Zoom. But that was an added bonus as people not living in Chicago, like me, could join in from all over the world, and the membership of the organization expanded.

In the meanwhile, Nena and I found we had so many synergies, way beyond fashion, with telephone chats about literature, film, history, and decor. I loved hearing about her relationship with the iconic

RIGHT Nena Ivon is a font of information about the fashion industry. Her decades of service at Saks Fifth Avenue Chicago, as its fashion director, make her the perfect fashion historian.

Chicago photographer Victor Skrebneski and her great friendship with the designer Bob Mackie. Her knowledge of Chicago's social hierarchy cannot be matched. Thinking about our relationship, I am reminded of the lyrics from the Gershwin song, "Isn't It a Pity": "Imagine all the lonely years we wasted / You with the neighbors, me at silly labors / Isn't it a pity we never ever met before?"

What I think I love most is how Nena's sensibility, while thoroughly modern, also harkens back to a time when civility, great manners, and politeness reigned. And I, for one, am all for it.

Isn't it amazing when somehow life sends you to people who, over time, become the actual fabric of your life and you simply cannot remember what life was like before they came into it? My great friend Doria de La Chapelle is a prime example of that kind of person. I first met Doria when, as a young designer with no staff or assistants, I was all by myself backstage, trying to dress many male models, in my first fur collection. The other designers in this Alixandre show, all of whom had a cadre of help, were Hubert de Givenchy, Yves Saint Laurent, Calvin Klein, and Viola Sylbert. Doria and her small public

LEFT My beloved partner in crime, Doria de La Chapelle, was photographed with her husband Philippe. I would never have ventured on my literary path were it not for Doria.

relations firm, Hathaway/de La Chapelle, had been hired to help some of these designers, but unfortunately, not me. Doria saw me flailing and *schvitz*ing and took pity on me. Thus began one of the most important friendships of my life. Doria and her partner, Mallory Hathaway, ended up working on public relations and fashion shows for me for several years afterward as my fortunes rose. Eventually, when Mallory left to go live in Spain, the company closed, and Doria came to work with me on my Jeffrey Banks collections and Merona Sport, writing press releases and dealing with fashion editors. Doria's witty and breezy writing style always intrigued me as it was so different from most public relations flacks of the time.

When taking a work-hiatus to spend more time with her young sons, her husband Philippe implored me to put her back to work. I had been thinking about a book about tartan plaid, an obsession of mine since childhood. Nearly every one of the books I had read about tartan was the same—about how to find your family's clan or signature tartan plaid. I wanted to dig much deeper. Where did tartan come from? What was its history? Its cultural significance? Why not write the book I wanted to read? The trouble was, what did I know about writing a book? Nothing. And Doria had never written a book either. She had done advertising copy for Henri Bendel and tons of designer press releases, but had no book-writing experience. Then I thought, why not? And who else to do it with but Doria?

Truth be told, I was more like a project manager on this venture. I did the research—my favorite thing—I found and selected the art. I acted as the editor of Doria's prose. I met with the potential publishers. I bought a book at Barnes & Noble called *How to Write a Book* and Doria and I followed it to the letter, with one exception. The book advised to develop a one-page marketing plan. Well, I thought, I am a designer, I know a lot about marketing, so I produced a 15-page plan. Every potential publisher remarked that they had never seen first-time authors come up with such an extensive marketing plan. Eventually, Rizzoli, my first choice, decided to publish it.

I think Doria and I were both shocked at the size of the initial print run and the favorable critical reaction to the book. However, having taken five long years to write it, we vowed never to write one again. Famous last words. I guess writing books is a lot like childbirth, eventually you forget the pain and have a go at another one.

Actually, we did five more. With each one, we grew more confident in our abilities and the reception to each book grew exponentially. We found that working together, we were an unbeatable team. But just as I was planning to write this memoir, fate reared its ugly head, and Doria was diagnosed with the beginnings of dementia. What a cruel sentence for someone whose whole existence is marked by a torrent of imaginative words, words she can no longer utter due to the diagnosis of aphasia, a language disorder that affects a person's ability to understand and communicate.

On a recent visit to her at her home in the Hamptons, I was saddened to see how diminished Doria was by her inability to use language. For years, she was an avid tennis player and her body has retained its taut physique, but her hollow eyes betrayed the pain of not being able to communicate as she once had done. She restlessly roamed the living room unable to find peace in a single spot. At times, she fondled my heavy overcoat repeatedly, as if trying to contact me. When I finally got her to sit next to me on the sofa, she rested her head on my shoulder and gently held my hand. I felt a glimmer of my old friend desperately trying to reach through and connect with me. She was still there somehow, deep inside, but not outwardly present.

As I write this memoir, I do so completely on my own, without Doria for the very first time. I hope that she is still there, guiding me along, arguing over syntax or meaning, but loving the process nonetheless.

As difficult as it is for me to accept the unfair card that Doria has been dealt, I am somewhat placated by the tremendous memories we have shared for decades and the work that will hopefully live on past our time here on Earth.

VII. GIVING BACK

I feel so blessed to have been able to earn a living and have a career in the fashion industry, the thing I love the most. Having been so lucky, I have always felt a certain responsibility to give back and/or pay it forward for the good fortune I have repeatedly received. Only a few years after meeting Marvin Feldman, the president of the Fashion Institute of Technology, after going out on my own, he called me and asked me to join the board of trustees. I was flabbergasted and flattered but protested that I was in no financial position to join an important board. Marvin was persistent that money did not matter, that the reason he wanted me was for my expertise on curriculum. I eventually succumbed, and it was one of the best things I ever did. First, I met my lifelong friends Richard Streiter and Vikki Barbero at FIT because of my board service. Second, the 14 years of being on the board made me grow up and become an adult.

Stan Herman asking me to join the board of the CFDA was another wonderful life lesson. I felt I got more out of working for the betterment of my fellow designers than they got from me. Our campaigns to benefit research in breast cancer and AIDS, and the scholarships for fashion students were challenging and enriching at the same time.

I was also very fortunate early on, to meet Damian Martin and Emery Hetrick who founded the Hetrick-Martin Institute, the first public high school created specifically for gay teenagers. These kids, many of whom had been thrown out of their homes by their parents, often ended up living on the street. Until Damian and Emery, a gay couple, who were educators themselves, started HMI, the kids had no possible way to finish their education. I ended up joining the HMI board for decades, eventually becoming vice-chair and meeting Verna Eggleston, the executive director, who now works for Bloomberg's charitable arm that focuses on Africa.

One of the greatest things that Stan did as president of the CFDA was to take the copious amounts of money raised at 7th On Sale and have the New York City AIDS Fund distribute it to worthwhile AIDS-related organizations. I was vice-chair of the Hetrick-Martin Institute and brought him to a recital that the kids of the school were doing of works they had written at the Public Theater. Having been helped by Stan's great friend Terrence McNally, the work was so impressive that as I looked over at Stan during the performance, he had tears in his eyes and whispered that we must give HMI a good chunk of money. As it turns out, we gave them the largest single grant of our fund, which allowed them to move into a new, larger, safe place. Other boards I have been privileged to serve on include my alma mater, the Parsons School of Design, and the board of the

OPPOSITE A corporate group marched for the Hetrick-Martin Institute during the Gay Pride Parade in New York.

OVERLEAF Gordon Munro shot a series of group photographs of the first fashion-related AIDS benefits that were held in New York at the Jacob K. Javits Convention Center on April 29, 1986. Ticket sales were lagging until Calvin Klein announced he was bringing Elizabeth Taylor, *third from the right in the front row, next to* Calvin Klein, to the event. I am standing in front of Grace Jones and Azzedine Alaia. In front of me is Ryan White, who was the first person in the United States to contract AIDS from a blood transfusion. To my right is Kenzo with Tina Chow behind him. Perry Ellis behind Calvin is next to Geraldine Stutz. I was very proud to be there to represent friends I had lost and the fashion industry in general.

HMI

To Care
is
To Cure
AmFAR American Foundation For AIDS Research

To Care
is
To Cure

OPPPOSITE TOP Ruth Shuman, far right, with Cindy Lewis next to her, was surrounded by the kids she serves at Publicolor, her educational youth development organization.

OPPPOSITE BOTTOM This is one of the many public spaces that Publicolor beautifies with paint all over New York.

Ali Forney Center, which arranges housing for indigent gay youth. Selfless, altruistic, compassionate, and generous are all words I would use to describe Ruth Shuman, the founder of Publicolor, an organization I have volunteered with for many years. Created to help underserved youth in the five boroughs of New York, many of these public-school kids get to high school without the basic reading and mathematics skills that so many of us take for granted. They also do not know how to confidently present themselves to the world. Publicolor, a voluntary after-school program, helps these kids to not only successfully complete high school, but also to go on to excel in college. In many cases, these students are the first in their families to attend college. Graduates of the program have worked for large companies such as Estée Lauder, Verizon, and Bloomberg, and over half of the Publicolor staff today is comprised of former graduates of the program. After her unhappy marriage ended, Ruth became a board member of the Big Apple Circus. It was during that period that she realized the need to support the education of underserved kids by using art in an innovative way to teach math and reading.

I met Ruth at a dinner party held by my friends and neighbors Peter Stamberg and Paul Aferiat. I was immediately taken by her abundant passion and drive for her work with young people. Over breakfast the very next morning, she asked if I would join the Publicolor board. Although I felt by this time that my numerous board services were behind me, I did agree to help the not-for-profit, an arrangement that continues to this very day.

It is marvelous to see how these young people, many from broken homes with incarcerated parents, flourish from what they learn from Publicolor's various outstanding programs and the nurturing and loving care Ruth lavishes on every child, often becoming in many ways a surrogate parent, always going above and beyond the call of duty of merely teaching. In addition to the curriculum, the kids are taught practical painting skills that they can monetize to help themselves and their families. Ruth's work has become her life, and although the kids of Publicolor benefit from her largesse, I often wish that Ruth would apply more of that loving care to herself, travel more extensively, something she truly loves, or spend more time painting, visit more of the museums she finds so interesting, and ultimately find a life partner who shares her values. She certainly deserves that.

VIII. BIG DEAL

Since I was a young person, New York's Metropolitan Museum of Art has always represented the ultimate repository for historical artifacts, documents, and art. As a design student, I was fortunate enough to attend a weekly class at the Costume Institute of the Met, during which we were privileged to examine actual iconic garments. These included the wedding dress by the English couturier Norman Hartnell that Wallis Simpson wore at her marriage to the Duke of Windsor, as well as the extraordinary clothes and jewelry that once belonged to the socialite and heiress Millicent Rogers.

While I was in college, I attended the after-parties of the annual Met Galas on a student ticket, which was a great way to see the exhibitions as well as the elegant members of society who wore the designer clothes and jewelry that were the subject of articles in the press. As I started my career, the exhibitions I was most excited about were helmed by Diana Vreeland, such as *Man and the Horse*, *Romantic and Glamorous Hollywood Design, 1913–1947*, *The Imperial Style: Fashions of the Habsburg Era*, *The Glory of Russian Costume,* and *The World of Balenciaga*.

But never in my wildest dreams did I think that one day my clothing might be included in one of the Costume Institute's shows. This year, inspired by Monica L. Miller's book *Slaves to Fashion*, the Met show was titled *Superfine: Tailoring Black Style*, the first all-menswear show in over 20 years. Focusing on Black dandyism through the ages the exhibition was a venture to which I was beyond excited to contribute. It was like a full-circle moment for the kid from Washington, DC, who dreamed of someday being a designer.

In an article about my clothing in the *New York Times* on April 30, 2025, Professor Miller said: "He often describes his work as 'classic with a twist,' noting the suit's soft silhouette and checkered pattern, layered under a bolder plaid overcoat. The Jeffrey Banks ensemble appears in a section of the exhibition that examines the suit as a symbol both of pride and of protection in environments that could be hostile to Black men."

I have been overwhelmed by all the people who have wished me well and congratulated me since the exhibit opened. Many friends have photographed themselves next to my outfit and sent me the pictures to prove they have visited the Met. It has been a thrilling and humbling experience to be lauded by so many, and I am truly grateful.

OPPOSITE Doria de La Chapelle, wearing one of my designs, and I attended the Metropoilitan Museum of Art's Costume Institute Gala for the exhibition *Man and the Horse*, that opened in 1984.

OVERLEAF LEFT The close-up detail of my plaid tweed coat and tic-weave tweed double-breasted suit appeared in the *New York Times* when the exhibition *Superfine: Tailoring Black Style* was revealed.

OVERLEAF RIGHT Tyler Mitchell Studio captured a full-length view of the completely dressed mannequin in the catalog that accompanied the exhibition.

Jeffrey Banks. *Ensemble*, ca. 1980

INDEX

PHOTOGRAPHY CREDITS

Every effort has been made to locate the holders of copyright; any omissions will be corrected in future editions.

JADE ALBERT 96, 111, 112-113, 130-131
EVE ARNOLD 72
PHOTOGRAPH BY RICHARD AVEDON, © THE RICHARD AVEDON FOUNDATION 202
CLARENCE BANKS 22, 27, 36 all, 52, 269
JEFFREY BANKS 8, 27, 88, 193, 229, 237, 269, 280, 283, 295, 297, 299, 308 top
JEFFREY BANKS ARCHIVE 2-3, 12, 17, 21, 25 top and bottom, 32, 35, 44, 51, 83, 116, 117, 121, 122, 124 all, 125, 126-127, 128 top and bottom, 129, 143, 147, 150, 152, 153, 159, 173, 174, 184-185, 186, 187, 189, 198, 205, 210, 212, 214, 216, 230, 248-249, 253, 256-257, 262, 264, 265, 273, 279, 284, 286-287, 300, back endpapers
ANTOINE BOOTZ Front endpapers, 86-87, 142 newspaper, 292-293, 315 book
COURTESY OF BURGUNDY FARM COUNTRY DAY SCHOOL 43
CALVIN KLEIN, INC. 104
COURTESY OF SAL CESARANI 180-181, 218, 219
COURTESY OF WALLACE COLVARD 274-275, 276-277
BILL CUNNINGHAM 222
ARTHUR ELGORT/COURTESY OF RIZZOLI 291
COURTESY OF TOM FALLON 98, 100-101 all, 261
ZACHARY FREYMAN/CONDÉ NAST VIA GETTY IMAGES 59
GENESCO ARCHIVE 60
THOM GILBERT 133 all, 138 all, 139
OBERTO GILI 238-239, 240, 241
LES GOLDBERG 179, 182
STAN HERMAN ARCHIVE 223
COURTESY OF THE HETRICK-MARTIN INSTITUTE 305
© THE AL HIRSCHFELD FOUNDATION. WWW.ALHIRSCHFELDFOUNDATION.ORG 64, 208-209
HORST P. HORST 140, 141, 142
HULTON ARCHIVE/GETTY IMAGES 115
THOMAS IANNACCONE/STAR BLACK/WWD/ PENSKE MEDIA VIA GETTY IMAGES 313
FRANK JEDDA 232
WILLIAM KARAM 192
COURTESY OF TOM KIRDAHY 271
LYNN KOHLMANN Cover, 118, 119
COURTESY OF PETER KUNZ 92-93, 94
BRUCE LAURENCE 10
ERICA LENNARD/COURTESY OF FRED J. DEVITO 91
COURTESY GIUSEPPE LONGO 75
KATHRYN GAMBLE LOZIER 52
COURTESY OF FERN MALLIS 242
COURTESY OF THE SANDRA MARTIN COLLECTION 144-145
PHOTOGRAPH © PATRICK MCMULLAN 243
MEDIAPUNCH/SHUTTERSTOCK 76
TYLER MITCHELL 315
GORDON MUNRO 306-307
COURTESY OF THE NATIONAL MUSEUM OF AMERICAN HISTORY 63
COURTESY OF THE NEW SCHOOL ARCHIVE AND SPECIAL COLLECTIONS 79, 80, 81, 82
From The New York Times, March 2nd © 1980. The New York Times. All rights reserved. Used by permission and protected by the Copyright Laws of the United States. The printing, copying, redistribution, or retransmission of this Content without express written permission is prohibited., 142
EVANGELINE PEARSON ARCHIVE 29, 30, 31
HAL PHYFE/COURTESY OF MARK BOZEK, 190
MATTEO PRANDONI/BFA.COM 227
COURTESY OF PUBLICOLOR 308 bottom
COURTESY OF MARK RYKKEN 46, 48-49
LAWRENCE SCHILLER/POLARIS COMMUNICATIONS/GETTY IMAGES 68-69
SNAP/SHUTTERSTOCK 207
PETER STAMBERG 266
VINCENT TULLO/THE NEW YORK TIMES/ REDUX 314
COURTESY OF SUZANNA WARD-WELDON 258
ALBERT WATSON 4
BRUCE WEBER: BACK OF FRONT ENDPAPERS 1, 6, 7 all, 103, 107, 123, 134, 135, 136, 137, 148-149, 154, 156-157, 160, 163, 164, 166, 167, 194, 197, 201

CAPTIONS

FRONT AND BACK COVERS One of my favorite portraits was taken by my late friend, the model and photographer Lynn Kohlmann.

FRONT ENDPAPERS I was very proud of the construction and handwork in my Jeffrey Banks tailored clothing. The suits were made to last right down to the real horn buttons.

HALF TITLE Inspired by Ernest Hemingway's Key West, this range of tailored clothing and sportswear was done in a mix of cotton, linen, and silk, all in cream and ivory tones.
PAGES 2–3 In the Merona Sport collection my cotton pieces predated the athleisure movement by 10 years. Thom Fleming, Michael Ives, and Jon Wiedemann exuded handsome athleticism.

OPPOSITE TITLE The Scottish photographer Albert Watson captured my collection for the advertising of a new Jeffrey Banks shop at Macy's. The models and I, *from the left*, are Mark Shapiro, in a shearling coat, Tony Yurgaitis in a Shetland plaid sports coat, Denis La Marsh in a barathea tuxedo, Rob Yoh in a double-breasted suit, and Tony Sanchez in a dark flannel suit.

PAGE 6 I have always loved the mix of pattern on pattern for the lush texture and visual interest it provides. Shown on the left is Renauld White in a parquet-patterned tweed Balmacaan coat over a guncheck tweed sportcoat, plaid shirt,and woven necktie.

PAGE 7 Various textures from lambswool to canvas to suede and tweed are worn by David Gilman in a plaid sweater, *top left*, Steve Lundquist in a Fair Isle sweater, *top right*, David Womack in a patterned sweater, *bottom left*, and David Gilman in a checked suit, *bottom right*.

OPPOSITE DEDICATION My mother's predilection for "of the moment" clothing has never failed her. Not many women over 90 years of age would don knee-high skintight boots.

OPPOSITE CONTENTS In 1973 the photographer Bruce Laurence caught me unawares behind the scenes at Ralph Lauren's second Coty show. A call from him, and I quickly looked over my shoulder, and it was done.

PAGE 12 At three years old, I remember climbing the stairs to the photographer's studio off F Street in Washington, DC, to have my picture taken. My mother said that I chose my outfit myself, down to the white, yellow, and brown socks. Maybe I was destined to be a designer after all.

BACK ENDPAPERS Some of the many people who have touched my life.

ACKNOWLEDGMENTS

Vikki Barbero, **Richard Streiter**, and **Nena Ivon** for listening patiently to my musings on the past over the past year. **Bruce Weber**, for the very generous use of his beautiful images. **Jade Alpert**, for foraging up vintage images I didn't even know existed. **Paul Hands** and **Wallace Colvard**, for magically restoring faded keepsake images. **Stan Herman**, whose constant encouragement and laptop computer kept my juices flowing. **Thom Gilbert**, whose photographs helped to brilliantly illuminate this tome. **Rick Hindin** and **David Pensky**, for their always-reliable remembrances of the early days of Britches. **Mark Rykken**, for his invaluable help and wonderful photographs. **Lygeia Grace**, whose culinary skills helped to sharpen my technique. **Antoine Bootz**, whose photographic skills are endless. **Audrey Smaltz** and **Sandra Martin**, for helping to find the unfindable. **Evangeline Pearson** and **Sharon Christophe Dunlap** whose family pictures helped fill in the blanks. **Suzanne Slesin**, my publisher and editor at Pointed Leaf Press, who wholeheartedly embraced this project from day one, along with **Frederico Farina**, the creative director, who created artful layouts and was able to use my humble cell phone photographs, and **Julian Cosma**, whose investigative skills helped to locate missing parts of the puzzle.
And to all my friends and colleagues, all along the way, who shared so much of themselves with me.

POSTSCRIPT

By now you have journeyed with me through several hundred pages and many decades of my life in fashion.
One of the hardest parts about doing this book was figuring out how to avoid it becoming encyclopedic. I am so lucky and blessed to have led such a rich and fulfilling life that including every person and telling every anecdote would have been impossible. In so doing, I would have run the risk of exceeding Barbra Streisand's 970-page autobiography!
I faced a similar problem going through the more than 80,000 photographs I had saved in my files, many of which I would have loved to have included in this book. I realized that I had to stay focused on the overwhelming role that fashion has played in my life. So for some of you, I have a bit of a surprise that I hope you will enjoy. Please turn the page for a look at the many wonderful people who have been in my life. Thank you all for joining me thus far.

From the left, 1. Leo Narducci; 2. Orlando Bloom; 3. Jonathan Ringel and Cary Brown; 4. Bernadette Peters; 5. John Conroy; 6. Charlotte Neuville and John Bartlett; 7. Emma Snowdon- Jones; 8. Evangeline Pearson; 9. Jim Lehrer; 10. William Ivey Long; 11. Chiun-Kai Shih; 12. Dan Scheffey and Howard Zar; 13. Giuseppe Longo; 14. Bruce Weber and Nan Bush; 15. Buffy Birrittella; 16. Peggy and Myron Polenberg; 17. Barbara and Don Kurzman; 18. Daniel, Emily, and Elizabeth Horowitz; 19. Audrey Smaltz and Gail Marquis; 20. Holly Adam; 21. Tony Testa, Vikki Barbero, Nick Athanail, and Richard Streiter; 22. Steve Gold and Jane Hertzmark-Hudis; 23. Sam Shahid; 24. Nelly Moudime; 25. Jon Giswold; 26. Susan Sidor; 27. Chaz Stevens and Marty Kovacevich; 28. Craig Sotres, Joe Baldi, and Kevin O'Malley; 29. Phil and Lucy Suarez; 30. Billy Porter and Glenn Close; 31. David Landay; 32. Chuck Thomas and Michael Kretchmar; 33. Philip Greenberg; 34. Louis Falcone; 35. Thomas and Amy Lea Raglin; 36. Jeffrey Felner; 37. Mark Starr; 38. Ted Muehling; 39. Andy Jubelt, Effie Zeyra; 40. Joe Baldi; 41. Oprah Winfrey; 42. Rob Eichberg and Honey Ward; 43. Rachel Crespin and John Calcagno; 44. Chaz Stevens and Fameed Khalique; 45. Pamela Fiori; 46. Julie C. Britt and Tim Easton; 47. Deanna Littell; 48. Michael Ward and Manel Garcia-Espejo; 49. Jennifer Houser; 50. Gordon Henderson and Naomi Campbell; 51. Gerard Leddy; 52. Dustin Pittman and Jeffrey Felner; 53. Arthur Elgort and Grethe Holby; 54. Yeohlee Teng and Susan Scafidi; 55. Donald and Holly Loftus; 56. Shepard Vineburg; 57. Bethann Hardison; 58. Steven Kolb; 59. Andrew Carter; 60. Bibhu Mohapatra; 61. Mark Beard and Jim Manfredi; 62. Georgann Crudup; 63. Pamela Stephenson and Billy Connolly.

PUBLISHER Suzanne Slesin
CREATIVE DIRECTOR Frederico Farina
EDITORIAL ASSISTANT Julian Cosma
COPY EDITOR Amelia Kutschbach
ISBN 978-1-938461-71-2
L.O.C. NUMBER 2025906493
First Edition
Printed in Spain

Pointed Leaf Press LLC, 136 Baxter Street, Suite 1C, New York, NY 10013.

1
2
3
4
5
13
14
15
NYFW The Shows
NYFWFeb20
16
22
NEW FEST
THE 35
23
24
25
32
33
34
35
42
43
44
45
52
53
54
55
56